AMERICANS AND THEIR SERVANTS

AMERICANS
AND THEIR SERVANTS

Domestic Service in the United States
from 1800 to 1920

DANIEL E. SUTHERLAND

Louisiana State University Press
BATON ROUGE AND LONDON

Designer: Joanna Hill
Typeface: Century
Typesetter: G & S Typesetters, Inc.
Printer: Thomson-Shore, Inc.
Binder: John H. Dekker and Sons, Inc.

The author gratefully acknowledges permission to reprint a portion of his article, "The Servant Problem: An Index of Antebellum Americanism," which appeared in *Southern Studies*, XVII (Winter, 1979).

Library of Congress Cataloging in Publication Data

Sutherland, Daniel E.
Americans and their servants.

Bibliography: p.
Includes index.
1. Women servants—United States—History. I. Title.
HD6072.2.U5S94   331.4'8164046'0973   80-29689
ISBN 0-8071-0860-X

To Grady McWhiney

CONTENTS

ILLUSTRATIONS

PREFACE

My purpose in the following pages is to describe and clarify the forces shaping the occupation of domestic service and the lives of domestic servants in the United States between 1800 and 1920. This is no easy task. Myth and anecdote have stamped a distorted but enduring image on service and servants. Yet, if one of the historian's most useful functions is to expose myths about the past, an accurate picture of domestic service must be attempted. This occupation, which yearly touched the lives of millions of people, is worthy of close attention.

Traditionally, the "servant problem" has been perceived as the challenge of finding and retaining good servants. This one-sided view from the employers' perspective has warped our impressions of service and prejudiced our opinions of servants. My inquiry, by focusing on the "servant problems," will show that servants had grievances that were fully as frustrating as those of employers and equally worthy of being called "problems." The troubles of servants and employers were really parts of a single dilemma. I will rivet attention on that fact. I will also focus on domestic service reformers, well-meaning individuals who tried to mediate differences between Americans and their servants. Although largely unsuccessful, they played an important role in the history of American service.

The central difficulty of the servant problems—and, thus, an important theme in the following story—was the "belated" nature of service. From the very start of the nineteenth century, service was out of date, behind the times. American attitudes towards service, servants' conditions of labor, and above all, the master-servant relationship made it so, marking domestic service as one of the nation's slowest changing, least attractive occupations. A resultant and related problem was the isolation of service and servants. Service stood as a world apart, its workers cut off from one another and the mainstream of American life. Servants, employers, and reformers, each group in its own way, battled to improve this situation, but to no avail. Even when one of the main obstacles to modernizing service—the need for live-in servants—was severely undermined after 1920, the servant problems continued.

Within this framework, *servants* will be defined as free laborers, as opposed to slaves and indentured workers, performing household or personal service in private homes, boarding houses, and hotels. Indoor house servants, as opposed to chauffeurs, gardeners, and handymen, will be the main concern. Indoor servants represented the largest percentage, generally at least 80 percent, of all servants. Hotel servants are included because they were affected by many of the same problems plaguing domestics and, thus, provide a broader sampling of servants and their problems. Moreover, hotel workers, such as chambermaids and bellboys, were true servants during the nineteenth century. Even dining-room waiters (waitresses remained rarities for most of the century) were identified as servants far more readily than are twentieth-century restaurant workers. Where differences existed between hotel and household workers, they are explained. Finally, *servants* will be distinguished from *Americans* in order to dramatize the gaping social chasm between servants and their fellow citizens. The nature of their work and their failure to conform to certain racial-ethnic-cultural standards associated with being "American" meant that servants, even when native-born, were often treated as aliens.

In chronological scope the time period extending from 1800 to 1920 provides a convenient framework for discussion. By 1800 the United States, outside the South, was well on its way to eliminating slavery and indentured servitude and had started adjusting to a system of free servants. By the 1920s, domestic service had finally, painfully evolved into something significantly different. In unraveling the history of domestic service over so long a time, I have chosen to stress its continuity. To do so is not to deny changes, even significant ones, in service.

Alterations in the size and character of the servant work force, American households, and methods of housekeeping transformed the entire nature of household labor between 1800 and 1920. Such changes, however, were so slow-paced, their immediate effects so uneven, that only after 1920 did they become apparent and widespread.

Geographically, I have considered the entire United States. My emphasis falls on the area east of the Mississippi River because Americans in that region employed the most servants. Likewise, servants in cities and towns, rather than in rural areas, are the focus. Such an approach has admitted drawbacks. By trying to describe domestic service across the nation, one could easily overlook significant differences that existed between service in Boston and Baton Rouge, between servants in Philadelphia and San Francisco, between employers in New York City and rural New York State. But differences, once recognized, should not obscure the many similarities in service or the prevailing notions of Americans about household labor and domestic workers. Service, servants, and employers, regardless of regional peculiarities, had more in common than otherwise, a fact that makes it possible and desirable to reach conclusions about the nation at large.

The story, then, is about American domestic service in its broadest sense: servants, employers, reformers, and their mutual servant problems. Problems create questions, and questions require answers. The question nagging Americans and their servants between 1800 and 1920 was clear: Could domestic service be changed? The answer was yes, but it was a timid and qualified response. For service, if changed, could not be changed suddenly, totally, or, in the opinion of many people, significantly. The 1920s marked not an end to the servant problems so much as the departure of some old problems and the advent of new ones; the problems were not solved so much as altered and diluted. Further diminishing the achievement, change emanated not so much from servants, employers, and reformers as from inventors, architects, and world war. The story of how, why, and to what effect that happened is an intriguing one.

I have accumulated many debts of gratitude during my research and writing. Dozens of people have given generously of their time, talent, and intellect. I am indebted especially to Grady McWhiney. It was while working for Professor McWhiney as a floundering, fledgling graduate student that the possibilities of domestic service as a research topic occurred to me. Professor McWhiney directed the early stages of my investigation, and I have completed a large part of my labors with his patient assistance. Oftentimes under very adverse circumstances, he has done his best to eliminate all outrageous foolishness from the following pages. Also providing valuable criticisms, suggestions, and queries were Goldwin Smith and Joe Gray Taylor. Both Professors Smith and Taylor read and made extensive comments on earlier drafts of this book. My remaining debts are too numerous to discuss in detail, but I am particularly grateful for the professional assistance and personal encouragement of Wayne Andrews, John E. Basset, Gary L. Browne, Charlotte Erickson, Henry L. Golemba, the late Alfred H. Kelly, Forrest McDonald, Blaine E. McKinley, Penelope K. Majeske, Philip P. Mason, Diane Kim Sutherland, and Vern Wagner.

Librarians and archivists, of course, proved themselves invaluable during the research phase of this project. I am grateful for the help of the staffs at the following institutions: in the United States, the Wayne State University Libraries; Archives of Labor History and Urban Affairs, Reuther Library, Wayne State University; Detroit Public Library; Burton Historical Collection, Detroit Public Library; University of Michigan Libraries; Clements Library, University of Michigan; Michigan State Archives; Cornell University Libraries; Collection of Regional History, Olin Library, Cornell University; Syracuse University Libraries; Manuscript Division, Arents Library, Syracuse University; New York Public Library; Manuscript Division, New York Public Library; Museum of the City of New York; Columbia University Libraries; New-York Historical Society; Vassar College Library; Manuscript Division, Vassar College Library; Harvard University Libraries; Schlesinger Library, Radcliffe College; Massachusetts Historical Society; University of North Carolina Libraries; Southern Historical Collection, University of North Carolina; Duke University Libraries; Manuscript Division, Perkins Library, Duke University; University of Alabama Library; McNeese State University Library; Louisiana State University Library; State Department of Archives and History, Louisiana State University; Calvin M. McClung Historical Collection, Knoxville–Knox County Public Library; Chicago Historical Society; Filson Club; University of Arkansas Library; Southwest Missouri State University Library; Washington University Library, Saint Louis; Historical Society of Pennsylvania; South Caroliniana Library, University of South Carolina. In Great Britain, I was aided by my friends at the British Library of Political and Economic Science, London School of Economics, and at the Public Records Office of Northern Ireland, Belfast.

I also owe a special thank you to the State of New York, Department of Correction and to its former commissioner, Peter Preiser, for allowing me to inspect restricted records of the New York House of Refuge and the New York Agricultural and Industrial School. These records are located in the Arents Library, Syracuse University.

AMERICANS AND THEIR SERVANTS

PROLOGUE

THE PROBLEMS OF DOMESTIC SERVICE

Imagine the following scene. An unskilled, nearly penniless waif of eighteen arrives in New York City from a Pennsylvania village. She is intelligent, chaste, of white, middle-class background. She goes to New York in trepidation yet confident of making her way in the world. After several days, however, she is still without work. Jobs are available, but they pay little. She holds out, waiting for her luck to change. It does not. Her cash reserve dwindles. She moves from a clean, respectable boarding house to a cheaper, less savory one. She becomes desperate, the terrifying thought flashing in her mind, "Work or Starve, Work or Starve!" She eventually secures a job making paper boxes at three dollars a week. Overjoyed, she dances home to tell her landlady, an understanding woman who has befriended her, only to find the boardinghouse in flames. In a few hours, she stands gazing at the ashes of the building and of her few worldly possessions. Her sympathetic landlady is dead. Dazed, the girl is unsure what to do. She has a job, but nothing else, nowhere to live, and little to live on until her first paycheck. After spending the night at a relief shelter, she explains her plight to the well-to-do woman operating the refuge and asks what she should do.

"You would not go into service, I suppose?" queries the woman.

The girl is astonished. She finds the question remarkable. As she later recalled, "I had never thought of such an alternative before, but I met it without a moment's hesitation. 'No, I would not care to go into service,' I replied, and as I did so the lady's face showed mingled disappointment and disgust." Despite the knowledge that she may be throwing away her only means of survival, the girl is proud of her blunt refusal to wear "the definite badge of servitude."[1]

This episode is a parable of domestic service in the United States from 1800 to 1920. It illustrates the deep prejudices towards domestic service shared, or at least recognized, by all Americans. The answers to why the Pennsylvania girl so quickly and uncompromisingly rejected domestic service as an occupation and why the well-to-do woman accepted her refusal so routinely yet with undisguised "disappointment and disgust" explain the American servant problems and reveal much about Americans and their history.

Between 1800 and 1920, most Americans were unaware of the seriousness and complexity of the nation's servant problem. Many people considered it a great joke, fair game for cartoonists, satirists, and wits of all stripes. But for millions of employers and servants it was a major social issue and serious business indeed. Properly speaking, there was no servant "problem" but, rather, multiple servant "problems," a maze of interrelated riddles that bedeviled both employers and servants. The origins of these problems were unknown, buried in the murk of unrecorded time and pitted with contradictions and unfathomable mysteries. The fact that many servant problems could be self-perpetuating, the complaints of one side causing or aggravating the grumblings of the other, heightened their complexity. A delicate balance of human relations governed domestic service. Problems occurred when that balance was upset, when good servants encountered bad employers and good employers clashed with unruly servants. Yet, even this oversimplifies matters. Real heroes or villains seldom existed. Most of the players were merely comic or tragic. Neither employer nor servant understood the problems of the other; even momentary glimmers of mutual sympathy were too often extinguished by the exigency of an "us-versus-them" mentality.

Furthering these already perplexing problems were the stereotypes each side had of the other. Domestic service, even in 1800, had so long been a subject of fiction and gossip that myths and types already categorized both employers and servants. Servants were portrayed as either loyal saints or devious rascals, employers as benevolent guard-

---

1. Dorothy Richardson, "The Long Day," in William L. O'Neill (ed.), *Women at Work* (New York: Quadrangle Books, 1972), 3–57.

ians or ill-natured tyrants. There was no middle ground, no room for reality. Worse still, employers and servants too often prejudged one another according to their least endearing traits. Each generation inherited and perpetuated an exaggerated impression of the master-servant "war." People reacted to even slightly disagreeable experiences, to both genuinely and only seemingly unfair or self-willed antagonists, in the melodramatic fashion called for by tradition. Small wonder that appeals to reason went unheard amidst the din of slamming doors, horrible curses, and heartrending pleas for deliverance. Small wonder the servant problems remained to a large extent unsolved and insolvable. Changes and even some improvements occurred in domestic service, but they were slow-developing, unimpressive, stopgap measures that never confronted the real issues. The most lasting reforms proved to be those that reduced the dependency of Americans on household workers. In other words, the only way to solve the servant problems was, apparently, to eliminate servants.

The indelible nature of these problems resulted from three unhappy circumstances: the terrible social stigma on domestic service and servants, the remnants of a feudal master-servant relationship, and the touchingly naïve belief of employers and reformers in a mythical golden age. America's servant problems were molded, nourished, and made impregnable by these three closely related and mutually reinforcing conditions. Enhancing the seriousness of these circumstances were their long pedigrees. Nearly every strand of nineteenth- and early twentieth-century servant problems could be traced back at least as far as the seventeenth and eighteenth centuries, so that as early as 1800, the basis of all future problems was firmly entrenched and not to be easily dislodged. It was within this context that servants and employers reacted to one another, their own situations, and the world they lived in.

First in importance was the social stigma. Traditionally, domestic service was regarded as a menial, even degrading occupation, filled with ignorant, immoral, and incompetent folk who could not earn their living at any honorable trade. Americans inherited this view from the British and legitimized it through their own experience. Colonial Americans accepted English connotations of the word *servant*. This alone may have proved adequate to degrade service in American eyes, but then American servants—including indentured workers, redemptioners, and apprentices—gave the stigma genuine meaning. All bound laborers in British America were called servants, and even

though many of them worked in occupations other than domestic service, their varying degrees of servitude added odium to the word's
general sense. Nor did the disagreeable origins and behavior of many
of these servants help matters. Arrogant, drunken, and runaway servants abounded, and along with those "colonists in bondage" serving
punishments for crimes and debts, they made poor advertisements for
domestic service as an honorable vocation. As indentured servants
and redemptioners gradually disappeared after the American Revolution, their legacy was inherited by domestics.[2]

It was the American experience with Negroes and immigrants,
however, that firmly entrenched the social stigma. Negroes supplied
the most odium. American racial prejudice against blacks began to
form during the last half of the seventeenth century. As it spread, this
black bias became both a cause and an effect of Negro slavery. Negro
slavery and racial prejudice legitimized and reinforced each other, becoming nearly inseparable during the eighteenth century as blacks,
the "servile descendants of Ham," became associated with servitude
generally. This association proved disastrous in the nineteenth century, for wherever blacks served, domestic service was labeled "nig-
ger's work." In 1899 a respected Negro historian continued to explain
the problems of service as springing from the legacy of black slavery
and the addition of "a despised race to a despised calling."[3]

Xenophobia further branded domestic service. Immigrants, from
the early nineteenth century into the twentieth century, occupied a
subordinate position and an unenviable reputation in the United
States. Unfortunately, they also supplied large numbers of workers

2. Useful works for the colonial period are Marcus Wilson Jernegan, *Laboring and Dependent Classes in Colonial America, 1607–1783* (Chicago: University of Chicago Press, 1931); Richard B. Morris, *Government and Labor in Early America* (New York: Columbia University Press, 1946); Edmund Morgan, *The Puritan Family: Religion and Domestic Relations in Seventeenth Century New England* (New York: Harper and Row, 1966); Julia Cherry Spruill, *Women's Life and Work in the Southern Colonies* (Chapel Hill: University of North Carolina Press, 1938); Laurence W. Towner, " 'A Fondness for Freedom': Servant Protest in Puritan Society," *William and Mary Quarterly*, XIX (1962), 201–219.

3. Winthrop D. Jordan, *White over Black: American Attitudes Toward the Negro, 1550–1812* (Baltimore: Johns Hopkins University Press, 1969), 80–81, 123; James Curtis Ballagh, *White Servitude in the Colony of Virginia* (New York: Burt Franklin, 1969), 65, 68–69, 73; Cheesman A. Herrick, *White Servitude in Pennsylvania: Indentured and Redemption Labor in Colony and Commonwealth* (New York: Negro Universities Press, 1969), 274; Lorenzo Greene, *The Negro in Colonial New England* (New York: Atheneum, 1969), 108–109, 290, 350; Edgar J. McManus, *Black Bondage in the North* (New York: Syracuse University Press, 1973), 41–42, 57; W. E. B. DuBois, *The Philadelphia Negro: A Social Study* (New York: Benjamin Blom, 1899), 136–37.

for American households, at most times outnumbering even Negro servants. Two of the most scorned groups of foreigners, the Irish and the Chinese, became widely recognized symbols of the American servant. As such, they attached all of their supposed vice, ignorance, and poverty to service, further degrading it and disqualifying it as a civilized, respectable, Christian calling.

This ancestry boded ill for service and servants. Americans described service as "disgraceful," "dishonorable," "degrading," "repugnant," "undignified." The Boston census of 1845 categorized servants as part of the "unclassified residue of the population." Etiquette books assured Americans that to close a letter as "your obedient servant" did not compromise the writer or signify an inferior position. "Disguise it as we may, under all specious forms of reasoning," wrote a shrewd British oberver of antebellum America, "there is something in the mind of every man which tells him he is humiliated in doing personal service to another." Likewise, an American woman admitted in 1915, "Who of us would join their [servants'] ranks if it were possible to do anything else for a living. . . . And although there are splendid, able, dignified women working, and to be hired, as servants, the fact remains that they are *in* this class—if not of it—where the occupation is believed to be menial drudgery, and the form of Contract Semi-Slavery."[4]

In addition to the social stigma, a second factor contributed to the formidable nature of America's servant problems. Nineteenth-century Americans were burdened with an anachronistic master-servant (as opposed to employer-employee) relationship in which servants lived with employers and depended upon them for food, shelter, and sometimes clothing. This somewhat feudal arrangement required that employers assume the obligation of managing both the working and private lives of their servants. Unlike modern contractual agreements based on economics, service arrangements remained largely informal, based on social relationships or "status."

The feudal connection was at once a theoretical product of the social stigma and a living spur to it. This dualism functioned in the same way that Negro slavery both strengthened and was stimulated by racial

4. Lemuel Shattuck, *Report to the Committee of the City Council Appointed to Obtain the Census of Boston for the Year 1845* (Boston: n.p., 1846), 43Y; A Gentleman, *The Laws of Etiquette; or, Short Rules and Reflections for Conduct in Society* (Philadelphia: Carey, Lea, and Blanchard, 1836), 89; Thomas C. Gratten, *Civilized America* (2 vols.; London: Bradbury and Evans, 1859), I, 258; Mary Pattison, *The Business of Home Management* (New York: Robert M. McBride & Co., 1918), 56–57.

prejudice. Americans believed that their servants were descended from serfs, indentured servants, and slaves. In all of these forms of bondage, a servant's time, or "freedom," was entirely at the master's disposal. Thus, even though the conditions of American service were not comparable to slavery, and the degree of feudalism present in its system of free labor was not as extreme as that found in serfdom or indentured servitude, Americans continued to accept and defend a relationship that irredeemably stigmatized servants and service. As late as 1910, reformers insisted that the "crux" of the servant problems was the "medievalism" of the home.[5]

A third factor perpetuating the servant problems was the belief of employers and reformers in a golden age of service. Employers and reformers reminisced about a time when American service was based on a truly paternalistic relationship. They looked back nostalgically to the days when American servants were efficient, cheerful, and obedient. They insisted that revival of such a period was possible if workers would only be more loyal and respectful. But confusion reigned as to when this glorious era had existed. No matter where one stood in time, it was always a generation or two in the past, out of reach yet tantalizingly retrievable. For many years, the ideal servant had supposedly lived at the time of the American Revolution or during the early years of the Republic. But the date kept inching forward. By the mid-1870s, the golden age was estimated to be around 1850, a calculation that would have amazed antebellum employers. In the twentieth century, those halcyon days were remembered as being in the decade after the Civil War, and by 1920, they had progressed as far as 1900. Thus employers in all periods mourned the loss of their mothers' cooks and sought "old-fashioned" servants.

The only Americans to fix upon a single golden age were post–Civil War southerners. After 1865 the golden age in southern domestic service, as in so much else, became and remained the antebellum years. Slavery, so the legend went, had supplied southerners with happy, loyal, efficient servants. With emancipation, these once contented servants were incited to revolt by rabble-rousing Union soldiers and smooth-talking carpetbaggers. Southerners enjoyed a brief reprieve in that many older slaves retained or eventually regained their senses and continued to serve their old masters faithfully. But there were none to replace this generation, and southerners were soon complain-

5. I. M. Rubinow and Daniel Durant, "The Depth and Breadth of the Servant Problem," *McClure's Magazine*, XXXIV (March, 1910), 580–81.

ing bitterly about the " 'new issue,'—negroes who have grown up in freedom, utterly untrained as cooks, housemaids, and nurses." By the early twentieth century, the highest compliment a southern employer could give a servant was to call him or her "an old time, before the war darkey."[6]

Such insistence thwarted practical reform. So long as employers and reformers believed in the existence of the perfect servant, they could never be content with this best of all possible worlds. They became dissatisfied with the mere mortals who cleaned their houses and cooked their meals. Muttering and grumbling about their problem, they freely scolded and dismissed servants who did not measure up to expectations. This ruthlessness only further eroded the quality of service. Servants passing through the hands of such employers became more hostile and more belligerent than ever. Seeing little hope of fair treatment, they too remained brooding and out of sorts.

Another version of the golden age myth held that, just as the best servants had lived a generation in the past, so surviving "treasures" had fled to other parts of the country. With few exceptions, southern housekeepers maintained that the best servants lived in the North, while northern housekeepers stood just as convinced that the reverse situation reflected reality. The same was true for employers everywhere. "You southern ladies have no idea how we western ladies have to work," wrote an Indiana woman to her friend in Virginia. "Imagine yourself . . . with but one servant and that a very inefficient one, who cannot get even breakfast without assistance and indolent, unprincipaled [sic], and yet demand two dollars a week." She concluded, "O! how I wish I could transport a cargo of some of your well trained house servants. I could soon find homes for them in our small town very easily." We do not know what her Virginia friend thought about this, but from down in Alabama a woman wrote, "Every body says *this* is the worst place in the world for servants."[7]

These three circumstances—the social stigma, the feudal relationship, and the myth of the golden age—explain why Americans failed to solve their servant problems. The traditions, customs, and habits of

6. Orra Langhorne, "Domestic Service in the South," *Journal of Social Science,* XXXIX (1901), 170; Patience Pennington [Elizabeth Waites (Allston) Pringle], *A Woman Rice Planter,* ed. Cornelius O. Cathey (Cambridge: Harvard University Press, 1961), 7–8, 165–66.

7. Lizzie Davidson to Mary E. Schooler, June 4, 1877, in Mary Eliza Schooler Papers, Perkins Library, Duke University; Laura C. Phillips to Cornelia P. Spencer, December 20, 1890, in Cornelia Phillips Spencer Papers, Southern Historical Collection, Library of the University of North Carolina at Chapel Hill.

centuries were not easily changed. At one time or another, sometimes singly, sometimes in combination, these forces conspired to reduce the likelihood that Americans would ever find satisfactory solutions. The human element was too powerful a force within domestic service to admit of easy answers, and Americans were either too impatient or too proud to try the hard ones. Traditionally, the servant problem had been defined as a shortage of good servants. But there was also a shortage of good employers. Both servants and employers expected too much, both gave too little. This created servant problems without end.

CHAPTER ONE

A SPECIES OF DODO
The Servant Shortage

Adam Smith was wrong. Supply does not always equal demand. Between 1800 and 1920, Americans needed servants. Necessity, real and imagined, dictated that middle- and upper-class Americans employ servants to feed them, dress them, clean their houses, and take care of their children. Yet, despite the hundreds of thousands of men and women willing to work as servants, employers complained of a shortage. Americans wanted not just servants but good servants, and by their standards such creatures were truly rare. This fact lent an expression of gloom to an otherwise cheerful nation. A Philadelphia gentleman, reviewing at least two decades of personal frustration, lamented in 1822, "In these United States nothing would be wanting to make life perfectly happy (humanly speaking) had we good servants." Over half a century later, a rural Nebraska woman echoed his words: "if only I could be so fortunate as to get a competent girl I should be the happiest of mortals." These two remarks indicate the extent, both geographically and chronologically, of the servant shortage. People with good servants considered themselves fortunate. The majority chanted a forlorn chorus that droned across the United States: good servants were becoming "extinct—a species of dodo."[1]

1. H. E. Scudder (ed.), *Recollections of Samuel Breck* (Philadelphia: Porter and Coates, 1877), 296, 299; Elizabeth N. Harding to Lucy M. Salmon [1889], in Lucy Maynard Salmon Papers, Vassar College Library; Mrs. M. E. W. Sherwood, "The Lack of Good Servants," *North American Review*, CLIII (November, 1891), 555.

The demand for servants came from the middle and upper classes, and it was impressive. Nearly everybody who could afford a servant employed one during the nineteenth century. Exact numbers are uncertain, especially before 1850, but approximately one servant was available to every eight American families between 1800 and 1920. Of course, the number of families actually employing servants was smaller than this potential demand, but that cannot detract from the widespread craving for domestic workers. Most families kept modest staffs. The majority—probably three-fourths—had only one or two servants. Still, about one-third of all servants worked in establishments, including hotels, with staffs of three or more. Some private householders employed as many as twenty servants before the Civil War, and retinues of twenty-five to forty were not unheard of by 1890.[2]

Americans required servants for several reasons. The physical strain of housework was the principal one. Many women simply could not accomplish their innumerable household tasks without help. Almost as important were the roles and responsibilities assigned to American women, especially their roles as "housekeepers" and "ladies." Status was a third reason for having servants, tradition yet another. All of these reasons were interconnected, and more than one might have influenced any single employer. Some reasons were also more valid than others at different times and places. But all helped to create an insatiable desire for servants.

The dominant reason for employing servants during most of the nineteenth century was the exhausting, backbreaking, unceasing nature of household labor. Housekeeping exacted dozens of daily, monotonous chores. Few housekeepers fluttered merrily through their duties of dusting, mopping, scrubbing, and cooking. Even women who enjoyed housework found their multiple responsibilities a rather tough

2. U.S. Bureau of the Census, *The Statistical History of the United States from Colonial Times to the Present* (New York: Basic Books, 1976), Series A288–319, D167–81, *Ninth Census of the United States: Population* (Washington, D.C.: Government Printing Office, 1872), I, 598, 755–804, *Tenth Census of the United States: Population* (Washington, D.C.: Government Printing Office, 1883), I, 670–77, 860–909, *Eleventh Census of the United States: Population* (Washington, D.C.: Government Printing Office, 1893–95; XV, Part 1, pp. 932–47, XVI, Part 2, pp. 630–743, *Twelfth Census of the United States: Population* (Washington, D.C.: Government Printing Office, 1902), II, Part 2, pp. 640–59, *Twelfth Census of the United States: Special Report on Occupations* (Washington, D.C.: Government Printing Office, 1902), 428–79, *Thirteenth Census of the United States: Population* (Washington, D.C.: Government Printing Office, 1913–14), I, 1289–291, IV, 152–291, *Fourteenth Census of the United States: Population* (Washington, D.C.: Government Printing Office, 1921–23), I, 1268–270, IV, 1049–1257.

business, and some tasks, such as emptying chamberpots, changing infants, and cleaning up after pets and people with weak bladders and upset stomachs, were downright unpleasant. Servants were needed to spare American women the dirt, monotony, and drudgery of their own homes.

The exhausting nature of housework provided many sobering experiences. Women with large families or spacious houses usually regretted trying to do without servants. They were victimized by the strain of housekeeping, prematurely losing the bloom of youth and acquiring a drawn, tired, beleaguered look. One woman who managed without a cook for just one week found herself "broken down, sick & in bed." People who contemplated going servantless were advised against such folly by their friends. Experience had proven that if one had to be temporarily without servants, it was best to let the work go. Better to leave kitchen floors unmopped and to eat cold suppers than to suffer a "train of aches and pains" from overwork.[3]

Distaste for the drudgery of housework was made more terrible by the social roles assigned to middle- and upper-class American women. The dominant female role during most of the nineteenth century was that of housekeeper, a function demanding specific, unquestioned responsibilities established by custom and morality. American women were expected to be exemplary household workers. They were supposed to be knowledgeable in all phases of housework, from cooking turnips to removing blueberry stains from linen. But only those women who could not afford servants were expected to perform these tasks themselves. The traditional image of the servant and the grubby nature of household labor exempted American housekeepers from menial chores. The housekeeper was a "regulator and manager." The secret to keeping a tidy house, or even a hotel for that matter, was not the hard work invested in scrubbing, cleaning, and polishing but the "administrative skill" that coordinated those tasks. A housekeeper's role was limited to training and directing her servants, keeping household accounts, and organizing household work. Mothers, in preparing daughters for the day they would oversee their own homes, stressed

3. Calvin H. Wiley Diary (MS in Calvin Henderson Wiley Papers, Southern Historical Collection, Library of the University of North Carolina at Chapel Hill), May 4, 1885; F. S. Ellas to Sister, June 7, 1864, in Ellas Family Papers, Collection of Regional History, Cornell University. See also Anna C. L. Mills to Elisabeth D. Cabot, February 19, 1860, in Hugh Cabot Family Collection, Schlesinger Library, Radcliffe College, and Mrs. Hunckley Williams to Clarinda B. Boltwood, December 15, 1889, in Boltwood Family Papers, Burton Historical Collection, Detroit Public Library.

mastery of managerial skills. This was the prescribed role, and if the reality for few, it was the dream of many.

But a housekeeper's duties went far beyond keeping house. She was also the moral and spiritual guardian of her home. Her "higher duties" as wife and mother allowed no time for manual labor. A wife and mother was not expected to toil in dust and cinders. She was to serve as "the enlightened instructor and guide of awakening minds, her husband's counselor, the guardian and purifier of the morals of her household." Moreover, American housekeepers had a moral and spiritual responsibility to the nation. The middle-class American home was the essence of democratic virtue; each home represented the United States in miniature. It was in the home that morality, virtue, and republicanism were to be learned by rising generations. Responsibility for instilling these values fell naturally upon the American wife and mother. Protecting the nation's morals, sheltering the "inner spirit" of society, and infusing the home with "moral goodness" and "moral happiness" was her "sacred mission."[4]

Ideally, the American housekeeper was also a "lady," an equally demanding but less easily defined role. The nineteenth century was the grand age of the lady, and American women wanted more than anything else to be so regarded. A necessary step towards this goal was to be a perfect housekeeper, but the true lady was something more. She was a superb administrator, but she was also cultured and genteel. Historians generally represent the "ornamental" woman of the nineteenth century as an incompetent social butterfly. But a woman's failure to engage in the manual labor of her home did not make her idle. Any leisure time she gained from having servants was to be spent not in idleness or self-indulgence, but in self-improvement and philanthropic activities. She required time for reading, writing, and if circumstances permitted, practicing and patronizing the arts, attending lectures and lyceums. Reformers who criticized the idleness of American women, especially those writing before 1890, most often addressed themselves to housekeepers who shirked their duties as administrators and moral guardians. Incumbent upon the wealthiest and most leisured ladies was the obligation of assuming duties outside the home. Ladies were civic and social leaders, humanitarians, and altru-

4. Mrs. A. J. [Margaret] Graves, *Woman in America* (New York: Harper and Brothers, 1843), 29–30, 55–57, 72; Mary Sargent Potter, "The Proposed Tax on Servants," *North American Review*, CCVIII (November, 1918), 745–46. See also Nancy F. Cott, *The Bonds of Womanhood: "Woman's Sphere" in New England, 1780–1835* (New Haven: Yale University Press, 1977), 44–48, 71–74.

ists. Temperance meetings, charity bazaars, and organizations promoting relief of the homeless and indigent all demanded a lady's attention. Admittedly, some women pursued these activities out of boredom rather than a desire to be considered ladies, but the results were the same. Cultural and benevolent duties drew women outside the home, requiring that they have help in accomplishing household chores. The difference between ladies and servants was most evident in the fact that servants had "no social duties, no intellectual, no benevolent ones."[5]

American women were encouraged to be ladies by their fathers and husbands. To be a gentleman was as dear to American men as being a lady was to the women-folk, but no man could be a gentleman while his wife and daughters slaved as domestic drudges. In 1846 a North Carolina doctor advised his daughter of the necessity and the difficulty of combining a housekeeper's skill with a lady's grace. If not properly managed, he warned, housework could be "dirty, demoralizing & debasing," confining one to "low pursuits," "filthy drudgery," and "disgusting slovenliness." A lady in that position had "little time for study or quiet meditation, & very little for improving conversation or refined society."[6] No matter how expensive or troublesome servants became, they were necessary in the home of a lady.

After the Civil War, middle- and upper-class women expanded their traditional roles of housekeeper and lady. Their earlier responsibilities remained intact, but the increasing wealth and leisure time of the Gilded Age and early twentieth century presented new opportunities. The new roles varied, but like those of housekeeper and lady, they were characterized by hostility to the manual labor of housekeeping. Some of the new roles allowed women to escape housekeeping entirely. New occupations opened to women, and fewer restrictions were placed on their chances for formal education. Middle-class women became working wives with their own jobs and careers; they entered

5. See, for example, Daniel T. Rogers, *The Work Ethic in Industrial America, 1850–1920* (Chicago: University of Chicago Press, 1978), 182–209, Susan Porter Benson, "Business Heads and Sympathizing Hearts: The Women of the Providence Employment Society, 1837–1858," *Journal of Social History*, XII (1978–79), 304, and Keith Melder, "Ladies Bountiful: Organized Women's Benevolence in 19th-Century America," *New York History*, XLVIII (1967), 231–54; E. Elcourt, "The Persecuted Woman," *Lippincott's Magazine*, V (January, 1870), 28–30. Finally, see Gerda Lerner, "The Lady and the Mill Girl: Changes in the Status of Women in the Age of Jackson," *Midcontinent American Studies Journal*, X (1969), 5–15, for the growing connotations of social class inherent in the word *lady*.

6. Quoted in Guion Griffis Johnson, *Ante-Bellum North Carolina: A Social History* (Chapel Hill: University of North Carolina Press, 1937), 231–32.

professions that delivered them from the kitchen forever. By the twentieth century, it could no longer be assumed as a matter of faith that American women had been directed by Providence to serve as wives, mothers, and housekeepers.

Fashion created a third reason for employing servants—as status symbols. Americans were materialistic. They dreamed of belonging to the leisured class and were stricken by a feverish desire for material comfort and symbols of affluence that knew no cure save gratification. Given their tendency to pursue traditional European symbols of wealth and social arrival, it was nearly inevitable that Americans should accept servants as the ultimate means of "conspicuous display."[7] Nor was this fancy confined to the nation's wealthy upper crust. It applied to the rising middle classes, too. Ambitious but as yet socially unrecognized young merchants and clerks, along with their wives, sought evidence of their improving social and economic fortunes. The old wealth and *nouveaux riches* may have been more spectacularly visible than the middle classes in exhibiting their fortunes, but all were equally vainglorious. All were willing to spend an inordinate proportion of their incomes—as much as one-third among less well-to-do families—in order to secure servants.[8]

Americans reached the zenith of their craving for servants during the Gilded Age. It was reportedly an American who said, "Give me the luxuries of life and I will not ask for the necessities."[9] As E. L. Godkin's "chromo-civilization" emerged, Americans lived up to this philosophy by going on a binge of extravagance that lasted some thirty years. The heart of the Gilded Age, the 1870s and 1880s, witnessed a larger proportional increase in the number of servants than any other time in American history. The decade of greatest growth was the 1880s, when the number of servants increased by over 425,000. The 1880s also saw the largest numerical increase of male servants, some 73,000, perhaps an even more important indication of the value of servants as status symbols during those years.[10]

7. Thorstein Veblen, *Theory of the Leisure Class: An Economic Study of Institutions* (New York: Funk & Wagnalls, 1967), 41–51, 53–78, was the first attempt to articulate this idea in regard to servants.

8. "Hiring a Cook," *Ladies' Magazine and Literary Gazette*, VI (November, 1833), 517; Harriet Prescott Spofford, *The Servant Girl Question* (Boston: Houghton Mifflin, 1881), 88; Frances A. Kellor, "The Housewife and Her Helper," *Ladies' Home Journal*, XXIV (April, 1907), 42.

9. James Fullarton Muirhead, *America the Land of Contrasts: A Briton's View of His American Kin* (Boston: Lamson, Wolffe, and Co., 1898), 15.

10. See note 2 above.

Male servants (commonly known as flunkeys) became the ultimate status symbol. More often than females, male servants fulfilled a social role rather than an economic or productive one. They were paid for servility; their function was to emphasize the social position of employers. Male retainers received twice the wages of most female servants while doing about half as much work. This supposedly evinced their employers' lack of concern with expense. Likewise, while female servants were kept out of sight as much as possible, men were thrust into the spotlight at every opportunity, greeting callers, guarding hallways, serving meals, and delivering messages to parlor and sitting room. Men were also the ones decked out in livery, their glittering gold braid and glistening silk breeches heightening the effect of conspicuous display. Men were seldom employed in establishments with fewer than four servants. Most often they were found in hotels—especially as waiters—and large, expensively operated private households.[11]

A final reason for hiring servants was tradition. Families that had employed servants in one generation continued to enjoy their services in later generations. Women raised in such families became increasingly dependent on servants, and in time, family traditions became irrevocably enmeshed with ideas of status and fashionable living. Once accustomed to a life-style requiring servants, people found it hard to give them up. Even when the advent of modern household machines made housemaids obsolete on the practical level, status and tradition insured that some families would keep servants to operate the machines. More dramatically, even people who had lost their financial fortunes and otherwise claimed to be in poverty would often continue to employ servants, relinquishing this last possession only as they themselves were being trotted off to the poorhouse. The post–Civil War South offers many such examples.

The demand for servants was real enough, none could gainsay that. Yet, regardless of who they were or where they lived, Americans faced a servant shortage. The rich and not-so-rich in large cities, middling towns, small villages, and on isolated farms were alike puzzled by their inability to hire servants. Potential servants abounded in densely populated areas, but so did people requiring servants. Elsewhere, fewer people hired servants, but there were also fewer willing

---

11. Veblen, *Theory of the Leisure Class*, 44–45, 95; I. M. Rubinow, "The Problem of Domestic Service," *Journal of Political Economy*, XIV (1906), 504–505.

workers. Small wonder, then, that employers everywhere were ob-
sessed by the task of finding and keeping servants; it was the "one un-
varying subject" of conversation in every community. "You have no
idea," wrote a Tuscaloosa woman to her sister, "how much the difficulty in getting & keeping servants—cooks especially—has to do with
the social life of this place."[12] The same might have been written by
employers from Brooklyn to Walla Walla.

Many organized attempts were made to increase the supply of servants. The grandest schemes involved importation of immigrants.
Various government and privately financed projects were aimed at enticing domestic laborers from Europe and Asia. Before the Civil War,
the Irish Pioneer Emigration Fund was used to bring girls to Ohio.
A similar association operated in Maine during the 1860s. The American Emigrant Company and the Columbia Emigrant Company led a
host of post–Civil War organizations striving to attract domestics and
other laborers to the United States. Southerners joined the hunt for
free servants after the war, becoming especially excited about the possibilities of importing European and even Oriental labor. None of these
schemes was very successful, however, and neither exemption of servants from immigration restrictions in 1885 nor their inclusion in severe twentieth-century quotas seemed to influence the number of foreigners in service.[13]

On a less lavish but probably more successful scale, migration of
servants within the United States was encouraged. For example, the
Women's Protective Emigrant Society was organized in 1857 to draw
"destitute young women and girls" from eastern cities to the sparsely
settled West. Similar efforts were organized by post–Civil War northerners seeking to entice southern Negroes into northern households,
hotels, and boarding houses. They did not have to try very hard. Discontented blacks were "wild to come Norf," where they expected to

12. A Sufferer, "Domestic Servitude," *Knickerbocker*, XIX (June, 1842), 521; Laura
C. Phillips to Cornelia P. Spencer, February 20, 1892, in Cornelia Phillips Spencer Pa-
pers, Southern Historical Collection, Library of the University of North Carolina at
Chapel Hill.
13. Carl Wittke, *We Who Built America: The Saga of the Immigrant* (New York:
Prentice-Hall, 1939), 104, 108–109; Just M. Caén and J. C. Wright to John Esten Cooke,
July 25, 1866, in John Esten Cooke Papers, Perkins Library, Duke University; Henry
Nutt to Peter Mallett, November 23, 1869, in Peter Mallett Papers, Southern Historical
Collection, Library of the University of North Carolina at Chapel Hill; Rowland T.
Berthoff, "Southern Attitudes Towards Immigration, 1865–1914," *Journal of Southern
History*, XVIII (1951), 328–60.

work a short time and then retire on their fat Yankee earnings.[14] Still, these maneuverings did little to relieve the general distress.

The variety of methods used by individuals to obtain servants further testifies to the desperate nature of the search. Particularly distraught middle-class employers were not above stopping people in the streets to ask if they were looking for a place at service or knew of anyone who was. Immigrants, always an important source of American servants, were propositioned at the wharves of port cities, where both urban and rural housekeepers, or their agents, eagerly awaited the arrival of each immigrant-laden ship.[15] Most methods, however, proved more orthodox, and recommendations from friends and trusted servants, newspaper advertisements, and employment bureaus became the principal means of supply.

The safest plan was to obtain recommendations from friends or reliable relatives. This was the only sure way of obtaining a true account of a servant's virtues and vices. Written references offered by servants were too often forged to be entirely trustworthy. Even genuine references, when provided by former employers who did not wish to injure a servant's chances for a job, sometimes failed to reveal all. On the other hand, vindictive employers could use references to hinder servants seeking employment. Thus, reformers stressed the importance of honest references as a safeguard for both servants and employers.[16] Meanwhile, friends relied on one another to negotiate for available servants and to pass on rumors of where good servants might be found. Pleas for help filled the private correspondence of employers, and no one can tell how many bargains were made or rumors exchanged over backyard fences and at afternoon teas.

14. David M. Katzman, *Seven Days a Week: Women and Domestic Service in Industrializing America* (New York: Oxford University Press, 1978), 204–209; Carter Goodrich and Sol Davison, "The Wage-Earner in the Westward Movement," *Political Science Quarterly*, LI (1936), 94–96; New York *Times* , January 26, 1874, p. 8, September 13, 1874, p. 4; Frances A. Kellor, "Assisted Emigration from the South," *Charities*, XV (October 7, 1905), 11–14; R. R. Wright, Jr., "The Negro in Unskilled Labor," American Academy of Political and Social Science *Annals*, XLIX (1913), 19–27.

15. William Hickey [Martin Doyle], *Hints on Emigration to Upper Canada* (Dublin: William Curry, Jr., and Co., 1832), 74; John C. Guldin to Mary Williams, March 24, 1852, in Josiah Butler Williams Family Papers, Collection of Regional History, Cornell University; John W. Cunningham to Calvin H. Wiley, September 28, 1872, Calvin Henderson Wiley Papers, Southern Historical Collection, Library of the University of North Carolina at Chapel Hill.

16. See Domestic Reform League reference form (MS in Women's Educational and Industrial Union Records, Schlesinger Library, Radcliffe College), Box 3, Folder 23.

Servants, too, could sometimes be relied on to fill vacancies. Conscientious workers, when leaving positions, might recommend suitable replacements for themselves. One employer boasted that she had used an employment agency only three times in twenty-three years because her servants had been "self-replacing." Some servants had a knack for finding reliable help whatever the occasion. For instance, Susan Hale, of the Boston Hales, had a remarkable servant who seemingly "invented" needed replacements. In fact, wrote Miss Hale, of her "General Purveyor of Help," "when I lift up mine eyes, it is not to the hills whence cometh my help, but to Mrs. O'Brien, a coachman's wife with a large family, cross-eyed, acquainted not only with grief (her husband drinks—some), but with all the gilt-edged ladies who work on Back Bay."[17]

Newspaper advertisements were also used but not so often as might be assumed. Experienced employers generally ignored newspapers, both as a means of locating available servants and of announcing their own needs, for several reasons. Many employers doubted that good servants placed or responded to newspaper advertisements. Good servants, it was said, were known by reputation and had a dozen standing offers for employment. Many employers also ignored employee ads because of the inconvenience involved. In answering ads, employers were usually required—particularly before telephones became common—to run all over town tracking down suitable workers. Then too, employers were sometimes victimized by practical jokers advertising nonexistent services. As for proclaiming their own needs, employers felt embarrassed at publicly revealing their inability to find and keep satisfactory domestics. Servants advertised more often than employers, but even then it was usually only the better-educated servants and those wise to the ways of "city life" who sought work by this means. Early newspaper ads lumped the pleas of both employers and servants in a single "Wanted" column, but it was clearly the notices of servants that dominated. By the mid-1850s, when "Situations Wanted" were listed separately from employer "Wants," the former consistently outnumbered the latter. A survey of advertisements in two New York City newspapers as late as 1908 shows that, while 3,166 ser-

17. Antoinette B. Hervey, "The Saints in My Kitchen," *Outlook*, C (February 17, 1912), 368; Susan Hale to Mary Dinsmoor, June, 1904, in Caroline P. Atkinson (ed.), *The Letters of Susan Hale* (Boston: Marshall Jones, 1921), 389.

vants sought jobs through newspapers that year, only 257 employers sought servants by this means.[18]

The employment bureau, or commercial "intelligence office," was the largest supplier of servants in towns, cities, and their suburbs. Intelligence offices, as opposed to regular employment agencies, furnished only servants. Towns of five to ten thousand population usually had at least one office, and large cities had dozens, sometimes hundreds, of such depots. Probably the first American intelligence office was established at New York City in 1774, patterned after similar offices in England and Ireland. It was opened, according to its founder, Solomon Griffiths, "because great inconveniences [sic] hath and does frequently happen to masters and mistresses of families for want of knowing where to apply for good servants; and likewise servants where they may get good places."[19] By the mid–nineteenth century, intelligence offices were an accepted part of city life in the northeast, and western cities opened offices as soon as their populations warranted. In the South, offices provided both free black and white servants before the Civil War. Southerners, however, even after the abolition of slavery, preferred other sources of supply to intelligence agencies.

Intelligence offices became the center of any town's servant trade. It was there that servants registered, proclaiming their qualifications, employment preferences, and availability. It was there that employers made known their needs and interviewed candidates meeting their requirements. For a small fee, sometimes free to servants, compatible parties were introduced to one another. If time or inconvenience prevented a meeting between parties at the agency, servants could be sent to employers' homes to be interviewed. If in a hurry, employers sometimes called on servants. Rarely did intelligence offices concern themselves with resulting contracts; they acted only as a means of introducing employers and employees.

The variety of commercial intelligence offices was startling. A type of office existed for every species of servant. One type catered strictly to immigrants, enlisting them on the docks and occasionally operating

18. Edward T. Devine, *Report on the Desirability of Establishing an Employment Bureau in the City of New York* (New York: Russell Sage Foundation, 1909), 145. For a comment on the resentment harbored by many employers against this unorthodox method of finding workers see New York *Times*, October 15, 1871, p. 4.

19. Quoted in Samuel McKee, Jr., *Labor in Colonial New York, 1664–1776* (New York: Columbia University Press, 1935), 50.

a modest importation service. Some immigrant agencies specialized in particular nationalities, but most found it profitable to keep a variety in stock. In any case, their laborers were usually untrained as servants and desperate for work. Another type of office, which handled only experienced servants, catered to the wealthy in both town and country. A third specialized in hotel help, and yet another placed only Negroes. This fourth type was especially active in bringing southern blacks north after the Civil War. Finally, there was the general agency, usually found in small towns, that welcomed all comers.[20]

Offices were equally varied in appearance and business methods. The vast majority of offices, about three-fourths, were one-person operations, representing varying degrees of respectability. Since little operating capital was required, the intelligence office frequently became a side job for janitors, saloonkeepers, shopkeepers, and employees of railroads and shipping companies. Their "offices" were of the table-and-chair variety, squeezed into back rooms of warehouses, stores, and rented tenement space. Most such offices were located near their supply of servants; immigrant offices, for example, were close to the docks. Records of clients and engagements, if kept at all, were generally logged in old, dog-eared notebooks. At the other extreme and in the minority were the highly respectable offices—formal, businesslike, reliable, located in fashionable sections of downtown business districts. Their equipment and methods, including, by the twentieth century, cross-referenced filing systems manned by efficient secretarial staffs, were refreshingly sophisticated. They also occupied clean, comfortable quarters, often whole suites of rooms furnished with carpets, draperies, and attractive furniture. Thus offices ranged in appearance and operation from "pushcart to department store." Most were probably somewhere in between, but far too many resembled the former type.

Offices also varied in honesty and morality. Many agents were unscrupulous in their methods of hiring and placing servants. Servants, as will be seen, bore the brunt of this exploitation, but employers also had reason for complaint. For example, in order to collect registration fees, which were their one source of profit, nearly all agents over-registered and overpromised. Even the best offices led employers to

20. Frances A. Kellor was the nation's leading authority on intelligence offices in the early twentieth century. Her consummate work on the subject is found in *Out of Work: A Study of Unemployment* (New York: G. P. Putnam's Sons, 1915), 194–235. Her remarks, upon which the following discussion is based, apply to earlier years, too.

expect first-class servants at a moment's notice. Once they had an employer's money, however, such promises were often forgotten, and employers complained bitterly about the poor-quality servants foisted upon them. Employers also accused offices of conspiring with servants to maintain wages at inflated levels. It was a practice of some offices to collect a percentage of each servant's first month's pay as compensation for placing them. Such offices, employers charged, encouraged servants to demand high wages so that agents in turn could collect large fees.[21]

Small wonder employers distrusted commercial intelligence offices and had a low regard for the servants they supplied. Employers believed that only servants of "low character" or questionable ability frequented commercial offices and that respectable workers avoided them. The experience of one New York employer illustrates why this was so. This particular gentleman paid a year's subscription of five dollars to a city intelligence office only to watch a procession of nine unsatisfactory employees pass through his home during the twelve months. The first of these servants he dismissed as a thief after one week; the second was sacked for dishonesty after the same period. The third lasted three months, but then fell to the temptation of demon rum, as did the fourth after only three days. The fifth was dismissed after two months (cause not specified). The sixth was also an alcoholic, but lasted five months before becoming incapacitated. A seventh fell to drink after two months. The eighth stayed one day, had a "Fit," and could no longer work. The ninth left on account of ill health after one and one-half months. Not a very illustrious crew. Small wonder general opinion condemned commercial intelligence offices as the "most disheartening and least reliable" means of getting servants.[22] And yet, because these offices controlled much of the servant supply, employers found them a necessary evil.

Labor exchanges were alternatives to commercial offices. These government-operated clearinghouses for immigrants in American port cities were designed, as often as not, to remove aimlessly wandering aliens from city doles and place them in self-sustaining jobs. Probably

21. A Gentleman, *The Laws of Etiquette; or, Short Rules and Reflections for Conduct in Society* (Philadelphia: Carey, Lea, and Blanchard, 1836), 120–21; "House Servants," *Harper's Weekly*, I (May 9, 1857), 289. For still other ploys, see New York *Times*, September 16, 1874, p. 3, September 18, 1874, p. 2, and December 10, 1882, p. 4.

22. James Bogert, Jr., Account Book with Hired Servants (MS in Museum of the City of New York), inside front cover; Mrs. Henry Ward Beecher, *Motherly Talks with Young Housekeepers* (New York: J. B. Ford and Co., 1873), 247.

the first and certainly the most important exchange was at New York City. It was established in 1850 by the New York Commissioners of Emigration, and it formed, after 1855, part of the immigrant-processing facility at Castle Garden. The exchange provided employers with all sorts of laborers, free of charge, but it was especially helpful in supplying domestic servants. At its peak of activity in the 1860s, the New York exchange placed over 25,000 female immigrants during a two-year period. Unfortunately, the exchange fell into disuse by the mid-1880s apparently because not enough immigrants were aware of its services.[23]

Other alternatives to commercial offices were charitable and philanthropic agencies. Operated by churches, benevolent societies, and immigrant aid societies, these organizations sought to combat the exploitation of workers. Their agents, sometimes known as "missionaries," were characterized by their humaneness, a trait rarely found among commercial agents and only latent among officials at labor exchanges. Likewise, the YWCA and many post-1870 domestic service reform organizations supplied reliable workers to both households and hotels. Employers disgusted with commercial offices also organized philanthropic ventures in hopes of managing their own cooperative agencies. The first such office appeared at New York City in 1825.

Finally, in their desperation to acquire servants, some employers stooped to theft. Unscrupulous persons bargained on the sly with servants of friends, neighbors, and strangers, hoping to entice workers into employment with promises of high wages and easy living. Some cases of theft were less blatant than others, being more nearly questions of etiquette than outright felonies. For example, was it proper for one employer to hire a girl who had left another employer of her own free will but over whom the two employers had previously competed? This was a common problem, and bad feelings were bound to result when the servant in question made a choice between the contending parties. Also, when were employers ethically free to approach a servant about a new position? Was it right to bid for the services of a worker who was on a leave of absence from her job but who was expected to return? Such instances barely skirted the borders of legality, and passions could be aroused when two employers believed they had equally valid claims to the same servant.

23. Friedrich Kapp, *Immigration and the Commissioners of Emigration of the State of New York* (New York: The Nation Press, 1870), 115–16, 238n; Charlotte G. O'Brien, "The Emigrant in New York," *Nineteenth Century*, XVI (1884), 537–38.

A well-documented case of conflicting claims is that of Lucius M. Boltwood of Hartford, Connecticut, versus Edward Dickinson of Amherst, Massachusetts. The servant in question, Maggie Maher, was a twenty-year-old Irish girl who had worked in the Boltwood family for several years. Maggie was happy with the Boltwoods, but in 1867 a series of family crises forced Maggie to return home to Amherst. She honestly intended to return to the Boltwoods, but in the midst of her family's troubles, Maggie was obliged to take a number of temporary jobs. One of those jobs was in the home of Edward Dickinson, father of the poet Emily Dickinson. That was when the trouble began.

After Maggie had been with the Dickinsons for a few weeks, Mr. Boltwood's parents, also of Amherst, found themselves in need of temporary help. Naturally, they turned to Maggie. But Maggie declined their summons, explaining that she felt duty-bound to remain with the Dickinsons for as long as they needed her. The Amherst Boltwoods were astonished not only at Maggie's refusal to serve them but because her refusal had implied that she would not now return to Hartford without Mr. Dickinson's consent. The Dickinsons and the Boltwoods never discussed this incident, but tensions began to build, and poor Maggie found herself in the midst of a furious tug-of-war. Maggie herself was emotionally torn between her loyalty to the Boltwoods and her promise to the Dickinsons. Told by the Amherst Boltwoods that they never wanted to see her again, Maggie sought to explain her predicament to the Hartford Boltwoods: "You know that I dont want to disapoint any person or Brake my word if i be Poor and working for my living. I will always try to be rite if [I] can let me be blamed as I will."[24]

A month later, Maggie was writing again to the Boltwoods, promising to return in a few months. She had been trying to find a replacement for herself, but Mr. Dickinson had refused to accept any substitutes. "Mr Dickinson said he would Pay me as much more wages soner then let me go," wrote Maggie, "so that I have desided to stay for the Preasant." She beseeched the Boltwoods not to blame her for failing to return. "If I would lave Now and go to you," she explained, "it would caus them [the Dickinsons] to be angry with us all so we will wait for a nother time. The[y] get very excited when you write to me for fere that [I] will go to you."[25]

24. Maggie Maher to Clarinda B. Boltwood, March 2, 1869, in Boltwood Family Papers.
25. Maggie Maher to Clarinda B. Boltwood, April 6, 1869, in Boltwood Family Papers.

After several months of such haggling, Mr. Boltwood became disgusted with the tyrannical Edward Dickinson. He attributed Maggie's prolonged absence to Dickinson's forbidding her to leave. "It is a speciman of the arrogance of the man," fumed Boltwood, "but he has no claim on Margaret whatever. She has lived with us for years. . . . It is nothing but impertinence on the part of Mr. Dickinson to try to brow beat & threaten her into staying with him." In the end Maggie remained with the Dickinsons. She did not, however, seem to suffer unduly from her captivity. She spent many years in the Dickinson household and became devoted to the family.[26]

Despite frequent occurrences, servant stealing remained socially unacceptable. Etiquette books sometimes included entire chapters discouraging this deplorable practice. Servants, readers were told, had a right to work wherever they could earn the highest wages, but negotiations for their services must be made openly, not behind their employers' backs. Furthermore, it was argued, stealing gave servants false impressions of proper behavior and inflated their already overblown egos. "Much of the discomfort and disturbance in our households springs from this evil spirit," maintained one authority, "making servants fickle and unfaithful, and their mistresses' life a burden." Ultimately, it was a "species of kidnapping" that went against God's law, "Thou shalt not covet." Still, the practice flourished, leading one wag to comment, "To 'all is fair in love and war' must be added 'and in servant hunting.'"[27]

Despite all of these resources, legitimate and otherwise, employers could not find enough good servants. One man's efforts to hire a cook-laundress typifies the perplexities. He was a suburbanite who, being unable to capture his quarry near home, went to the city to pursue the hunt. He stalked the streets, tracking down and interviewing likely candidates for the job who had been recommended by the city's intelligence offices. He walked six and one-half unproductive hours on the first day. Cooks were available, but they were either unsatisfactory to him or he to them. One refused to work in the suburbs, another

26. Lucius M. Boltwood to Clarinda B. Boltwood, June 24, 1869, in Boltwood Family Papers. For an outline of Maggie's career with the Boltwoods and Dickinsons, see Jay Leyda, "Miss Emily's Maggie," in *New World Writings* (3rd Mentor Selection; New York: New American Library, 1953), 255–67.

27. Beecher, *Motherly Talks*, 112–16; Managers of the Society for the Encouragement of Faithful Domestic Servants in New York, *First Annual Report* (New York: D. Fanshaw, 1826), 13; Frances A. Kellor, "The Intelligence Office," *Atlantic Monthly*, XCIV (October, 1904), 461.

wanted to work in a smaller family, still another would not wash clothes in addition to cooking. And so it went. He returned to his hotel footsore and exhausted. That evening he wrote a letter to his patiently waiting wife, vowing not to return home without the needed cook but explaining that his search would take longer than anticipated. Betraying his frustration, he whispered in a postscript, "Don't let the *servants* know there is any trouble in getting new ones." He was to the hunt next day—and the next. Finally, his diligence rewarded, he found a suitable woman. But alas, some curse seemed to haunt the fellow. He was suddenly struck down by fever and confined to his hotel room, unable to meet his new employee for the trip home. When he failed to appear at the scheduled time, she took another position.[28]

Americans obviously had problems. They required servants for several reasons, and yet good servants were scarce. The supply was not equal to the demand. Nor was this scarcity a simple numerical shortage. The ironic part about the servant "shortage" was the perpetual pool of unemployed workers. Most people could find servants, but they were often dissatisfied with what they found. This discontent had two explanations: the class consciousness of employers and their peculiar definition of a good servant. Employers were particular. They sought specific qualities in their servants, and only workers meeting those rigid standards could satisfy them. Their fastidiousness caused more trouble.

28. Henry Watson, Jr., to Sophia Watson, August 17, 20, 1860, in Henry Watson, Jr. Papers, Perkins Library, Duke University.

CHAPTER TWO

THE EYE OF THE BEHOLDER
Employers Define a Good Servant

Employers were at least partly to blame for the dearth of domestics. They erred, first of all, in their treatment of servants. Assuming servants to be reprobates and rebels, far too many employers were condescending and haughty. Many people were downright contemptuous, almost brutish, and even the best, most understanding of them recognized insurmountable "class" differences between masters and servants. Employers also erred by limiting the number of "good" servants by definition. *Good* meant more than being efficient; it implied a specific race, nationality, religion, and personality. No servant could be christened *good* without qualifying on each point. Further confusing the issue, employers defined each of these magic requirements in terms of their own backgrounds. Since few servants could meet all of their rigid standards, employers continued to regard service as a contemptible business and servants as misbegotten creatures.

Many employers narrowed their chances of obtaining and retaining good servants by their determination to maintain class lines. Although American social classes—defined by a hotchpotch of factors, including income, education, and religion—were comparatively more fluid and less visible than those of Europe, they were no less real. Americans were very sensitive about their social positions. Alert to the slightest hint of disrespect, they challenged the lordly airs of social superiors while jealously guarding their own social prerogatives against encroachment from below. Americans inherited many traditions from their British and European ancestors, but deference was not among them.

Nearly all employers believed in their servants' inferiority—social, intellectual, and otherwise. The stigma on domestic service and the traditional master-servant relationship made this the only logical view. If employers had once regarded servants as social equals, or if servants had once assumed such equality, the spell would have been broken, the system proved a fraud. To eliminate this danger, employers kept servants at a respectable social distance and demanded at least token subservience. Of course, insecure, callous, and power-crazed masters needed to lord it over a retinue of vassals, but most people only wanted to preserve a delicate social balance. The contrast between America's democratic political tradition and its less democratic social habits made this balance all the more precarious.

Employers differed, however, on the degree of vigor and the type of tactics to be used in defending class lines. One group, hoping to influence servants through reason, submerged its blatant class interests in a sincerely felt moral obligation. Most middle- and upper-class Americans were social conservatives who placed great stock in traditional moral values and class structure. They felt obligated to defend those values and class lines and believed that the survival of civilization depended upon their success or failure. One of their principal obligations was to direct the social and spiritual improvement of the nation's lower and, thus, morally depraved classes. Servants, of course, were part of this group, and so employers undertook to indoctrinate these "poor ignorant creatures" in middle-class moral values. Many housekeepers embarked upon this task with a sincere religious fervor. Determined to protect their families from the contagion of unclean minds and bodies, they quoted verses of Scripture for their servants' guidance, required their attendance at family prayer meetings, and counseled them in matters of personal cleanliness. "Ladies," who tended to confuse manners with morals, felt obliged by the "laws of etiquette" to impress the same lessons. In either case, employers saw no contradiction in describing servants as cattle in one breath and then going on to speak of them as human beings worthy of benevolence. Cattle, too, were God's creatures, and if lacking man's intelligence, were all the more to be pitied and cared for.

A second group, probably the majority, was more pragmatic. These people sought to preserve class distinctions, but they did so more nearly by instinct than from dedication to moral or social theory. True, a thousand servants affecting hundreds of homes could wreak havoc in a community and threaten revolt and decay in society generally, but in the heat of battle, most employers lost sight of the connection between this fact and the immediate crises of having their meals cooked and their clothes washed. Their view was narrow, some would say selfish, but it was all that circumstances allowed.

For a third group, those possessing some defect of character, those drained of benevolence by a string of unbearable servants, or those drawing their religious motivation from the Old Testament's wrathful Yahweh rather than from Jesus, old-fashioned discipline was the only way to deal with servants. Servants were so spoiled by high wages and notions of equality, believed these employers, that the only way to control them was by imposing an absolute dictatorship. Servants, after all, were servants; they always had been, and with God's blessing, they always would be. Rigid rules and strict discipline, even if they caused rebellion or resulted in the loss of a servant or two, were the only ways to acquire and retain good servants. One midwestern woman, for instance, believed her married daughter's servant problems resulted from lack of discipline. She reprimanded her daughter for treating her servants with "too much consideration." Even good servants, advised this concerned mother, must never be praised, lest they become "uppish." [1]

Yet disciplinarians did not consider themselves unjust. They appraised the problems rationally, considering their own demands and their servants' needs. If circumstances dictated that servants be treated sternly, so be it. Wrote a Staten Island housekeeper:

> The trouble with the servants is no new thing, but a persistent disregard of our rules regarding company, time of being in in the evening and of locking the house and retiring, (notwithstanding repeated reminders on my part). I feel it has gone quite far enough, though on many accounts I shall be very sorry to make a change, I think one thing or the other must be done, either they must conform to what are by no means unusually strict rules, or find some other place. I do not feel it right to them nor to myself and the children here either to go to bed myself, leaving the house open, with anything they may please going on in the kitchen below stairs, nor that I should be kept on watch for them

1. Elizabeth E. Stuart to William Baker, May 4, 1853, in Helen Stuart Mackay-Smith Marlatt (ed.), *Stuart Letters of Robert and Elizabeth Stuart and Their Children, 1819–1864* (2 vols.; New York: Harbor Press, 1961), I, 523–24.

night after night any where from 10.30 to 12 o'clock. I think for the proper and peaceful running of the household it is important such rules be observed.[2]

Whatever their perspective on the problems, employers continually reminded servants of their lowly position. The means of accomplishing this were usually silent, even symbolic, but the declaration was unmistakable: the social abyss between master and servant must not be bridged. For example, servants must use crockery and ironware to eat their meals, not china and silver. They must never, whatever their desires, eat meals with the family. Their proper place was in the kitchen. Livery for men and uniforms for women were required in all upper-class households. Even some middle-class employers dressed female servants in a "modest" black dress and white cap to insure that a servant was not "mistaken for a member of the family." If need be, nearly all employers used these and similarly subtle devices to remind servants of their "place."[3]

Employers enforced social distinctions outside the home, too. For example, employer and servant did not mingle socially. Employers avoided public entertainments attended by their servants, and servants were supposed to do likewise. This was an unstated rule to which both employers and servants were expected to conform. "I suppose nothing is ever said about it," confessed one employer, "but it is always an understood thing that the lady and the girl do not know each other outside." For an employer to consort openly with a servant or, the ultimate horror, to marry one was unforgivable. Rumors of such affairs were scandalous and hoped to be incorrect. If confirmed, prayers were said for the children who might suffer the disgrace of such a union. Some question even existed about whether a gentleman should offer his seat to a female servant on a public conveyance.[4]

Employers also tried to maintain a dress code among servants, es-

2. Charlotte E. Tanner to Mary Williams, February 9, 1897, in Josiah Butler Williams Family Papers, Collection of Regional History, Cornell University.
3. For example, see Misses Mendall and Hosmer, *Notes of Travel and Life* (New York: Privately printed, 1854), 148–49; "Domestic Service," *Old and New*, VI (September, 1872), 365; Alden W. Quimby, "The Housekeeper's Stone," *Forum*, XXXI (June, 1901), 455.
4. Quoted in Lillian Pettengill, *Toilers of the Home: The Record of a College Woman's Experience as a Domestic Servant* (New York: Doubleday, Page, and Co., 1903), 374–76; Harold Earl Hammond (ed.), *Diary of a Union Lady, 1861–1865* (New York: Funk & Wagnalls, 1962), 93–94; Sarah L. Wadley Diaries (MS in Southern Historical Collection, Library of the University of North Carolina at Chapel Hill), I, 91; Elizabeth Drexel

pecially female servants, but servant girls were infatuated by fashionable dress. Fancy clothes made girls feel elegant and gave them a sense of equality with employers. This upset employers. They accused servants of "wasteful and disgraceful extravagance," of "squandering" their money on "finery" when they should have been buying "necessities," by which employers meant such unglamorous apparel as underclothes, aprons, and thick-soled shoes.[5] Servants' pathetic attempts at imitation threatened the security of their employers' own hard-earned social positions. To have kitchen maids dressing like a banker's wife diluted every vestige of middle-class respectability and prestige. What was the use of striving for economic and social success if servants acted and looked like their social betters? One might just as well give up the fight and enjoy the easy, carefree life (so it seemed to employers) of servants.

Perhaps the most fascinating attempt to impress servants with class distinctions involved the architecture of American houses. The American "house" was divided in order to minimize contact between employers and servants, to insulate as much as possible the American "home." Those parts of the house occupied by servants were physically isolated from family compartments so that employers and servants formed "two separate communities." Back entrances, back stairways, bedrooms tucked away in rear portions of houses and attics, and service areas partitioned from living quarters by halls, pantries, and doors allowed servants to travel inconspicuously from cellar to attic and to enter and leave a house unseen. Some servants, such as scullery maids, never entered family quarters, for they worked in isolation and ate and slept in nooks and crannies reserved for themselves and the household mice. Such segregation was more easily accomplished in mansions than in middle-class households. Wealthy employers could exile servants to entirely disconnected wings. But in all cases, separation was deemed necessary for the "concealment of those aspects of domestic life which should be concealed." Even in modest-sized farm

Lehr, *"King Lehr" and the Gilded Age* (Philadelphia: J. B. Lippincott, 1935), 110–11; Blaine Edward McKinley, " 'Strangers in the Gates': Employer Reactions Towards Domestic Servants in America, 1825–1875" (Ph.D. dissertation, Michigan State University, 1969), 207–10.
    5. H. E. Scudder (ed.), *Recollections of Samuel Breck* (Philadelphia: Porter and Coates, 1877), 298–99; William A. Alcott, *The Young Wife; or, Duties of Women in the Marriage Relation* (New York: J. C. Derby, 1837, 1855), 222–24; Sarah J. Hale, *Manners; or, Happy Homes and Good Society All the Year Round* (Boston: J. E. Tilton and Co., 1868), 236–43; Polly Sprague, "The Hired Girl in the Home," *Ladies' Home Journal*, XXXIII (September, 1916), 54.

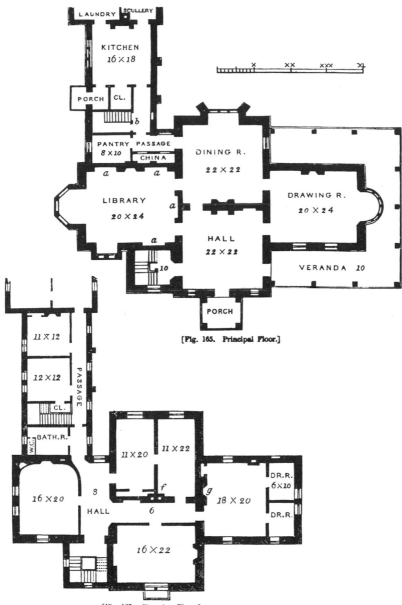

[Fig. 165. Principal Floor.]

[Fig. 167. Chamber Floor.]

This design by Andrew Jackson Downing provides an excellent example of
how servants were separated from their employers. The house includes what
is very nearly a servants' wing with bedrooms directly above the kitchen area.
Andrew Jackson Downing, *The Architecture of Country Houses* (New York: D. Appleton and Co.,
1850).

houses, the problem of what to do with the hired help was considered "a knotty one."[6]

The positioning of kitchen and dining room was one of the most serious considerations.[7] Ideally, the kitchen was located in a separate wing of the house, connected to family quarters by a long passageway. In southern homes, especially in rural areas, the problem was solved by locating the kitchen in a separate building. Basement kitchens characterized many urban houses for much of the nineteenth century, with dining rooms one floor above. In crowded cities, where land prices, building costs, and taxes allowed only the well-to-do to construct even modest-sized houses, builders had to use all available space. The arrangement provided a safe, natural separation of servants and family. Some kitchens appeared on the first floor by 1840, but the change was slow. If kitchen and dining room were adjacent, precautions were taken. The most widespread solution was to divide kitchen and dining room by means of a butler's pantry or short hallway, closed off at the kitchen by a swinging door. A sliding panel between dining room and pantry or kitchen was another answer. This effectively spared employers the kitchen's indelicate environment and preserved family privacy from intrusion by its coarse inhabitants. Having the kitchen within sight was more efficient and permitted closer surveillance of servants, but employers disliked the "occasionally annoying . . . sound, sight, and smells" of the kitchen intruding upon their meals. A butler's pantry also guarded against servants' assumed dishonesty and carelessness by serving as a way station between dining room and kitchen. Unlike the kitchen pantry, which was

6. James M. White, "Architecture of Country Houses," *American Kitchen Magazine*, XVII (January, 1902), 135–37; Isabel Bevier, *The House: Its Plan, Decoration, and Care* (Chicago: American School of Economics, 1907), 56–57; Harry W. Desmond and Herbert Croly, *Stately Homes in America: From Colonial Times to the Present Day* (New York: D. Appleton and Co., 1903), 510–15; David H. Jacques, *The House: A Manual of Rural Architecture* (New York: George E. and F. E. Woodward, 1867), 96; Jeanne Hunnicutt Delgado (ed.), "Nellie Kedzie Jone's Advice to Farm Women: Letters from Wisconsin, 1912–1916," *Wisconsin Magazine of History*, LVII (1973), 12. For evidence that architects accepted popular ideas about servants and the home, see Henry W. Cleaveland, William Backus, and Samuel D. Backus, *Village and Farm Cottages* (New York: D. Appleton and Co., 1856), 1–4; and Eugene C. Gardner, *Illustrated Homes: A Series of Papers Describing Real Homes and Real People* (Boston: James R. Osgood and Co., 1875), 150–51.

7. Examples of this and of all the architectural innovations described in the following pages may be found in the dozens of architectural handbooks that appeared during the century. A helpful sampling is provided in the Bibliographical Essay. Also helpful is McKinley, "'Strangers in the Gates,'" 236–65.

simply a large closet for storage of provisions, the butler's pantry was a workshop. There, salads were made, wines and liquors decanted, food transferred from pot to plate, and china, silverware, and crystal washed and stored. The butler's pantry made it unnecessary to send china, silver, glass, and "little delicacies of the larder" to the kitchen. These valuables remained under the eye of employers or a trusted servant, and the risk of theft or breakage was reduced.[8]

A Detroit housekeeper went even further. The woman's property was utterly exposed to the obnoxious sights and sounds of her neighbor's kitchen and back porch. During warm weather, open windows made this a genuine "nuisance" and sometimes offended delicate sensibilities. As she described it: "In the afternoons the servants would take their sewing & sit out in the gallery & occasionally have a haw or two. . . . Then on 'Washing & Ironing Day' all was done under our supervision—every piece be they what they might, were displayed to us and our guests." On one particularly humid July afternoon, the servants became so "loud & impertinently boisterous" that the woman was forced to close her windows. That was the last straw. She ordered a high fence erected between the houses "to shut out the appearance as well as the nuisance." But that was not the end. She soon found it necessary to add shutters to her windows, to lay a walk alongside the fence, and to modify the fence itself. In the end, she paid eighty-five dollars for her privacy.[9]

Employers shielded themselves from the daily comings and goings of servants, too. Servants, for instance, always entered and left the house through a service entrance, which was usually at the rear or side of the house, although in many townhouses it was located beneath the front stoop. In any case, it opened into the kitchen or an adjacent hallway, thus lessening the family's risk of undesired encounters. Employers also designated back stairs for servants' use. These were not found in the average townhouse before about 1850, but thereafter, the growing size of American houses and the need for privacy made them indispensable. At the very bottom or the very top of back stairways one found servants' living quarters. Attic and cellar commonly served as sleeping space in middle-class households. Even large houses rarely

8. Andrew Jackson Downing, *Cottage Residences, Rural Architecture, and Landscape Gardening* (New York: D. Appleton and Co., 1847), 2–4, 52, 130.
9. Elizabeth E. Stuart to Kate Baker, July 6, July 29, 1850, both in Marlatt (ed.), *Stuart Letters*, I, 99–100, 113. For the solution of an equally desperate property owner, see New York *Times*, March 30, 1879, p. 9.

included rooms meant expressly for servants, and if they did, the rooms were isolated aft. If on the same floor as family chambers, servants' bedrooms were placed, whenever possible, at the far end of the hall, eliminating the need for servants to pass through family quarters. All such arrangements narrowed the chances of intrusion upon the family.

An interesting twist to this situation was the housing of black servants. Most blacks lived outside of their employers' homes. In the South this tradition had originated during slavery. Southerners in plantation house and townhouse alike discovered that the best way to protect themselves from inconvenience and annoyance was to keep as few servants as possible—usually only body servants—in the house overnight. The same situation existed wherever blacks were employed, although in the North unmarried black girls seem to have lived-in more frequently than those of the South. The system was very convenient for employers since it significantly reduced the problems of separation. The only potential drawback was the lack of employer supervision over servants, but this danger was not so great as it seems. Even though many black servants lived in their own homes or with their parents, they usually remained within easy reach of their employers. In rural areas they might live as tenants or sharecroppers on their employers' land or, perhaps, reside in outbuildings very near the main house. In cities black servants often lived in shanties built behind their employers' houses like the extended wings of a mansion. This detachment gave many black servants an unusual degree of freedom during their off-duty hours, but it did not effectively reduce employer control.[10]

Thus, servants were in the household but not of it; they were, in the language of a popular, sympathetic description of the servant's plight, "strangers within the gates." Employers regarded servants as "aliens" and "sphinxes," unknown and unknowable. At times, this was literally

10. Ira Berlin, *Slaves Without Masters: The Free Negro in the Antebellum South* (New York: Pantheon Books, 1974), 251; Howard N. Rabinowitz, *Race Relations in the Urban South, 1865–1890* (New York: Oxford University Press, 1978), 113, 119; From Harriet Ware, April 29, 1862, in Elizabeth Ware Pearson (ed.), *Letters from Port Royal, 1862–1868* (Boston: W. B. Clarke, 1906), 23–24; Robert Somers, *The Southern States Since the War, 1870–1871* (University: University of Alabama Press, 1965), 118–119; Isabel Eaton, "Special Report on Negro Domestic Service in the Seventh Ward Philadelphia," in W. E. B. DuBois, *The Philadelphia Negro: A Social Study* (New York: Benjamin Blom, 1899), 454–55; Mary White Ovington, "The Colored Woman in Domestic Service in New York City," *Bulletin of Inter-Municipal Committee on Household Research*, I (May, 1905), 10.

true. Immigrant domestics, often so different in dress, customs, and language from Americans, made employers nervous, apprehensive, and suspicious. The same was true when lower-class Americans, totally unfamiliar with middle-class customs and manners, were employed. One historian has maintained that, because most southern black servants lived outside of their employers' homes, "the presence of black servants did not represent an intrusion into the privacy of the family" and that southern whites "did not experience any discomfort or anxiety at the presence of 'strangers within the gates.'" It is true that fewer cultural traditions stood between whites and blacks in the South than was the case with northerners and many immigrant servants, although the differences between racism and xenophobia are few. It is also true that most southern employers preferred black labor to white labor. But this does not mean that southern employers were any less dedicated to keeping servants in their place than were northerners. Employers always accepted servants on a trial basis, taking time to evaluate them as workers and as people. Yet, given their preconceptions and prejudices, it was nearly impossible for them to regard servants as equals. The very fact that people expected servants to discharge duties that they had neither the time nor desire to perform for themselves established a social barrier. Neither employers nor servants were to blame for this situation; it was merely a fact of American life. The home was the "most exclusive institution in the world" and had no place for strangers, aliens, and sphinxes. Good servants were expected to accept this fact.[11]

Employers limited the possibilities of finding good servants in other ways, too. Rather than allowing *good* service to mean *efficient* service, employers demanded numerous provisos and amendments. Efficiency was important, of course, and many workers were disqualified on that score alone, but efficiency dwelled in the eye of the beholder. Each housekeeper had her unique method of operating a household, which

11. Emily L. Watkins to Mary Watkins, May 17, 1854, in Abiathar and Emily L. Watkins Papers, Manuscripts and Archives Division, New York Public Library, Astor, Lenox, and Tilden Foundations; Nicholas B. Wainwright (ed.), *A Philadelphia Perspective: The Diary of Sidney George Fisher Covering the Years 1834–1871* (Philadelphia: Historical Society of Pennsylvania, 1967), 532; "The Stranger in the Gates," *Harper's Bazar*, VI (July 19, 1873), 450; "The Sphinx in the Household," *Scribner's Magazine*, XLIX (September, 1911), 379–80; Helen Ekin Starrett, "The Housekeeping of the Future," *Forum*, VIII (September, 1889), 111–12; David M. Katzman, *Seven Days a Week: Women and Domestic Service in Industrializing America* (New York: Oxford University Press, 1978), 200.

shaped her individual image of the perfect servant. Workers unable or unwilling to conform to a particular housekeeper's methods, standards, and idiosyncracies were cast off. Servants who may have delighted one person were considered incompetent by another. Some employers deemed even well-trained foreign servants worthless if they were unfamiliar with American modes of housekeeping. Likewise, native servants going from one part of the country to another might experience difficulties. This was true, for example, of southern Negroes going North, where household management was "so radically different." Even competent workers could be accused of laziness, indifference, and carelessness. Servants, said employers, were never in a hurry. They were always going, never arriving. They seemed to be in a perpetual trance, conjuring up new ways of avoiding work. Many became practiced "eye servants," "pleasant, knowing, and doing as little as may be," and that little only when employers were watching.[12]

Yet, at the same time, employers disliked changing servants, especially people to whom they had grown accustomed. They fired servants with hesitancy and grew perturbed when servants left of their own accord. Because training new servants was tiresome, employers often paid wages they could ill afford and endured behavior they abhorred in order to keep even mediocre workers. Finding servants who answered one's requirements was difficult, and employers always feared going from bad to worse. Ironically, this also explains why many employers were willing to hire "green," inexperienced girls. They hoped that if a girl was docile, had a "good disposition and a reasonable degree of handiness," she might be made into a good servant. In other words, employers often assumed that they would have to create their servants, molding them to fit personal needs.[13]

12. Mrs. Clavers [Caroline Matilda Kirkland], *A New Home—Who'll Follow Me?* (New York: C. S. Francis, 1839), 73; A. A. B. to Eleanor A. Whiteside, February 11, [1869], in Shattuck Family Papers, Massachusetts Historical Society; Anna L. Williams to Elizabeth F. Camp, May 5, 1890, in Camp Family Papers, Collection of Regional History, Cornell University; Mrs. Henry Ward Beecher, *Motherly Talks with Young Housekeepers* (New York: J. B. Ford and Co., 1873), 248–49; Frances A. Kellor, "Assisted Emigration from the South," *Charities*, XV (October 7, 1905), 12–13; Henry Dana Ward Diary, 1850–57 (MS in Manuscripts and Archives Division, New York Public Library, Astor, Lenox, and Tilden Foundations), June 10, 1855, April 26, 1856.

13. Wainwright (ed.), *A Philadelphia Perspective*, 524; E. A. Williams to Clarinda B. Boltwood, October 9, 1871, in Boltwood Family Papers, Burton Historical Collection, Detroit Public Library; Evelyn Ordway to Lucy M. Salmon, March 10, 1889, in Lucy Maynard Salmon Papers, Vassar College Library; Catherine E. Beecher and Harriet B. Stowe, *The American Woman's Home; or, Principles of Domestic Economy* (New York: J. B. Ford and Co., 1869), 315–16; To Dear Sister, June 7, 1866, in David Weeks and Family Papers, State Department of Archives and History, Louisiana State University.

The waiter at this expensive dinner party seems intent on proving the employer adage that servants were *always* getting in the way.
Courtesy of the Burton Historical Collection of the Detroit Public Library.

Good servants also had to play the role of humble subordinate. Employers wanted obedient workers, people contented with their place in the Great Chain of Being. Should servants prove willing and dutiful, much could be forgiven. They may have been terrible cooks or abominable waiters, but if submissive and smiling, they were retained and called "good." On the other hand, if obedience was lacking, servants could be wizards of the household arts yet be dismissed overnight.[14]

14. The fact that efficiency was not enough is illustrated by a survey of 574 employers taken about 1900. Even though 71.4 percent said that their servants gave "good" to "excellent" service, 67.6 percent complained that it was "difficult" to "impossible" to hire "competent" workers. Gail Laughlin, "Domestic Service," in *Report of the United States*

Degrees existed in this demand for obedience. Some employers were satisfied with quiet, polite, well-intentioned, pleasant servants. An Albany woman seemed happy with a girl who was "cheerful" and wore a "pleasant face." One slow, careless maid was deemed a good servant because she was "honest, sweet tempered, patient, . . . very respectful in her manners, and respectable in her ways." Servants so described often had nothing else to recommend them, but their docility appealed to harried housekeepers. Such servants may be termed "but" servants: "She is sluggish & slow-motioned—but decent & cleanly & honest." "Nancy is . . . not skilled, but clean civil & well meaning." Employers so easily satisfied must have known what truly bad servants were like. Other people, more stringent in their demands, sought not pleasantness, but deference; not politeness, but homage. These employers distrusted excessively independent or clever servants. They wanted dull, unimaginative drudges who performed their work with no questions asked. Thinking servants were apt to be overly familiar, blurring class lines. One woman admitted that her maid was efficient and swore that she would not exchange her for any other worker in the neighborhood. Yet the woman also thought her servant too "naturally independent." She would have preferred "some one not quite so *smart* and more kind and retiring."[15]

Religious, ethnic, and racial preferences further defined a good servant. Here, caprice played a role, for taste, prejudice, and fashion influenced the popularity of one race or nationality over another. Heated debates raged over which races and nationalities made the best servants, but most Americans wanted native-white Protestants. This was not so vital in hotels since the owner and his guests did not actually live with the help, but even so, some owners sponsored "Americanization" programs for alien employees. In private households, most of them Anglo-Saxon Protestant homes where, like it or not, servants lived in intimate contact with the family, it became highly desirable to

---

Industrial Commission on the Relations and Conditions of Capital and Labor (19 vols.; Washington, D.C.: Government Printing Office, 1901), XIV, 751–53.

15. Martha Chauncey to Mary Williams, August 3, 1885, in Williams Family Papers; Eliza DeRosset to Katherine Meares, October 1, 1857, in DeRosset Family Papers, Southern Historical Collection, Library of the University of North Carolina at Chapel Hill; Ward Diary, May 4, 1850; Cornelia P. Spencer to Fanny Phillips, June 14, 1868, in Cornelia Phillips Spencer Papers, Southern Historical Collection, Library of the University of North Carolina at Chapel Hill; Wainwright (ed.), *A Philadelphia Perspective*, 527; Mrs. D. W. Fiske to Hannah Terry, December 1 [1838], in Boltwood Family Papers. See also To Sister, April 6, 1868, in Weeks and Family Papers.

have servants of similar background. When employers were not Anglo-Saxon or Protestant, they often preferred servants of their own
nationality or religion.[16] Unfortunately for the majority, native-white
Protestants willing to work as servants were hard to find and likely to
be excessively arrogant when obtained. Most employers, therefore,
settled for Protestants of any available nationality.

Protestants, by American definition, were modest, sober, chaste,
cleanly, and hardworking, the very qualities demanded by employers.
Employers frequently described servants in terms of religion, recom-
mending a "protestant girl" to a friend, or rejoicing when successfully
hiring an "Irish Protestant," as though religion somehow enhanced a
servant's abilities. They generally asked prospective servants their religion, and employment bureau applications invariably demanded a response to this key question. Servants, aware of this Protestant preference, often asserted in newspaper advertisements that they were
among the blessed.[17]

Protestant demand stemmed from a strong anti-Catholic prejudice
that far exceeded petty distinctions between good and bad servants. It
was part of the widespread nativism that has bedeviled the nation in
varying degrees throughout its history. Reaching its peak in the
mid–nineteenth century, prejudice against Catholic servants continued into the twentieth century. Catholic servants could not be
trusted. They were spies of the Pope sent to infiltrate American homes
and to brainwash American children in a seemingly never-ending plot
to make the United States a papal province. Irish immigrants bore the
brunt of this suspicion, but only because there were so many of them.
Catholic Germans, French, and Swiss were equally discriminated
against, although perhaps less vehemently.

16. Frank W. Bering, "Giving Orders in English," *Hotel Management*, I (March,
1922), 85–86; Veronica Frank to Pastor Frank, July, 1854, in Louis F. Frank (comp.),
*German-American Pioneers in Wisconsin and Michigan: The Frank-Kerler Letters,
1849–1864*, trans. Margaret Wolff, ed. Harry H. Anderson (Milwaukee: Milwaukee
County Historical Society, 1971), 296; Irving Howe, *World of Our Fathers* (New York:
Harcourt Brace Jovanovich, 1976), 268–69.

17. Mrs. A. Porter to Mary Williams, August 8, 1848, Martha Chauncey to Mary
Williams, September 10, 1855, Mary Williams to Charlotte E. Tanner, June [1876?], all
in Williams Family Papers; Annie Dewey to Lucy M. Salmon, November 11, 1889, in
Salmon papers; Pettengill, *Toilers of the Home*, 8, 121, 243; Employment Bureau of
Boston YWCA application form (MS dated 189_ in Salmon Papers). For examples of
both employer and employee ads, see New York *Tribune*, January 20, 1846, March 4,
1876, Chicago *Tribune*, May 7, 1858, January 24, 1866, New York *Times*, January 6,
1880.

Irish Catholics were accused of being dirty, greasy, uneducated, undisciplined, immoral, and a host of other unpleasantries. Not one in one hundred was capable of learning the intricacies of domestic service or of adjusting to life in a civilized, Christian home (Catholics were not Christians). "They defile, they corrupt, they encourage one another in sin," sputtered one Presbyterian minister with a household flock of Irish servants, "and, if they have any scruple of conscience, by confession to the priest, he puts all right." "Who is sufficient for these things," asked a weary housekeeper facing the task of converting a Catholic girl into a respectable citizen and tolerable servant. "Our holliest [sic] wisest Missionaries say 'tis easier to go to the Heathen than to the Catholics."[18]

The Irish had defenders, but they were almost defensive in pointing out Irish virtues and in trying to ignore their Catholicism. The biggest plus for the Irish was their pleasantness; they were perfect "but" servants. The stereotype of dirty, ignorant Paddy and Bridget was often overshadowed by that of the genial, fun-loving lad and lass who attracted sympathy and won hearts wherever they went. The Irish were awkward and unrefined, admitted one defender, but they were "invincibly good-natured" and had "the merit of good intentions, plenty of mother wit, and an ever amusing faculty of blarney."[19]

The most notable exception to the preference for white servants was in the South. The majority of American blacks lived in the South, where they had their own niche in history and tradition and where, regardless of their level of efficiency, they remained the primary source of domestic labor. This only made sense, for servants were drawn from a community's lowest social and economic classes. In the South, this meant Negroes. Then too, the threat to white supremacy loomed larger in the South than elsewhere in the United States. Consequently, it was thought unwise to have southern whites working in menial, traditionally black occupations. Even after the Civil War, when many more southerners than previously experimented with white servants, employers felt uncomfortable with menials of their own color. "Many of us are trying white servants," explained a North Carolina woman, "but they are not likely to become popular with the

18. Ward Diary, November 5, 1854, June 10, 1855; Elizabeth E. Stuart to Kate Baker, August 21, 1852, in Marlatt (ed.), *Stuart Letters*, I, 395.
19. Thomas Low Nichols, *Forty Years of American Life* (2 vols.; London: John Maxwell and Company, 1864), II, 10.

present generation of mistresses. We don't know how to treat them as servants, nor where to put them; neither do they themselves know where to stand."[20]

But the Chinese were the real losers. They were not only further from being Protestant or possessing Protestant virtues than even the Irish, they were the wrong color, wore funny clothes, spoke an unknown language, and ate impossible food. Negroes, if the wrong color, were at least Protestant and native-born. Though few in number before the Civil War and confined largely to the area west of the Rocky Mountains, the Chinese, by 1870, were disdained throughout the nation as "barbarians," whose chief attributes were "their fitness for servile duties and their want of social ambition." The anti-Chinese agitation of the 1870s and 1880s proved more intense than even that against Catholics, and the Chinese Exclusion Act, which capped this period of raging xenophobia, was the only antiimmigration legislation passed against a specific nationality before 1920. Oddly enough, Americans did not display this same prejudice against the Japanese, perhaps because there were fewer of them in the United States. Americans believed the Japanese to be more intelligent, moral, and ambitious than the Chinese.[21]

Like the Irish, the Chinese had their defenders, but they were none too complimentary. Chinese "imitativeness" was one of their most admirable traits. Unlike the slow, dull-witted Irish, the Chinese learned household duties quickly and never forgot them. They performed their work with meticulousness and machinelike efficiency. Equally praiseworthy was their docility. Chinese servants performed their work when, where, and as they were told without question. They bore "the instinct of centuries of submission" and were so "bred in servility" that they could hardly "fail in respect." They, like the Irish and the Negro, served the very useful function of preserving traditional master-ser-

20. Richard C. Wade, *Slavery in the Cities: The South, 1820–1860* (New York: Oxford University Press, 1964), 274; Cornelia P. Spencer, "Hiring-Time," *North Carolina Presbyterian*, January 13, 1869, and "Young Ladies' Column," *North Carolina Presbyterian*, August 31, 1870. See also Julian Ralph, *Dixie; or, Southern Scenes and Sketches* (New York: Harper and Brothers, 1897), 385–87.
21. Stuart Creighton Miller, *The Unwelcome Immigrant: The American Image of the Chinese, 1765–1882* (Berkeley: University of California Press, 1969), 168; Harriet Prescott Spofford, *The Servant Girl Question* (Boston: Houghton Mifflin, 1881), 164–81; Helen Starr, "The Pacific Coast Makes Ready," *Collier's Magazine*, LI (May 10, 1913), 21, 24.

vant relationships. "John Chinaman" was so inferior to white Protestant employers that the latter were protected from "imposition" and reassured of their social position.[22]

Insofar as other nationalities were concerned, a generally recognized hierarchy in the order of English, Scots, Scandinavians, Germans, Welsh, and Swiss existed, but there was no clear preference. Newspaper advertisements indicated the variety. Servants boasted of their nationality in personal ads, just as they did of their Protestantism, whenever they thought it would earn them a job. Intelligence offices also made known their wide selections of available nationalities. "Abundance of Good Servants," announced a New York agency in 1863; "English, German, Irish, Scotch, American, and Protestant help, civil and capable, to suit all. Also small Girls. Good places every day." Language differences could be a drawback, but this was generally outweighed by good recommendations or crying need. Here again, intelligence offices catered to public demand by offering "a great abundance and variety of spoken languages."[23]

Various miscellaneous attributes helped round out the perfect servant. Physique was important to some employers. Different jobs required different body types. Among the "smart set" of the post-1870s, for instance, an imposing looking butler was a must. A "good" five-foot, three-hundred-pound, balding butler was impossible. Nor did anyone want an anemic washerwoman. A strong back, broad shoulders, and an extra ration of stamina were necessary in the days before automatic washing machines became widespread. On the other hand, no one wanted a squat, thickset chambermaid; tall, comely ones were required in wealthy homes. Good health was a related and vital characteristic. One of the reasons people hired servants was to save their own health. It thus served no purpose to have domestics who were continually ill and missing work.

Yet, despite the presence of every conceivable size, shape, race, and religion among servants, many Americans were dissatisfied and dismally pessimistic about the future of domestic service in the United States. Black, white, or yellow, all seemed equally inefficient; none

22. Mary E. Blake, *On the Wing: Rambling Notes of a Trip to the Pacific* (Boston: Lee and Shepard, 1883), 176; C. C. Coffin, "China in Our Kitchens," *Atlantic Monthly,* XXIII (June, 1869), 750; *Report on Chinese Immigration, Senate Reports,* 44th Cong., 2nd sess., no. 689, p. 48. This report contains mixed opinions concerning the honesty, cleanliness, and morality of Chinese servants.
23. New York *Tribune,* April 24, March 16, 1863.

A cook and a waitress of the most reliable and esteemed Irish type

One of the few native American houseworkers to be found in these days. "Margaret" is a hired housekeeper. The picture at the side is only an artist's fancy, and has nothing to do with the case. The women whose portraits are shown are not that kind

Scotch lassies make excellent nurses and are generally intelligent and steady in all kinds of domestic service

These photos from *Good Housekeeping* illustrate American stereotypes of servants. They include two Irish girls of the reliable and educated variety, a rare native-white American, and an "intelligent and steady" Scots lassie.
Good Housekeeping, LV (September, 1912).

was congenial or capable of becoming a member of "a real household." Finding good servants was likened to "buying tickets in a lottery."[24] Whichever way employers turned, they met ignorance, arrogance, and immorality. Not only did the servant shortage make nonsense of Adam Smith's law of supply and demand, it proved Thomas Malthus had been capricious in selecting the most dismal science.

Employers had largely themselves to blame for the servant shortage, the gravest of their servant problems. Their impossibly high and arbitrary standards narrowed the chances of finding good servants. Their undisguised haughtiness alienated many who might otherwise have served them long and faithfully. At times, employers were justified in their prejudices. Some servants were pretty scurvy characters. But such prejudices were usually unfounded, and employers only aggravated their problems by persisting in them. Employers made service an undesirable occupation. They made more odious the already tainted image of service. In other words, they helped to create the servants' side of the servant problems.

24. Goldwin Smith, "The Passing of the Household," *Independent*, LIX (August 24, 1905), 424; Beecher, *Motherly Talks*, 250.

CHAPTER THREE

SERVANTS, SERVANTS EVERYWHERE
A Statistical Description

From an objective point of view, talk of a servant shortage was ridiculous. The number of servants was staggering, rising from about 40,000 in 1800 to nearly 2,300,000 by 1910. Servants represented 5 to 6 percent of the total labor force during the first half of the nineteenth century, a figure that crept to 7 percent in 1860, when the servant force counted 600,000 strong. By 1870 the figure was 8 percent, the addition of freed southern slaves helping to boost the total number of servants to one million. Service was especially important as a female occupation, for 90 percent of all servants were women, and until 1870, at least 50 percent of America's gainfully employed women were servants. Only after 1890 did service seriously decline as a female occupation.[1] Within this growing work force, some aspects of service, such as the geographic distribution of servants, the type of people who became servants, and reasons for entering service, remained fairly constant. Some things, however, particularly the personal characteristics of the typical servant, changed. After 1870 the race, nationality, age, and marital status of the average servant evolved in order to meet new needs and demands. A description of what changed and what remained the same is revealing.

1. See Chapter One, Note 2. Statistical description of the servant force is difficult because of a lack of reliable data. For the problems involved, see the Bibliographical Essay and George J. Stigler, *Domestic Servants in the United States, 1900–1940*, Occasional Paper No. 24 of the National Bureau of Economic Research (New York: National Bureau of Economic Research, 1946), 37–40.

Servants, like most of their employers, were urban creatures. Throughout the period 1800 to 1920, well over half of the nation's servants worked in cities. Before the Civil War, this meant that most servants were employed east of the Mississippi River, many of them along the Atlantic coast. The growth of western cities like Saint Louis, Chicago, Denver, and San Francisco broadened the scope of servant employment, and although the demand for servants in western cities never equaled that of the East, it indicated the pattern. America's servant-employing class was an urban class, and it would remain so. Most of the nation's rich and "lesser rich" earned their incomes from urban-oriented occupations. Merchants, financiers, industrialists, professional men, and large speculators were urbanites, living and spending their money in cities. As villages became towns and towns blossomed into cities, their inhabitants adopted well-established social traditions and affectations. As more Americans of comfortable means began enjoying the pleasures of civilized life, the demand for servants kept pace. Likewise, commercial and resort centers required hundreds of waiters, porters, cooks, and chambermaids in dozens of boarding-houses and hotels.

A few statistics will illustrate this pattern. In 1845 the citizens of Boston enjoyed the benefit of one servant for every four families. This ratio was far above the national figure of one to ten. By 1870 when the national ratio was one to eight, Bostonians could boast of one servant for every three and one-half families, the highest ratio of any northern city. Elsewhere, during that same year, New York City and Philadelphia managed one-to-four and one-to-five ratios, respectively. Western cities were doing equally well, as demonstrated by Chicago (1 : 5), Saint Louis (1 : 6), and San Francisco (1 : 4). Southern cities had the nation's highest servant-family ratios, as evidenced by Charleston (1 : 2), New Orleans (1 : 3), and Baltimore (1 : 4). This urban trend continued into the 1920s.[2]

But the way a city earned its money was important, too. Where manufacturing provided the basis of a city's economy, mere population was deceiving. Even cities with high per capita incomes might utilize few servants if they were blue collar towns. Places like Lowell, Fall River, Camden, Paterson, and Pittsburgh emerged as industrial-manufacturing towns as the nineteenth century progressed. All of these

2. Lemuel Shattuck, *Report to the Committee of the City Council Appointed to Obtain the Census of Boston for the Year 1845* (Boston: n.p., 1846), 84. Shattuck's statistics do not include hotel servants. See Chapter One, Note 2.

towns had lower percentages of servants per family than nonindustrial cities with similar sized populations and incomes. The most dramatic demonstration of this is Detroit. In 1880 one servant was available to every six Detroit families. This ratio compared favorably with other midwestern cities like Chicago and Cincinnati, and it was well above the national ratio of one to nine. But upon introduction of the automobile industry, Detroit's demand for servants plunged more rapidly than that of any other major American city. By 1920 when it claimed the nation's largest industrial population, the Motor City could muster only one servant for every twenty-one families, well below the national ratio of one to sixteen.[3]

As to the personal characteristics of servants, several factors must be considered. Racially and ethnically, servants were a mixed lot, but they could be classified in four racial-ethnic groups: native whites of native parentage, native whites of foreign or mixed parentage, foreign born, and native blacks. Yet, because native whites of foreign parentage were considered immigrants, it is convenient to speak of only three groups: "Americans," immigrants, and Negroes. The size of each group fluctuated in time and place, but from at least the mid-1840s until 1920, first- and second-generation immigrants had the edge in numbers. The striking characteristic shared by the majority of these people, regardless of race or nationality, was their lower-class origins. They were cultural and racial nonconformists, social outcasts, and economic misfits who could not obtain respectable employment.

Before 1870 probably three-fourths of the servants outside the slave states were white. It is notable that before 1840 a large number of these white servants were native Americans. Working most often in small towns and rural areas, where blacks and immigrants were fewer than in cities, native-white girls "hired out" to neighboring families in order to earn a few dollars for family coffers, their own doweries, and personal expenses. Likewise, wives and daughters worked in family hotels and taverns. Most of these women considered their positions to be temporary as, indeed, they usually were. Some young women took service posts merely as a means of getting away from home during the interval before marriage. These circumstances created the golden age of service for nonsouthern, rural and small-town Americans, an age of

3. Lucy M. Salmon, *Domestic Service* (New York: Macmillan, 1897), 80–88. Salmon correctly identifies the economic basis of a city or state as an important factor in explaining *decreasing* numbers of servants. Yet when explaining *increasing* numbers, she unaccountably discounts this factor for cities. See Chapter One, Note 2.

intelligent, efficient, living-as-part-of-the-family native-white "help."

The proportion of native-white servants continued higher in rural areas and small towns than in cities throughout the nineteenth century, but by the mid-1830s, rural Americans were complaining about the scarcity of workers. The number of native whites willing to labor as servants could not keep pace with demand, and alternative employment, such as factory work for girls in the northeastern United States, further diminished the supply. Luckily for rural employers, increased demand coincided with increased numbers of immigrants entering the United States. Like native-white servants, immigrants turned to domestic service for employment, although for the foreign born, this choice was more often required for personal survival. Most of these new arrivals served to bolster the ever-growing urban work force, but rural employers drafted many immigrants for duty in the countryside.[4]

The history of free, nonsouthern black servants took a similar turn after 1830. Working most often in northeastern cities, blacks generally supplied respectable numbers of servants wherever they represented large segments of the population. Thus, during the first decades of the nineteenth century, northern blacks were firmly entrenched not only in cities like Philadelphia where they would always be numerous but in places like New York and Boston where Europeans would later dominate. After 1830, however, the employment of blacks in private households decreased and, in some regions, had nearly ceased by the 1850s. The trend was evident by 1842, when a popular handbook for domestics was admittedly written for "white servants." Wealthy families continued to use blacks whenever it was fashionable, and a few Negro men with reputations for impeccable service retained their positions, but blacks were employed most often in hotels (usually second-class ones), as extra attendants at special social events, and as laundresses.[5]

4. David E. Schob, *Hired Hands and Plowboys: Farm Labor in the Midwest, 1815–1860* (Urbana: University of Illinois Press, 1975), 192–95; Caroline F. Ware, *The Early New England Cotton Manufacture: A Study in Industrial Beginnings* (New York: Russell and Russell, 1966), 240–41; Ann D. Gordon and Mari Jo Buhle, "Sex and Class in Colonial and Nineteenth-Century America," in Bernice A. Carroll (ed.), *Liberating Women's History: Theoretical and Critical Essays* (Urbana: University of Illinois Press, 1976), 289; Laurence A. Glasco, "The Life Cycles and Household Structure of American Ethnic Groups: Irish, Germans, and Native-born Whites in Buffalo, New York, 1855," in Nancy F. Cott and Elizabeth H. Pleck (eds.), *A Heritage of Her Own: Towards a New Social History of American Women* (New York: Simon and Schuster, 1979), 279.
5. Thomas C. Gratten, *Civilized America* (2 vols.; London: Bradbury and Evans, 1859), I, 17, 263; William Chambers, *Things as They Are in America* (Edinburgh: William and Robert Chambers, 1857), 188–89; Catherine E. Beecher, *Letters to Persons Who Are Engaged in Domestic Service* (New York: Leavitt and Trow, 1842), 166.

This shift, too, coincided with the influx of immigrants into service, but unlike the resultant decline in the number of native-white servants, the reduction in black servants was involuntary and relative. As large numbers of foreign immigrants began to pile up in American port cities, they competed with blacks for jobs in service. As the immigrant population surpassed black population in numbers, and as the demand for servants increased, immigrants were called upon more often to perform America's domestic chores. Immigrants thus gradually replaced blacks in service. They did not, however, displace Negroes. Even though the black proportion of the servant work force declined, a large part of the black community still labored in service. For example, by mid-century about three-fourths of New York City's female servants were Irish. Irish servants outnumbered Gotham's entire black population ten to one. Yet fully one-half of gainfully employed New York Negroes worked in service occupations.[6] The pattern was repeated elsewhere in the East, and as immigrants began drifting westward, they helped fill the demand for servants in America's ever-expanding and ever-multiplying western towns and cities replacing both native whites and blacks.

An important difference existed, however, between East and West. More often than in the East, nationalities other than Irish tended to dominate in western regions. Irish servants were numerous in places like New York because they represented the largest share of the immigrant population. But where other nationalities were numerically superior, it was they who contributed the largest numbers of servants. In the Middle West, at Saint Louis, and on the Plains, Germans dominated. In Minnesota, Illinois, and Wisconsin, Scandinavians proved most helpful. On the Pacific Coast, Chinese immigrants filled much of the need for servants. In the Southwest, Mexicans and even Indians became welcome sources of service. The Irish were still present in all of these places, and one traveler insisted that Paddy could be seen in his "truest and most emerald colors" in the West, in this instance meaning Chicago. But when one considers the roster of an Indiana hotel, in 1851, listing a Dutch chambermaid, two Irishmen, a Scotswoman, six "white" boys, a black cook, and an Asiatic, the danger of overgeneralizing is evident.[7]

6. Robert Ernst, *Immigrant Life in New York City, 1825–1853* (Port Washington, N.Y.: Ira J. Friedman, 1965), 65–66, 215; New York *Daily Tribune*, November 6, 1845.
7. J. Milton Mackie, *From Cape Cod to Dixie and the Tropics* (New York: G. P. Putnam, 1864), 196; John D. Beste, *The Wabash* (2 vols.; London: Hurst and Blackett, 1855), II, 74–76.

By 1850 the internationally recognized stereotype of the American servant was the immigrant, an image that prevailed into the 1920s. Most servants were not immigrants, but the illusion persisted primarily because of the glut of immigrants in American cities, particularly northeastern cities. There, a popular image of the servant was created by the writings of journalists, reformers, and popular writers of both fact and fiction.[8] Another factor was the peculiar American definition of *immigrant*. Because Americans refused to recognize the children of immigrants as native Americans, the large number of native-white servants was never appreciated. It is safe to assume that the percentage of native-white servants of native parentage rarely slipped below 20 percent. When native whites of foreign parentage, usually 15 to 20 percent, are added to this figure, American-born whites account for the largest single racial and ethnic group of servants. Contemporaries ignored this fact.[9]

Another stereotype persisted. Of all immigrant groups, the Irish symbolized the typical American servant. Even in the South, where traditions of Negro servitude held sway, the Irish were recognized as the typical white servant. The Irish seemed to be everywhere and to have "solved an immense difficulty" by supplying a substantial number of servants.[10] Several circumstances account for this impression. The Irish, first of all, were the largest unskilled immigrant group in the nation and, until the twentieth century, provided two to three times more servants than any other foreign nationality. Additionally, Irish servants worked in every section of the country and so, unlike the Chinese or even Negroes, became familiar as servants to large numbers of Americans through personal contact. Popular writers created an image that solidified this identification. American newspapers and magazines featured the colorful Hibernians, characterized as Paddy and Bridget, as stock subjects in jokes, cartoons, and anecdotes about servants. The impact of this impression was powerful and lasting.

The typical antebellum southern servant, both in fact and legend, was the Negro. This did not mean, however, that all antebellum southern servants were slaves or even black. By 1860 over 89,000 free ser-

8. Scott and Nellie Nearing, *Woman and Social Progress* (New York: Macmillan, 1912), 188. A similar stereotype existed among industrial workers. See David Montgomery, *Beyond Equality: Labor and the Radical Republicans, 1862–1872* (New York: Alfred A. Knopf, 1967), 37.
9. Francis A. Walker, "Our Domestic Service," *Scribner's Monthly*, XI (December, 1875), 273–78.
10. Chambers, *Things As They Are in America*, 188–89.

vants worked in fourteen slave states. North Carolina had the largest number, over 21,000, only 750 fewer than the total number of servants in New Jersey. Most free servants were probably black since by 1860 nearly 55 percent of the nation's half-million free Negroes lived in the South. Most free-black servants probably worked in cities, too, laboring wherever slaves were in short supply or deemed undesirable. But free blacks were not popular with all southerners. Many people preferred slave labor to free black labor because slaves could be more easily controlled. The shortage of good servants forced southerners to take whatever they could get. Consequently, many whites, mostly immigrants, were employed.[11]

Immigrants dominated among southern white servants for two reasons. First, the powerful Negro stigma on domestic service prevented native whites from entering the occupation except to serve as governesses or hired housekeepers. Equally important, most southern employers balked at using native whites as servants. As explained, the need to maintain white supremacy made it dangerous to degrade whites unnecessarily. Likewise, being unaccustomed to white servants, southerners remained unsure how to treat them and were uncomfortable in their presence. Their trauma, however, was evidently less when dealing with foreigners, for as in the North, immigrants began entering occupations native whites avoided and for which the supply of good black workers was inadequate. This trend, beginning in the 1820s, hit full stride by the late 1840s. By then, all southern states had at least some white servants, with the largest numbers working in Atlantic and Gulf Coast port cities.

New Orleans supported the largest number of white servants in the South. With its busy international port, the Crescent City played host to thousands of Irish and German immigrants. By the 1850s both groups worked in New Orleans households and inspired the creation of northernlike intelligence offices.[12] Owners of the city's several magnificent hotels also satisfied their need for employees by drafting immigrants. The Saint Charles and Saint Louis hotels replaced most of

11. U.S. Bureau of the Census, *Population of the United States in 1860* (Washington, D.C.: Government Printing Office, 1864), 674–75, and *The Statistical History of the United States from Colonial Times to the Present* (New York: Basic Books, 1976), Series A119–34, A172–94; Ira Berlin, *Slaves Without Masters: The Free Negro in the Antebellum South* (New York: Pantheon Books, 1974), 218–22, 228–29, 231–32.

12. Earl F. Niehaus, *The Irish in New Orleans, 1800–1860* (Baton Rouge: Louisiana State University Press, 1965), 49–50, 173n; John Frederick Nau, *The German People of New Orleans, 1865–1900* (Leiden, Netherlands: E. J. Brill, 1958), 23, 60.

their hired slaves and free Negroes with Irish and German servants by the 1850s, although they also employed French, English, and Swiss workers.[13] This displacement may be attributed, in part, to the preference for white servants among the northern businessmen and European travelers who frequented these hotels.[14]

Other regions of the deep South, supposedly the bastion of slavery, also found it necessary to utilize white servants. At Charleston in 1848 over one hundred whites—most of them Irish—worked as servants, outnumbering free Negroes so employed three to one. The same was true at Savannah, where whites were used both in the city and on nearby plantations. At Mobile whites were employed in hotels and private homes, with the Irish again holding many of the jobs. In Texas, where German emigration societies planted several colonies, "Dutch" girls served as a last resort for those southerners who could not obtain black servants.[15]

White servants were scattered throughout the upper South, too. White waiters served some Virginia resort areas as early as the 1830s, and white housemaids worked in Alexandria homes by the 1840s. Hotels at Richmond and Wheeling employed immigrants, an establishment in the latter town keeping English, Irish, French, and "Dutch" servants on the payroll. Irish waiters worked in Baltimore hotels in the late 1820s, and by 1860 the city's servant force was a very mixed one, including slaves, free blacks, Germans, Irish, Scots, and native whites. The District of Columbia's two largest hotels, Willard's and Gadsby's, were a little slower in hiring whites, but by the 1850s, they too employed white labor, mostly Irish. Hotels in Kentucky and Tennessee used white waiters and valets, and in the former state, Henry

13. For example, see Charles Lyell, *A Second Visit to the United States of North America* (2 vols.; New York: Harper and Brothers, 1849), II, 91, 125, 376; Arthur Cunynghame, *A Glimpse of the Great Western Republic* (London: Richard Bentley, 1851), 217; Robert C. Reinders, "The Free Negro in the New Orleans Economy, 1850–1869," *Louisiana History*, VI (1965), 276.

14. Mrs. M. C. J. F. Houstoun, *Hesperos; or, Travels in the West* (2 vols.; London: John W. Parker, 1850), II, 57; Joseph Holt Ingraham, *The Sunny South* (Philadelphia: G. G. Evans, 1860), 504.

15. Richard Wade, *Slavery in the Cities: The South, 1820–1860* (New York: Oxford University Press, 1964), 32; James and Mary Toal to Daughter, January 14, 1845 (T-1543), in Public Records Office of Northern Ireland, Belfast; Mary Jones to C. C. Jones, November 25, 1859, C. C. Jones to Charles C. Jones, July 5, 1860, both in Robert Manson Myers (ed.), *The Children of Pride: A True Story of Georgia and the Civil War* (New Haven: Yale University Press, 1972), 542, 592–93; Mary J. Owen to Sister, April 7, 1857, Mary J. Owen to Alexander S. Withers, September 23, 1857, in Cabell Tavenner and Alexander Scott Withers Papers, Perkins Library, Duke University.

Clay's son employed an Irish washerwoman at the ancestral home Ashland. North Carolinians relied heavily on free black servants, but "destitute" whites were also willing to serve in some places. As seen, Missouri, although a slave state, also had many white servants because of its large immigrant population.[16]

Insofar as age was concerned, American servants, regardless of race or nationality, were young before 1870. The youthful vigor of America's servants occasioned frequent comment, and most servants were probably in their midteens to late twenties. Early servant and household manuals urged housekeepers to remedy their servant problems by hiring domestics over thirty years of age, implying that many employers did not already do so.[17] In fact, many servants were not only young but literally children. Servants under the age of fifteen may have accounted for up to 15 percent of the total servant force during the antebellum period. American youths sometimes worked as servants to help support their families, either by hiring out for wages or by helping in family-owned boarding houses. The former circumstance was anything but desirable, and parents forced to send their children out as servants tried to place them with friends or relatives in order to minimize the stigma. So horrible was the prospect of forcing one's children into service generally regarded that an old Scotswoman, her husband dead, the soil of her farm exhausted, pleaded with a visiting countryman to take one of her daughters with him because she soon expected to be "under the necessity" of hiring the girl out.[18]

The nineteenth-century custom of apprenticing orphans and delin-

16. George Lewis, *Impressions of America and the American Churches* (Edinburgh: W. P. Kennedy, 1848), 69, 257; Chambers, *Things as They Are in America*, 271; Frederick Law Olmsted, *A Journey in the Seaboard Slave States* (New York: Dix and Edwards, 1856), 3–5, 49, 99; Jacob A. Kline Account Book (MS in Southern Historical Collection, Library of the University of North Carolina at Chapel Hill), 1840s; Thomas Hamilton, *Men and Manners in America* (2 vols.; Edinburgh: William Blackwood, 1834), II, 139–40; Eliza DeRosset to Katherine D. Meares, September 23, October 1, 1857, both in DeRosset Family Papers, Southern Historical Collection, Library of the University of North Carolina at Chapel Hill.

17. An interesting case study is Glasco, "The Life Cycles and Household Structure of American Ethnic Groups," 279, 281–83, 285–86; Robert Roberts, *The House Servant's Directory* (Boston: Munroe and Francis, 1828), 156; Elizabeth Ellet, *The Practical Housekeeper: A Cyclopedia of Domestic Economy* (New York: Stringer and Townsend, 1857), 27.

18. Richard Weston, *A Visit to the United States and Canada* (Edinburgh: Richard Weston and Sons, 1836), 204. See also James F. Cooper to Mrs. Cooper, February 23, 27, 1849, both in James Franklin Beard (ed.), *The Letters and Journals of James Fenimore Cooper* (6 vols.; Cambridge: Harvard University Press, 1960–68), V, 406, VI, 6, and New York *Times*, January 9, 1879, p. 8.

quents as servants encouraged the use of children. Unwanted children had labored as indentured servants during the eighteenth century, and they played an important role in the transition from bound to free service in many states. Originating in the Northeast, a system for placing-out orphans, paupers, and delinquents spread throughout northern and western cities before the Civil War. Early orphanages and reformatories were privately operated, but after 1850 city and state governments played an increasing role in their financing and management. The South lacked any organized system of apprenticeship until the end of the century, although local and county courts often assumed responsibility for contracting orphans.[19]

Institutions varied in the length of time they kept children, but most tried to teach their wards some skill or trade before placing them out. Boys not trained or apprenticed in a handicraft were placed as farm laborers and seamen more often than as servants, but girls, most of them eleven to eighteen, were bound out for the purpose of learning "the art and mystery of housewifery." While at an institution, girls were exposed to the whole range of housekeeping skills, including cooking, washing, knitting, spinning, and sewing. It would be misleading, however, to suggest that girls were actually taught these skills. They were given little formal training before 1880. Learning housewifery meant doing the domestic chores of the institution, an employment which consumed most of the girls' waking hours. Directors of one of the best-known reform institutions, the New York House of Refuge, confessed that training was designed more to instill in the children "habits of industry, than with the object of giving them a thorough knowledge of the art."[20]

The acceptance of such children as servants would be rather strange were it not for two important circumstances. First of all, these children fit the image of the servant. The impression, for instance, that

19. Among the most useful studies on this subject are Joseph M. Hawes, *Children in Urban Society: Juvenile Delinquency in Nineteenth Century America* (New York: Oxford University Press, 1971), Miriam Z. Langsam, *Children West: A History of the Placing-Out System of the New York Children's Aid Society, 1853–1890* (Madison: State Historical Society of Wisconsin, 1964); Robert M. Mennel, *Thorns and Thistles: Juvenile Delinquents in the United States, 1825–1940* (Hanover, N.H.: University Press of New England, 1973); Robert S. Pickett, *House of Refuge: Origins of Juvenile Reform in New York State, 1815–1857* (Syracuse: Syracuse University Press, 1969). For the South, see Berlin, *Slaves Without Masters*, 226–27. For documentary evidence, both North and South, see Robert H. Bremner (ed.), *Children and Youth in America: A Documentary History*, (3 vols.; Cambridge: Harvard University Press, 1970–74).

20. New York House of Refuge, *Tenth Annual Report* (New York: n.p., 1834), 5.

most of the children were immigrants was a popular one, even though, as in the case of servants, it was an overstatement. Some of the children were also the offspring of servants, a factor that, for some reformers and employers, explained their lack of discipline, unsanitary habits, and immoral behavior. Then too, some of the children were former servants who had been placed in reformatories for theft, intemperance, vagrancy, and sexual immorality. The second point to be remembered is the powerful mystique surrounding the American home, particularly the rural American home. Reformers made every effort to place children in rural households because the rural environment was associated with moral purity, with fresh air and clean thoughts. It was in the countryside that the tradition of American "help" was born, and most Americans associated the golden age with native-born rural servants. The farmer's home was "the best of all Asylums," a place where the "children of crime and poverty" could be made useful members of society. By extension, the American home, regardless of geography, was the ideal setting for reforming such ragged, dirty, unkempt little vagabonds, and so to domestic service they went.[21]

The marital status of servants depended upon their sex, race, and nativity, but before 1870, although evidence is fragmentary, the general impression emerges that the vast majority of servants were unmarried. Young women often entered service just long enough to find husbands or to secure more respectable jobs. The result was a high turnover of young, unmarried female servants. Many widowed and divorced females, primarily native whites forced to make their living, also entered service. Exceptions to this unmarried status were found most often among immigrants and blacks. Many of these women continued working or began working after marriage in order to supplement family incomes. Still, the number of married women remained low. Because employers generally required servants to reside with them as live-in servants both for the sake of convenience and in order to shield servants from an immoral world, only those married women hard pressed by economic woes entered service. The pre-1870 image is less clear for men. Most male servants were also unmarried, but they were more likely than female servants to be married. A contributing

21. Philadelphia House of Refuge, *Sixth Annual Report* (Philadelphia: n.p., 1834), 26–28; New York House of Refuge Case Histories (MS in New York House of Refuge Documents, Arents Library, Syracuse University), II, 221, VII, 1643, XXIII, 6593, 6704, XXXV, 15,918, 16,346, LIII, 25,482; Charles Loring Brace, *The Dangerous Classes of New York and Twenty Years' Work Among Them* (New York: Wynkoop and Hallenbeck, 1880), 28, 132–46, 301–302.

factor here was the greater freedom allowed male servants. Married men were often allowed to live out or, in some cases, were provided with accommodations for themselves and their wives.[22]

After 1870 the racial and ethnic balances, age patterns, and marital status of American servants changed. Racial-ethnic divisions, for example, shifted in subtle ways. A slightly higher percentage—roughly a third—of servants were Negroes, about one-fourth native whites, and the remainder of foreign and mixed parentage. A definite racial imbalance thus continued, but a wider variety and greater balance of ethnic groups appeared. The Irish still dominated, with Germans placing a respectable second, but the percentage of British, British-American, and Scandinavian servants increased each decade after the Civil War. The proportion of other nationalities fluctuated according to immigration cycles. Thus, the number of Orientals, primarily Chinese, increased during the 1870s and 1880s; southern and eastern Europeans made increases, though on a comparatively small scale, in the late nineteenth and early twentieth centuries. Germans and Scandinavians also increased their share of domestic positions as their proportion of total immigration rose.

Specific nationalities continued to work as servants in geographic regions where they formed significant parts of the population. Foreign servants were most numerous in New England and the Mid-Atlantic states. In both areas, as well as in parts of the Midwest, the Irish tended to dominate. Germans were most noticeable in Indiana, Iowa, Ne¹ raska, Wisconsin, Michigan, Ohio, and Missouri. Scandinavians held sway in Minnesota and Kansas, although they were to be found throughout the region west of Lake Michigan because of heavy northwestern promotion of Scandinavian emigration. Interestingly enough, a higher percentage of Scandinavians in the United States worked as servants than among either the Irish or the Germans in 1880 and 1890. British-Americans seeking work drifted into states all along the Canadian border and proved valuable as servants in Michigan, Vermont, and Maine. Orientals were confined mostly to the Pacific coast, although they never dominated that region to the extent popularly believed. The majority of Chinese in the United States lived in California, yet only at their peak in 1880 did they account for as much as half

---

22. See chapters six and seven for verification of these impressions. Herbert G. Gutman, *The Black Family in Slavery and Freedom, 1750–1925* (New York: Pantheon Books, 1976), 628–32, shows that black female servants in four selected towns were quite young as late as 1880.

of California's servants. Even then, the bulk, who were male, worked as launderers, Irish girls being preferred for housework. French servants were rare in the United States. Most of the 2,874 French servants to be found in 1870 were cooks, and 39 percent of these worked in the nation's three recognized gourmet centers: New York City, New Orleans, and San Francisco. Even in 1900 French servants composed only 2 percent of America's servant force.[23]

Racially, the South remained black, but not so solidly as it had once been. After the Civil War, southerners were hard pressed for servants. Trying to find reliable Negro servants, especially in the first few years after emancipation, was likened to "fighting shadows." Many newly freed blacks, associating any sort of personal service with slavery, refused to be domestics. White southerners declared that the new mobility of blacks, coupled with their inherent laziness and dishonesty, had ruined the race as servants. The "negro as a hireling," they decided, would never answer the South's needs. With "no bond but dollars and cents," white servants were the only solution. They were to be obtained "at all hazards, at any price."[24]

It was soon obvious, however, that white servants would not suffice. There were simply too few of them. Many southerners who had abandoned hope of finding good black servants discovered that it was equally "all up hill" locating competent whites. Middle- and upper-class southerners may have hoped to acquire white servants, but lower-class white southerners were still haunted by the stigma of service. Native whites capable of doing anything else avoided service, and immigrants, once the great hope of restoring domestic normalcy, failed to respond in sufficient numbers. Thus, the early postwar trauma of obtaining and adapting to white servants came to naught. The majority of southern employers continued or resumed using blacks. Percentages were higher in the lower South than in the border states and upper South, but probably no less than 60 percent of southern ser-

23. Walker, "Our Domestic Service," 277–78; E. P. Hutchinson, *Immigrants and Their Children, 1850–1950* (New York: John Wiley and Sons, 1956), 101, 112–15.

24. Ella Gertrude Thomas Diary (MS in Perkins Library, Duke University), May 29, 1865; Martin L. Wilkins to John B. Grimball, August 5, 1865, in Grimball Family Papers, and Grace B. Elmore Diaries, May 30, 1865, both in Southern Historical Collection, Library of the University of North Carolina at Chapel Hill; Mary Jones to Eva B. Jones, August 5, 1865, in Myers (ed.), *Children of Pride*, 1287. For the South's postwar problems, see Leon F. Litwack, *Been in the Storm So Long: The Aftermath of Slavery* (New York: Alfred A. Knopf, 1979), and Daniel E. Sutherland, "A Special Kind of Freedom: The Response of Household Slaves and Their Masters to Emancipation," to be published in *Southern Studies*.

vants were black between 1870 and 1900, and this figure went as high as 90 percent in some states. By 1890, 75 percent of all Negro servants were employed in the South.[25]

Then a curious thing happened. During the first two decades of the twentieth century, the number and proportion of black servants increased in nearly every section of the country *except* the South. Before 1910 Negro servants outside the South had been proportionately important only in Pennsylvania, and even there they represented but 20 percent of the total number of servants. By 1920, however, many northern cities had significantly larger black populations, and their use of black servants expanded at an even faster rate than those population increases. New York City surged ahead of Philadelphia in total number of black servants for the first time, although Philadelphians still employed a larger percentage of their city's Negroes as servants—over 50 percent of all blacks and over 80 percent of black females by 1920. Cities that had employed few blacks before 1900 made huge increases. Detroit, for example, boosted its use of black female servants by 300 percent between 1910 and 1920. Most Negro servants continued to work in the South, but their number and percentage dropped dramatically in nearly every southern state.[26]

Amidst this confusing kaleidoscope of shifting composition, the 1880s serve as a watershed. Insofar as domestic service is concerned, this was the most cosmopolitan and racially balanced decade in American history. According to the census of 1890, 27.5 percent of servants were black, 26 percent were native white, and 45 percent were foreign born or of mixed parentage. Among the foreign born, the plurality, 39 percent, was Irish, but 22 percent were German, 13 percent Scandinavian, 8 percent English and Welsh, 7 percent British-American, and 14 percent "other" (primarily Oriental). The 1880s also marked the high point of white dominance. Thereafter, the percentage of white servants declined while that of blacks, which had been steadily dropping for several decades, revived. By 1920 Negroes represented 38 percent

25. U.S. Bureau of the Census, *Eleventh Census of the United States: Population* (Washington, D.C.: Government Printing Office, 1893–95), XVI, Part 2, pp. 530ff.

26. Joseph A. Hill, *Women in Gainful Occupations, 1870–1920*, Monograph No. 9 of U.S. Census Bureau (Washington, D.C.: Government Printing Office, 1929), tables 83 and 84; Barbara Klaczynka, "Why Women Work: A Comparison of Various Groups—Philadelphia, 1910–1930," *Labor History*, XVII (1976), 84–85; David M. Katzman, *Before the Ghetto: Black Detroit in the Nineteenth Century* (Urbana: University of Illinois Press, 1973), 61–65, 110–11.

of the servant force, compared to 24 percent native white, 22 percent foreign born, and 14 percent mixed parentage.[27]

Several circumstances accounted for rising Negro numerical superiority. One was the American attitude towards the "new immigration." After 1880 the traditional northern and western European immigration declined in proportion to the rising numbers of southern and eastern Europeans. By 1914 the latter groups composed 73 percent of American immigrants. But Americans despised these strange newcomers even more than they had the heathen Irish. Differences of culture and tradition became too great for Americans, as xenophobia reached new dimensions. Poles, Bohemians, Hungarians, Italians, and Jews of all nations were seldom employed as servants, in part because they scorned such work themselves, but equally because Americans disliked and distrusted them.[28] Also, while more nonservice occupations opened to native-white women after 1880, blacks continued to be excluded. Blacks, therefore, inherited jobs in domestic service abandoned by whites fleeing to factories, shops, and offices.[29]

The age of the average servant increased between 1870 and 1920, particularly after 1890. A decreasing percentage of children in service partly explains this change. Although the number of children in service increased until the twentieth century, the proportion of children in the total servant force declined significantly. Then, as compulsory school attendance and child-labor laws were put into effect after 1900, the number of children also dropped, lowering their proportion even

27. U.S. Bureau of the Census, *Tenth Census of the United States: Population* (Washington, D.C.: Government Printing Office, 1883), I, 729, 752–53, 756–57; *Eleventh Census: Population*, XVI, Part 2, pp. 354–55.

28. Mary Grove Smith, "Immigration as a Source of Supply for Domestic Workers," *Bulletin of Inter-Municipal Committee on Household Research*, II (May, 1906), 8; Rose Cohen, *Out of the Shadows* (New York: Jerome S. Ozer, 1971), 158–59, 171–72; Izola Forrester, "The 'Girl' Problem," *Good Housekeeping*, LV (September, 1912), 381; Virginia Yans McLaughlin, "Patterns of Work and Family Organization: Buffalo's Italians," *Journal of Interdisciplinary History*, II (1971–72), 306, 309–310; Elizabeth H. Pleck, "A Mother's Wages: Income Earning Among Married Italian and Black Women, 1896–1911," in Michael Gordon (ed.), *The American Family in Social-Historical Perspective* (New York: St. Martin's Press, 1978), 495.

29. Mary White Ovington, "The Colored Woman in Domestic Service in New York City," *Bulletin of Inter-Municipal Committee on Household Research*, I (May, 1905), 10–12. Judith A. McGaw, " 'A Good Place to Work': Industrial Workers and Occupational Choice. The Case of Berkshire Women," *Journal of Interdisciplinary History*, X (1979), 234–35, underscores the point that discrimination against blacks in northern mills was nothing new.

further. By 1920 only about 4 percent of servants were children.[30] In that same year, only about half of American servants were aged fifteen to thirty-four, and less than one-fifth were in their mid-teens to late twenties. Many more servants than before 1870—20 percent by 1920—were in their mid-forties or older. The average age had crept upwards into the late twenties and early thirties.[31]

Male servants tended to be older than females partly because fewer young men were willing or needed to enter service. The social pressure placed on American men to "succeed" made service more degrading for them than for women. Even unskilled young men had far more opportunities for alternative jobs than did women. Women were seldom credited with having talent for anything other than housework. If they had to work for a living, it was assumed that most women would enter service. Young men, if they had any gumption or self-respect, were expected to avoid personal service. Frequently, a man entered service only after he had passed his youth and failed at all else. Then too, many female servants escaped work through matrimony before they reached middle age. Consequently, the average male servant was not so young as his female counterpart. As the average age of all servants increased, that of male servants increased more rapidly. By 1920, one-fourth were over forty-five, a category filled by only 19 percent of the women.[32]

Insofar as marital status is concerned, few changes occurred until after 1890. Between 1890 and 1920, however, the percentage of married females tripled. By 1920, 23 percent of all female servants were married. This increase may be accounted for largely by the rising popularity of daily workers. Women who had been unable to enter domestic service in earlier years without deserting their families could now join the work force on an hourly basis. Eastern and southern Euro-

30. Raymond G. Fuller, *Child Labor and the Constitution* (New York: Thomas Y. Crowell, 1923), 215, 219–25, 311–12; Bremmer (ed.), *Children and Youth in America*, II, 605–749.

31. U.S. Bureau of the Census, *Eleventh Census: Population*, XVI, Part 2, pp. 372–73, *Twelfth Census of the United States: Special Report on Occupations* (Washington, D.C.: Government Printing Office, 1902), 16–39, *Thirteenth Census of the United States: Population* (Washington, D.C.: Government Printing Office, 1913–14), IV, 430–32, *Fourteenth Census of the United States: Population* (Washington, D.C.: Government Printing Office, 1921–23), IV, 394–95. Census data on servants' ages fluctuates in preciseness, becoming more detailed after 1890. Unfortunately, because age categories are inconsistent, it is difficult to compare ages from one census to the next. Nonetheless, trends are discernible, particularly when supplemented by other sources.

32. *Ibid.*

pean women, for example, whose cultural traditions dictated that they care for their own families rather than for strangers, seem to have worked more often as hotel servants and daily house workers than as live-in servants. It is also significant that black women—who became more numerous as the popularity of daily workers increased—supplied the majority of married female servants. Marriage among black female servants seems always to have been more frequent than it was among white servants. Whether as cause or effect, fewer black servants lived with their employers. Using the 1880 census rolls for four southern towns, one historian showed that married blacks with children worked as washerwomen more often than as domestics, a situation that allowed them to care for their children while working. As daily workers became more numerous, there occurred a simultaneous increase in the number of black servants and married servants. Likewise, the percentage of widowed and divorced servants increased, again with Negroes representing the largest numbers. Among men, also, blacks provided the highest percentages of widowed, divorced, and married servants, nearly one-third of black male servants being married by 1920.[33]

Generally, then, the typical servant changed between 1800 and 1920. At the beginning of the nineteenth century, she was likely to be a young (seventeen to thirty years old), unmarried female. Where she worked was often determined by her race and nationality, although, in any case, it was probably in an urban area. Outside the South, she was white, and it was likely that either she or one or both of her parents had been born outside the United States. After World War I, the typical servant was still unmarried, although she was more likely to be so, slightly older (twenty-five to forty), and, even outside the South, a Negro. In most cases, only people in desperate financial straits, those who considered service a brief interlude to better things, or those who could not find employment elsewhere became servants. The large number of widowed and divorced female servants is one indication of this. Left on their own, women with no real skills resorted to service. Widows sometimes went to service in preference to becoming financial

33. U.S. Bureau of the Census, *Eleventh Census: Population*, XVI, Part 2, pp. 414–29, *Twelfth Census: Special Report on Occupations*, 54–63, *Fourteenth Census: Population*, 699, 715, 723, 731, 738; Berlin, *Slaves Without Masters*, 220–21; Leslie Woodcock Tentler, *Wage-Earning Women: Industrial Work and Family Life in the United States, 1900–1930* (New York: Oxford University Press, 1979), 143–44, 146–47; Pleck, "A Mother's Wages," 495. Gutman, *The Black Family*, 628–32.

burdens on their grown children. Likewise, female immigrants and Negroes flocked to service to help support their families or as a matter of personal survival.

Such a description is enlightening, but it is far from complete. It is largely a statistical description, telling little about servants as people. For a fuller account of American servants, one must examine the more subjective aspects of their lives: intelligence, moral behavior, leisure-time activities, class structure, duties, hours of labor, wages, and living conditions. These provide a clearer and more human picture of American servants.

CHAPTER FOUR

THE PIOUS AND THE PROFANE
Intelligence, Morality, and Recreation

Some employers doubted it, but servants were remarkably like other folk. Servants laughed and cried, sinned and repented, committed the same follies and indulged in the same pleasures as their fellow citizens. As they strolled along city streets and paused to gossip in neighborhood parks, servants were indistinguishable from people in a hundred other occupations. They certainly did not form a "class," defined by universal characteristics, as many employers believed. Employers generalized—and in none too complimentary terms—about the intelligence, moral character, and recreations of servants. Yet careful examination of these three aspects of servants' lives show that few workers fit their employers' cherished stereotypes. Servants were smart and simple, pious and profane. They were all of these; they were none of them. The nation's domestic laborers were as diverse and undefinable as the average American.

Intellectually, servants ran the gamut, from don to dunce. Statistical measurements of intelligence are lacking for the nineteenth century, and generalization on this subject is, therefore, admittedly subjective. The only measurable standard, literacy, exposes nearly a quarter of all servants as deficient. As late as 1890, 23 percent of female house servants and nearly 19 percent of male house servants could neither read nor write. Both of these percentages exceeded national female and male illiteracy rates—22 and 13 percent respectively—as well as those of many other working-class occupations, but one should not generalize too broadly from this.[1] Low literacy rates are perhaps a better indication of lack of opportunity for formal education than of bald ignorance. Thus, not surprisingly, the statistics for 1890 also indicate that native whites, those people with the best opportunity for formal education, were generally the most literate servants, while blacks and certain groups of Europeans, most notably the Irish, were often uneducated and illiterate. Some servants lamented their lack of formal education. They spoke of returning to school or of taking correspondence courses in order to qualify for better jobs.[2] If stereotyped, they were determined not to remain so.

Moreover, what employers bemoaned as the "ignorance" of servants might better be termed lack of sophistication. Stories about witless servants, most of them blacks and immigrants, were legion and served as sources of amusement at tea parties, in employer correspondence, and in popular magazines. But the real problem was that many servants, handicapped by rural or lower-class American and European origins, were unaccustomed to "civilized ways." They were overawed by the complexities of even modest middle-class households. They became confused by the elaborate ritual of middle-class table settings and, towards the end of the century, by the operation of washing machines and other modern conveniences. Many people, perhaps never having seen a stove, lacked training in the most basic housekeeping skills. Some servants spoke no English and were unfamiliar with American customs. Some cases, such as that of the eighteen-year-old German girl whose "unfamiliarity" with gas lamps resulted in her asphyxiation, ended in tragedy.[3]

Of more concern to employers than intelligence, however, was servants' moral behavior. Here, the most common charge was dishonesty, a sin taking many forms and practiced in varying degrees but usually involving such transgressions as lying, snooping, and mild deceptions. In order to get jobs, for example, many servants wrote fraudulent

1. U.S. Bureau of the Census, *Eleventh Census of the United States: Population* (Washington, D.C.: Government Printing Office, 1893–95), XVI, Part 2, pp. 763, 791. For a local survey of literacy see Massachusetts Bureau of Statistics of Labor, "Social Conditions in Domestic Service," *Massachusetts Labor Bulletin*, No. 13 (February, 1900), 9.

2. Essie to Margaret Scott, October 6, 1887, Libbie to Margaret Scott, January 3, 1886, in Adrian (Michigan) Girls' Training School Records, Michigan State Archives. Another girl criticized employers for their lack of concern with servants' education. See New York *Times*, December 5, 1872, p. 3.

3. Chicago *Tribune*, October 11, 1901, p. 8.

"Why should I worry about the Boxers? Sure, I have trouble of my own in china." This typical Irish caricature was a recognized symbol of both the worker and the quality of work of American domestic service.
Harper's Bazar, XXXIII (August 25, 1900), 1086.

character references and swore to qualifications they did not possess. Once hired, some servants continued to deal in deceit. They engaged in such mischief as changing the hands of clocks to suit their purposes, lying about how they spent their off-duty hours, buying lottery tickets with employers' market money, and using employers' personal effects without permission. Some servants admitted their guilt and were forgiven, but others compounded their crimes by denying any wrongdoing. For more than a few, the result was dismissal.[4]

Most such deceptions were harmless enough, but some servants were genuine rogues. One fellow continued to flimflam his employer long after he had retired from service. Claiming to be a Civil War veteran, the man—Isaiah Thompson by name—had always enjoyed his employer's good will, respect, and trust. Upon retirement, Isaiah announced his intention of entering an old soldier's home and living on his pension. He and his employer parted on the most amiable terms. Soon, however, Isaiah was writing to his former employer requesting money. It seems that he had been unable to gain admittance to the soldier's home, and so had gone to live with his children. But they, he claimed, had mistreated and ignored him. To escape their tyranny, he now intended to support himself by working as a ditchdigger (he was then seventy-two years old) but needed a little cash to hold him over until he collected his first paycheck. His sympathetic employer, expressing concern, responded to this and several subsequent requests for funds by sending him various sums of money, usually five to fifteen dollars. Isaiah thanked the family each time, blessed them, and told them he was sure they would all meet again in Heaven, but he never repaid the money as he promised he would. Instead, he borrowed more money, as well as clothing and shoes.

Finally, his employers received a letter from the old fellow's son, informing them that Isaiah had been bamboozling them for years. In the first place, said the son, he had taken good care of his father while the old man was living with him, even forgiving him his past transgressions of strong drink and wife-beating (Isaiah's wife had died as the result of one of his kicks). Furthermore, he continued, his father had

4. See, for example, James Bogert, Jr., Account Book with Hired Servants (MS in Museum of the City of New York), September 5, 1823, April 14, 1825; Delia to Margaret Scott, March 22, 1886, in Adrian Records. One survey shows that, while 92.6 percent of the employers questioned believed that servants were "honest," two-thirds expressed no further confidence in them. See Gail Laughlin, "Domestic Service," in *Report of the United States Industrial Commission on the Relations and Conditions of Capital and Labor* (19 vols.; Washington, D.C.: Government Printing Office, 1901), XIV, 754–55.

"Bin Playing the Solger Racket" and working on their sympathies for years. Isaiah had deserted the army three weeks after enlisting, later obtaining spurious discharge papers. Hence his failure to gain admittance to the soldier's home and his inability to live on his "pension."[5]

If not dishonest, many servants were certainly inquisitive. This was perhaps unavoidable. Living in such close contact with their employers as they did, tidbits of family affairs, gossip, and scandal were bound to be overheard. Some servants, however, went out of their way to keep abreast of their employers' activities. They eavesdropped and regularly scrutinized their employers' personal papers, believing that information so acquired was imperative to their survival. When carried to extremes, such persistent curiosity could cost servants their jobs. "Industrious, but obstinate, Self-willed & meddles with things in which she has no right," regretfully recorded one employer upon dismissing an overly inquisitive housemaid. "Famous for going about the house at night with a lamp for want of employment," he continued, "and conciets that she Knows more of the arrangements of the family concerns than her employers." Still, servants continued to regard such information as insurance. Knowledge of employers' doings might some day save their jobs, or at least increase employer politeness and prudence in dealing with them.[6]

A more serious complaint lodged against servants was thievery. Servants were always the first ones under suspicion should a theft be committed. "The butler did it," was a common assumption among nineteenth-century law officers, who routinely began investigation of any robbery by asking the character of family servants. A few servants were worthy of scrutiny. Working in league with professional burglars, they briefed confederates on the internal arrangements of a household and family habits in return for a share of the boodle. They were also in an excellent position to engineer kidnappings. Yet petty thievery was far more likely than grand larceny among servants. Such articles as loose silverware, jewelry, clothing, and small sums of cash were their usual haul. When large thefts did occur—say, $1,500, as happened at Boston in 1849—they could send "quite a sensation"

5. Isaiah Thompson to Mary Williams, December 14, 1892, March 4, March 26, April 4, April 27, 1895, September 7, 1899, Mary Williams to T. P. Moore, March 5, 1895, A. A. Williams to Isaiah Thompson, April 10, 1895, and John Thompson to Mary Williams, 1895, all in Josiah Butler Williams Family Papers, Collection of Regional History, Cornell University.

6. Bogert Account Book, 1845; Eliza Potter, *A Hairdresser's Experience in High Life* (Cincinnati: n.p., 1859), 62–64, 67–69, 115–22.

through a town. Still, one employer, who had been nearly drained (financially and emotionally) by servant thefts, realized that his domestics never stole really costly items. "They none of them, would take any valuable thing," he maintained; "they are all honest, as they understand *honesty*."[7]

Perhaps the most frequently encountered form of thievery occurred in the kitchen, with servants liberating provisions from employers' larders and wine cellars. When consistent, such thefts could force a heavy toll on family means, and household reformers offering advice on the servant problems urged housekeepers to keep stores under lock and key. Southerners evidently faced the gravest situation because they had traditionally tolerated such thefts. Dating from the days of slavery, southern cooks had been allowed to smuggle leftover victuals out of the master's house. As long as such thefts remained small, they were winked at, but after the Civil War, southern housekeepers complained that this system of "tot'in" was getting out of hand. An extreme example is that of an "incorrigible" old cook who pilfered food and, occasionally, small family possessions by deftly depositing her contraband in flour sacks tied around her waist under her dress.[8] Generally, however, pantry thefts—a bit of meat one day, a slice of pie the next—were more of a nuisance than a plague.

Another form of thievery, perhaps better termed a confidence game, was the kickback from local tradespeople. The game was played as follows. In order to attract business, some grocers and merchants made financial deals with those servants who did their employers' marketing. In return for cash commissions or gifts in kind, servants purchased marked-up goods from these shops. The wealthier the em-

7. William H. Bell Diary (MS in New York Historical Society), January 6, 9, September 24, 1851; George Ellington [pseud.], *The Women of New York; or, The Under-World of the Great City* (New York: New York Book, 1869), 500–501; Helen Campbell, *et al.*, *Darkness and Daylight; or, Lights and Shadows of New York Life* (Hartford: A. D. Worthington and Co., 1891), 680; Chicago *Tribune*, December 8, 1901, p. 1; George C. Shattuck to George C. Shattuck, Jr., May 23, 1849, in Shattuck Papers, Massachusetts Historical Society; Henry Dana Ward Diary, 1850–57 (MS in Manuscripts and Archives Division, New York Public Library, Astor, Lenox, and Tilden Foundations), November 5, 1854, June 10, 1855.

8. Elizabeth Ellet, *The Practical Housekeeper: A Cyclopedia of Domestic Economy* (New York: Stringer and Townsend, 1857), 28; Clara E. Laughlin (ed.), *The Complete Home* (New York: D. Appleton and Co., 1912), 295–96; George P. Rawick (ed.), *The American Slave: A Composite Autobiography* (19 vols.; Westport, Conn.: Greenwood, 1972), XIII, Part 3, pp. 191–93. See also Harris Dickson, " 'Help! Help! Help!' The Bogy That Darkens the Sun of Southern Domesticity," *Delineator*, LXXX (July, 1912), 7, 66.

ployer, the larger the orders and the larger the kickback. Servants usually received 5 percent on each sale, but experienced bargainers made off with as much as 10 percent. They did not regard these commissions as ill-gotten gains. Indeed, domestics in wealthy households considered such commissions "fixed facts" of servant life, and buyers refused to deal with overly scrupulous merchants.[9]

Servants succumbed to thievery for several reasons. Kleptomania was probably one of them. Another was that servants regarded theft as a legitimate means of avenging the tongue-lashings of tyrannical employers. Likewise, some servants stole in order to supplement skimpy wages. Sometimes gambling debts and bar tabs provided the motive, but many cases proved more pitiable. For instance, many servants took food neither to fill their own stomachs nor to turn a profit on the black market. Servants were generally well fed, but they sometimes had friends and relatives who were not so well off and for whom they were the only means of support. "You just have to help de chillum to take things," explained a South Carolina cook, "and while you doin' dat for them, you take things for yourself. I never call it stealin'!"[10] This last statement was the key. Many servants seemed convinced that they were doing nothing wrong. Their interpretation of honesty differed from that of their employers. Confronted with their employers' seemingly limitless resources, servants reasoned that a bit of steak or a piece of jewelry would never be missed.

Yet, despite the aura of dishonesty and thievery that enveloped servants, abundant testimony defended their honesty. Many employers swore to their servants' good qualities and never found reason to believe their faith misplaced. Nor was it unusual for accusations of theft or deceit to be proven false or found totally devoid of evidence. When charged unjustly with wrongdoing, servants could be genuinely hurt and aggrieved. Some of them, even when cleared, preferred to quit their places rather than brook such insults.[11] Most servants were no

9. Mary Elizabeth Carter, *Millionaire Households and Their Domestic Economy* (New York: D. Appleton and Co., 1903), 51–52; Frances A. Kellor, "The Housewife and Her Helper," *Ladies' Home Journal*, XXII (December, 1905), 32.

10. Rawick (ed.), *The American Slave*, III, Part 4, p. 2. See also Rebecca Mandeville to John D. Scott, July 21, 1865, in Henry D. Mandeville and Family Papers, State Department of Archives and History, Louisiana State University.

11. Frances Wright, *Views of Society and Manners in America* (London: Longman, Hurst, Rees, Orme, and Brown, 1821), 462–63; Potter, *A Hairdresser's Experience in High Life*, 85–86.

more dishonest than other folks, and they certainly did not represent a criminal class.

A more serious moral charge against female servants was sexual immorality, and there was evidence of serious sexual promiscuity. Servant girls had reputations as flirts, but some girls graduated from harmless flirtations to living with men not their husbands and bearing illegitimate children. Statistical evidence from the 1850s to the 1920s demonstrates that, as an occupational group, domestic servants also ranked high in cases of venereal disease and in the number of girls who became prostitutes.[12]

Servants often succumbed to prostitution because they needed money. Although most servants were assured of a place to sleep and adequate food, some girls required such "necessities" as fashionable clothes and jewelry, for which their cash wages were inadequate. Girls who had a strong yearning for such things and were not particular about how they got them discovered that prostitution paid higher wages than domestic service, besides offering shorter hours and easier working conditions. There were also legitimate money problems. For instance, unemployed girls who had not saved enough money while working to support themselves during lean times might turn to prostitution in desperation. The psychological impact of seduction had a profound effect, as well. Girls were made to believe that they were evil, worthless creatures if seduced; it was their fault, not the man's. When one girl was raped by a boarder in the lodging house where she worked, her employer, insisting that "such things don't happen unless the girl is to blame," comforted the girl by discharging her. Such experiences led otherwise good girls astray. It should be mentioned, too, that contrary to popular impressions, few girls lost their virginity to employers. One southern nurse insisted that black female servants in the South were at the mercy of male employers, but she so overstates the case that it is difficult to accept her account as typical. Once in ser-

12. Brayton Family Journals (MS in Collection of Regional History, Cornell University), September 25, 1843; Ella Gertrude Thomas Diary (MS in Perkins Library, Duke University), May 7, 1869; Cornelia P. Spencer to June Love, December 18, 1892, in Cornelia Phillips Spencer Papers, Southern Historical Collection, Library of the University of North Carolina at Chapel Hill; Frances Donovan, *The Woman Who Waits* (Boston: Richard G. Badger, 1920), 228n; William S. Sanger, *The History of Prostitution* (New York: Harper and Brothers, 1859), 524; Carroll D. Wright, *The Working Girls of Boston* (Boston: Wright & Potter, 1889), 124–25.

vice, girls were far more likely to be seduced by male servants in the same establishment or by their boy friends.[13]

Intelligence offices frequently made innocent girls into fallen women. An intelligence office could be a traumatic introduction to service. As shown, many offices pursued unethical or immoral business practices that affected both employers and servants. But whereas this skulduggery rarely cost employers more than a few dollars or some inconvenience, servants could be made miserable and, in some cases, have their lives ravaged by profit-seeking agents.

In recruiting men and women to hire out as servants, some intelligence offices used techniques that were at least questionable and sometimes criminal. The methods seemed endlessly varied, but perhaps the most ignoble schemes were those used to attract Europeans and southern blacks to northeastern states. In the latter case, northern agents, beginning soon after the Civil War, journeyed south to enlist discontented southern workers. A favorite ploy was to promise young rural girls glamorous jobs, such as lady's maid, in big northern cities. Agents then advanced the girls money to travel north, explaining that the loans would be deducted from their salaries at a later date. They shipped the girls' baggage north, too, free of charge but directly to their offices. Upon arriving in the North, girls learned that their glamorous-sounding jobs had been a ruse, and that they must take lowly positions as scullions and maids-of-all-work. If they refused the jobs, girls were reminded of their unpaid train fares, for which they likely had been charged treble the actual cost, and of their baggage, which agents would hold until accounts had been settled. Girls had little choice. They were penniless, friendless, jobless, and stranded miles from home. Similar methods were used to shanghai immigrants and even rural native whites.[14]

Registration fees were another instrument of injustice. Employee fees, if required, could be charged as either a flat rate, ranging from

13. Helen Campbell, *Prisoners of Poverty: Woman Wage-Workers, Their Trades, and Their Lives* (Boston: Robert Brothers, 1887), 135; New York House of Refuge Case Histories (MS in New York House of Refuge Documents, Arents Library, Syracuse University), VII, 1643; Sanger, *History of Prostitution*, 533, 535; A Negro Nurse, "More Slavery at the South," *Independent*, LXXII (January 25, 1912), 197–98; Carter, *Millionaire Households*, 156.
14. Frances A. Kellor, *Out of Work: A Study of Unemployment* (New York: G. P. Putnam's Sons, 1915), 200–204; Ellington [pseud.], *Women of New York*, 503–504.

fifty cents to four dollars, or as a percentage of their first month's wages, usually 10 percent. Their fee entitled servants either to placement in a single job or to unlimited placement for a specified number of months. Unfortunately, servants dissatisfied with their assignments, rejected by employers, or never even given a place seldom had their fees returned.[15]

Once fees had been pocketed, servants were treated with scant respect. Unlike prospective employers, who received courteous attention and were sometimes provided with comfortable surroundings in which to interview likely candidates, servants, regardless of age or sex, were commonly herded into crowded, dingy, ill-ventilated rooms and hallways that, if furnished at all, contained only plain wooden benches. Employers and servants even entered an office by different doors, so that the only glimpse of comfort afforded servants was when ushered into the main office for inspection. In order to win a job, servants were often forced to accept whatever wage was offered, to lie about their age, religion, and abilities, even to accept positions they did not want. Offices also falsified servants' references by vouching for their honesty and sobriety when they possessed neither virtue and by swearing to the excellent references of servants without having seen or verified them. Employers eventually discovered these deceptions and, being further entrenched in their suspicions about the ethics of both servants and intelligence offices, fired the worker. This convinced servants that all employers were heartless.[16]

The interior and occupants of a respectable New York City intelligence office were graphically described in 1848 by a gentleman who had lived in the South for many years. His impression would have been quite similar had he visited the office seventy years later:

> The whole establishment was more like a slave market at the South than any thing else I can compare it with. There are three doors. Over one is inscribed 'Entrance for Men.' Over a second is 'Entrance for Women.' Over the other is 'Entrance for Employers.' When you get in you see in one apartment of the room fenced off like sheep and arranged along in rows upon benches a

15. Robert Ernst, *Immigrant Life in New York City, 1825–1853* (Port Washington, N.Y.: Ira J. Friedman, 1965), 67n, 43; Ellington [pseud.], *Women of New York*, 504–505; Kellor, *Out of Work*, 208–214; Elizabeth Ross Haynes, "Negroes in Domestic Service in the United States," *Journal of Negro History*, VIII (1923), 403.

16. Kellor, *Out of Work*, 214–23; Anne Forsyth, "Seven Times a Servant," *Delineator*, LXXVI (October, 1910), 252, and "Seven Times a Servant," *Delineator*, LXXVI (December, 1910), 469.

great number of men of all sizes, ages, and appearance, some dull, some sprightly, some bright, intelligent & active, others apparently ignorant and stupid. A few, probably those most anxious to find employment, will be at the very front railing eagerly scouring the face of every new one who enters the last mentioned door. Some appear in fine spirits, others are worn and sad. The women are more numerous still, arranged in the same manner in another pen. Some were coarse Irish women, who may aptly enough be compared with our field hands, then there were the sprightly well formed and good looking often handsome ones, more like our choice house servants. Like the men some are in fine spirits & full of sport, but many alas were care worn and heart broken. Some even were in tears, and the anxiety with which some of them eye you as you enter the door is distressing. Some will be huddled up to the railings nearest the desk of the proprietor, evidently striving to catch the words that pass between them. I visited 'Stewarts' [the department store] on the same day. I there saw the other extreme, the rich, the gaudy, the proud & the happy.[17]

The generally "noxious" atmosphere of less respectable offices was another problem. Tucked away, as they were, in the shabbiest parts of town, some offices were hotbeds of crime and immorality. Con men, pickpockets, pimps, prostitutes, and mashers prowled overcrowded, stuffy office waiting rooms, plying their trades. Worse yet were the lodging houses operated by some offices. While awaiting places, servants were rented cheap rooms, often of the most primitive sort, cramped and unsanitary. Other offices recommended various "working girls' homes" to their applicants. Agents rarely had any personal knowledge of these houses. They directed girls to them only because the proprietors had promised, in return for the agent's consideration, to send them girls seeking employment.[18]

Far more insidious was the immoral placement of female servants. Some agents—though probably never as many as was popularly supposed—procured girls for brothels by placing them there as servants. Some girls knew the nature of these establishments when they were sent but accepted the jobs because of the extremely good pay. Most

17. Henry Watson, Jr., to Sophia Watson, June 12, 1848, in Henry Watson, Jr., Papers, Perkins Library, Duke University. See also George S. Foster, *New York in Slices: By an Experienced Carver* (New York: W. F. Burgess, 1849), 37–40; Roy L. McCardell, "Help! Help! Help!" *Everybody's Magazine*, XV (October, 1906), 478–80.
18. Bell Diary, August 6, 1851; Kellor, *Out of Work*, 220–24.

girls, however, were ignorant of their destinations and were lured to their fate by a variety of tricks and schemes and then forced to remain. In either case, many girls were eventually seduced and forced to become employees of a different sort. Likewise, agents sent girls to "men of pleasure," saloons, sleazy boarding houses, and similarly legal but questionable establishments.[19]

A minority of offices practiced the worst of these villainies; the majority probably dealt honestly with both servants and employers. But the intelligence office's image as "the fountain-head of many abuses" remained strong, and correction of those abuses became a major objective of domestic service reform. Although technically a business agency, the commercial intelligence office was also a "social institution, dealing with human beings in very intimate and critical ways." As such, it shaped the conceptions of many servants about what was right and wrong, moral and immoral in service. Servants who had been cheated or dishonored by greedy agents became dishonest, immoral, and cynical. Their sense of decency was often blurred or destroyed by their experiences or by the experiences of friends. "A girl's whole moral point of view" could be molded in an intelligence-office waiting room.[20]

Despite this unsavory influence and the less than chaste behavior of many servants, the majority of girls were probably no more promiscuous than other people of their age and environment. The widespread concern for the morals of all working-class folk during the nineteenth and early twentieth centuries helped to exaggerate estimates of the depth of debauchery to which servants had supposedly fallen. People raised without the benefits of economic security and moral guidance, as was the case with many servants, were easily lured into moral transgressions. Therefore, an inordinate number of prostitutes probably did come from the ranks of service, but such girls did not represent the morality of the average servant girl. For every example of whoring among female servants shone one of virtue triumphant. Many female servants refused to venture into a man's bedroom while he occupied it. Others rewarded overly fresh gentlemen with a resounding

19. Foster, *New York in Slices*, 38–39; Kellor, *Out of Work*, 225–32; Grace Abbott, "The Chicago Employment Agency and the Immigrant Worker," *American Journal of Sociology*, XIV (1908), 291.
20. Florence Hunt, "The Intelligence Office," *American Kitchen Magazine*, IV (November, 1895), 70; Kellor, *Out of Work*, 214–15, and "The Intelligence Office," *Atlantic Monthly*, XCIV (October, 1904), 460–61.

slap, a good ear-boxing, or a piercing scream. One girl, realizing her natural weakness for members of the opposite sex, tried to avoid temptation by refusing to work in households employing men with un-chivalrous reputations.[21] Most girls accused of wanton behavior were guilty of nothing more than the flirtations and sexual explorations of youth. Girls who frequented dance houses and other "improper places" or who loitered on the streets after dark quickly earned unenviable reputations, regardless of how innocent their intentions or deeds. Em-ployers' fears helped to blur the line between immorality and question-able behavior, thus exaggerating many charges and converting indis-cretion into sin.

If, as Doctor Johnson claimed, no man is a hypocrite in his leisure time, then one of the most valuable pictures of servants is that which portrays them in their precious off-duty hours. Here again, servants were unpredictable. They amused themselves with pastimes ranging from the tranquil to the riotous. While some servants were noted for their quiet attendance and liberal contributions at church, others were romp loving, mischievous, and heedless of the morrow.

Among their more subdued amusements were sewing and reading. These became natural diversions for workers who, as will be shown, spent much of their time in employers' households. Reading was con-fined primarily to newspapers and popular magazines. Only a few ser-vants read books, and most of these were fictional, ranging from the classics, through "light novels," to "trash."[22] The musically inclined en-joyed strumming guitars and, if permitted, playing their employers' pianos. A "scrap of gossip" with their "cronies" was another simple yet important pleasure. Conversations over back fences, at market, church, and planned social gatherings were important means of shar-ing complaints, joys, and scandals.[23] Still other servants were content with peace and quiet. One such chap, an Irish hotel waiter, enjoyed

21. Isaac Candler, *A Summary View of America* (London: T. Codell, 1824), 75; Agnes M., "The True Life Story of a Nurse Girl," *Independent*, LV (September 24, 1903), 2264; Mary Alden Hopkins, "'Living in': A Glimpse Behind the Scenes in a Hotel," *Collier's Magazine*, XLVI (November 26, 1910), 20; Carrie to Margaret Scott, March 16, 1887, in Adrian Records.

22. Massachusetts Bureau of Statistics of Labor, "Social Conditions in Domestic Ser-vice," 10–12.

23. See, for example, Anna Osborn to Lizzie Osborn, December 19, 1853, in Camp Family Papers (Additional), Collection of Regional History, Cornell University, Clara W. Tanner to Charlotte E. Tanner, February 12, 1897, in Williams Family Papers, Eliza Pot-ter, *A Hairdresser's Experience in High Life*, 84–86, and "About Servants in Liveries—and in General," *Harper's Weekly*, XLVI (May 3, 1902), 567.

meditating in a secluded portion of his hotel's balcony. When evening enfolded the earth and day's work had ended, he would stroll onto the upper portico, "settle himself in an armchair, cock his feet over the railing, and quietly smoke his cigar." [24]

Cupid dominated the lives of other servants. Servant girls were of a decidedly social turn, with romance and dreams of romance filling their thoughts. In establishments where the sexes were mixed, *amours* sometimes blossomed between fellow servants. Elsewhere, boy friends—"followers" they were called—were frequent visitors at kitchen socials, and they were ever ready for back-porch rendezvous or more clandestine meetings. Some girls, believing steady boy friends only slowed them down, became coquettes. They honed their talents on mailmen and delivery boys and then unleashed them in earnest during Sunday promenades in the park. It was for this reason that many girls preferred service in cities to small towns and rural regions. Army posts were also popular places to work. Some observers said this was because army wives were generally good-tempered. A more likely reason was that most posts sponsored weekly dances to which girls from the surrounding area were invited, and even without such formal affairs, there was never a shortage of men with whom to talk and flirt. Romance was so important to some girls that they refused to work where denied male visitors. [25]

Unfortunately, the hearts of some servants played them false. One hopeful young girl was mortified to discover that the fashionable young men with whom she flirted in the park had never been serious in their attentions towards her. Worse yet was the affair of a rather plain looking Irish cook who, after trusting the man of her dreams with her life savings in anticipation of their marriage, found herself deserted by the villain and poorer by three hundred dollars. Men were no less vulnerable. One young footman, on the rise in the domestic hierarchy after twelve years of loyal service, was discharged for secretly marrying one of the household chambermaids. This might have been tolerated in

24. J. Milton Mackie, *From Cape Cod to Dixie and the Tropics* (New York: G. P. Putnam, 1864), 197–98.

25. Ward Diary, January 2, 1851; Elizabeth E. Dana Diaries (MS in Dana Family Papers, Schlesinger Library, Radcliffe College), April 21, 1869; Sarah Comstock, "The Mistress Problem," *Collier's Magazine*, L (February 1, 1913), 16; Mrs. A. J. [Margaret], Graves, *Woman in America* (New York: Harper and Brothers, 1843), 81; Cleveland Amory, *The Last Resorts* (New York: Harper and Brothers, 1952), 98–99.

a less fashionable establishment, but marriage between servants on the same staff was not considered "good form" in the best homes.[26]

For jilted lovers and others sick at heart or weary in body, John Barleycorn was a popular release. Employers seldom allowed servants to partake of spirits in the household, but they could hardly prevent their smuggling a bottle onto the premises or liberating a portion of the household's private stock. However they managed it, whether legally or illegally, whether on duty or off duty, servants enjoyed ample opportunities for satisfying their thirst. An occasional tipple was generally not harmful. In moderation it proved a good remedy for escaping the boredom and fatigue of the day. But in excess, it could cost servants their jobs. The list of workers discharged for drunkenness was long, an unfortunate situation because in all other respects many of these people were excellent servants.[27] Yet employers had no choice. Intoxicated servants were useless, and in instances where they started quarrels or incited violence, they threatened the moral tone and safety of the home.

Even without strong drink, near riots could result from the frolicking of some servants. One legendary episode involved the coachmen and grooms of wealthy Newporters. Attending their employers at a lavish summer dance, these worthies became restless, hungry, and thirsty during their long vigil in the warm night air. At some time between the first round of dancing and the start of dinner, their patience deserted them. They descended upon the dining room like mountain bandits, devouring long tablefuls of terrapin and champagne that awaited their employers and holding "high carnival." Guests, discovering their meal had been ravaged, had no recourse but to return home. Retiring to their coaches, most employers stifled an impulse to thrash their delinquent servitors, but one of them could not refrain from giving his man a good tongue-lashing. "Richard, I am astonished at you," gasped the gentleman; "the other men's rascally conduct does not sur-

26. Dana Diaries, April 21, 1869; Ellen McGowan Biddle, *Reminiscences of a Soldier's Wife* (Philadelphia: J. B. Lippincott, 1907), 87; Carter, *Millionaire Households*, 215.

27. See, for example, Margaret Bayard Smith to Mrs. Kirkpatrick, July 21, 1801, in Margaret Bayard Smith, *The First Forty Years of Washington Society*, ed. Gaillard Hunt (New York: Frederick Ungar, 1965), 32; Bogert Account Book, April, 1832; Sarah W. Dana Account Book (MS in Dana Family Papers, Schlesinger Library, Radcliffe College), March 4–April 27, 1871; Charlotte E. Tanner to Clara Williams, June 5, 1891, in Williams Family Papers.

prise me, but you, an old family servant, to so disgrace yourself shocks me." The reply was, "I own up, Major, but indade I am a weak craythur." [28]

More organized efforts at merrymaking included evening parties in the kitchen or servants' hall. These gatherings varied in size and hilarity from small groups chatting over tea to full scale "*domestic soirées.*" At the latter, entertainment was provided by gossip, card playing, dancing, singing, and general clowning. High spirits were occasionally made still higher by consumption of alcoholic refreshments, not always served with employer consent. The clamor at these festivals, whatever the number participating and regardless of the type of refreshment, sometimes reached such unrestrained levels as to invite the complaints of neighbors and to require the intervention of employers. No matter. The celebrants had enjoyed themselves for a while at least and had added to cherished "remembrances of jolly times." [29]

Organized group activities outside the home enjoyed some popularity. These were generally subdued affairs, carefully chaperoned and often sponsored by religious organizations. Sunday school, church socials, and prayer meetings attracted some servants. The YWCA began, after the Civil War, to organize social, educational, and religious activities for maids in urban areas. Independent servant clubs also blossomed at this time, organized by both local women's clubs and servants themselves. Some of these clubs, as will be seen, also served as pseudo labor unions, performing reform functions in addition to their social ones. [30]

Most servants, however, were not joiners. Indeed, many had an absolute aversion to formal organizations. Clubs and societies organized and controlled by benevolent employers had obvious drawbacks. Servants objected to such patronizing. They preferred less closely supervised, more spontaneous amusements. Perhaps surprisingly, servants also avoided clubs dedicated to service reform or benevolent activities, whether organized by employers or servants. Those who did join organizations preferred groups dedicated to "social purposes" rather than

28. Ward McAllister, *Society as I Have Found It* (New York: Cassell, 1890), 202–203.

29. Ward Diary, January 2, 1851; Eliza Potter, *A Hairdresser's Experience in High Life*, 87–88; Irwin Hood Hoover, *Forty-Two Years in the White House* (Boston: Houghton Mifflin, 1934), 289.

30. Carrie to Margaret Scott, August 20, 1886, Ella to Margaret Scott, March, 1886, and Libbie to Margaret Scott, January 3, 1886, all in Adrian Records; Isabel Eaton, "Special Report on Negro Domestic Service in the Seventh Ward Philadelphia," in W. E. B. DuBois, *The Philadelphia Negro: A Social Study* (New York: Benjamin Blom, 1899), 464–70.

STUDIES IN EXPRESSION
An imitation of the Lady of the house

Charles Dana Gibson captures the essence of the "*domestic soirée.*"
Charles Dana Gibson, *The Social Ladder* (New York: R. H. Russell, 1902).

"the immediate rightings of 'wrongs.' " Thus, of 231 Massachusetts female servants surveyed in 1898, only 20 belonged to any club, clan,
lodge, union, or fraternal order, and only an additional 15 attended educational or craft courses.[31]

Servants, either from preference or because of their long work
hours, spent their leisure time as individuals or in the company of one
or two companions. Of the Massachusetts group mentioned above,
sixty-five women had at least one male caller per week, and nearly
twice that number had at least one female caller. This indicates that

31. "A Servant on the Servant Problem," *American Magazine*, LXVIII (September,
1909), 504; Massachusetts Bureau of Statistics of Labor, "Social Conditions in Domestic
Service," 13, 15–16.

servants spent a lot of time at home or went out in limited company. Servants who found such closely regulated projects as YWCA picnics too tame for their tastes struck out on their own. One German girl and her friends, working in New York City, sought excitement on excursions through the city and its suburbs. The Bowery, Coney Island, Rockaway—these were their haunts, the centers of real fun and fascination. Such places were, as one girl described them, "just like what I see when I dream of heaven." [32] Country girls found the equivalent of city parks, beaches, and arcades in picnics, berry picking, and county fairs.

Limited company and limited pleasures had another connotation. Servants discovered that most of their companions must necessarily come from service, either from among fellow servants in the same household or from among workers in neighboring homes. Again, this was partly because of the long hours of service that restricted a servant's free time outside the home. Another important factor, however, was the ostracism of servants by workers in other occupations. They were banned, for example, from many working-girl clubs and unions, and acquaintances of both sexes sometimes avoided servants socially. Even relatives could be embarrassed by their lowly position. "My sister works in a downtown store," revealed one girl, "and she's ashamed to tell anyone her sister works out, so she don't ask me up when she's got young gentlemen callers, and she don't want me to show up at all." Servants simply were not regarded as being respectable company, and more than one worker left service to escape the "social pressure" of being a servant. This explains why many servants liked to work in large hotels and wealthy households. "Servants like the big places," explained one girl, "because there is more fun where there are men below stairs." It was also comforting to have any companion of either sex near at hand. [33]

32. Agnes M., "Life Story of a Nurse Girl," 2265–266.
33. Izola Forrester, "The 'Girl' Problem," *Good Housekeeping*, LV (September, 1912), 377; C. S. Angstan, "The Story of a Housekeeper," *Independent*, LXIII (July 11, 1907), 91–94. See also Lucy Larcom, *A New England Girlhood* (Boston: Houghton Mifflin, 1924), 200–201; Thomas Hamilton, *Men and Manners in America* (2 vols.; Edinburgh: William Blackwood, 1834), II, 178; Robert Tomes, "Your Humble Servant," *Harper's Monthly*, XXIX (June, 1864), 59; H. H., "A Houseworker's Experience," *American Kitchen Magazine*, XVIII (February, 1903), 192; Lucy M. Salmon, *Domestic Service* (New York: Macmillan, 1897), 154; Anne Forsyth, "Seven Times a Servant," *Delineator*, LXXVII (January, 1911), 13; Carter, *Millionaire Households*, 148–49; Mary Alden Hopkins and A. O. C., "A Letter and a Reply on the Servant Question," *Collier's Magazine*, XLVII (April 22, 1911), 36; Anna L. Williams to Aunt Nancy, September 4, 1870, in Camp Family Papers (Additional).

Similarly, most servants liked to work in cities. Urban areas provided servants with a wide variety of amusements. For the religiously inclined, cities offered an opportunity to attend a church of their own denomination. This was especially true for Catholics, who sometimes felt stranded in America's largely Protestant countryside. Perhaps most importantly, cities allowed servants to escape the dreariness and boredom of pastoral and small-town life. The fun and excitement, the amusements and pleasures (employers called them temptations) of the city were naturally attractive to the young, unmarried men and women in service. The city was where they could find congenial companions of both sexes. The city was where they could buy the latest fashions. Thus the city was where they could best escape the awful isolation that engulfed servants everywhere. Loneliness haunted the city, too, but in servants' eyes, it was potentially less fearful. The urban environment, as one observer discerned, offered more "sympathetic notice" of what was going on.[34]

Now the picture of the typical servant becomes a bit clearer. Her degree of education varied, depending on where and when she was born and her race, but she was generally as intelligent as other working-class Americans. Her moral conduct ranged from sainthood to devilry, with most servants falling somewhere in between. Likewise, the amusements of some servants won the smiling approval of priests while others would have caused a Cyprian to blush. Logically then, servants should have faded into the American maze, imperceptible among their fellow citizens, yet they were clearly visible. Servants followed a peculiar way of life, one in which they were treated differently from other Americans. They responded to this way of life and to their treatment in a unique fashion.

34. Bolton Hall, "The Servant Class on the Farm and in the Slums," *Arena*, XX (September, 1898), 374.

CHAPTER FIVE

A WAY OF LIFE
Class Structure, Duties, and Hours of Labor

Domestic service was a way of life for millions of American laborers. Servants awoke each morning, worked through the day, and retired at night, day after day for weeks, months, and years as *servants*. Whatever their differences of race, nationality, sex, and age, their lives were defined by an unalterable, inflexible, mechanized routine that ground ponderously on. Several inescapable brute facts of service, though differing in detail of circumstance and time, remained remarkably similar for all of them. The most important of these facts, the servants' "class" structure, duties, and hours of labor, helped to define the boundaries of a servant's life. Although they affected individual servants in different ways, their combined impact produced a recognizable pattern.

Once in the domestic ranks, servants became conscripts in an army with its own regulations and leaders. Despite their contempt for middle- and upper-class pretensions, servants adopted their own class system and hierarchy. This operated on two levels. First was the occupational hierarchy, an arrangement essential in establishments with more than one servant since it provided a chain of command by which some semblance of discipline could be maintained. At another level, servants ranked themselves by race, nativity, employer status, and personal background. This hierarchy was more unofficial than that based on occupation, but it could be even more decisive in determining personal relationships among servants. These two methods of ranking servants sometimes ran counter to each other, but they were more often in agreement.

Occupationally, servants fell into one of three groups, depending on the type of work performed. First came an elite of administrators, including hired housekeepers and butlers. Chefs, as opposed to "plain" cooks, also belonged to this upper crust. Just below them stood body servants: valets, lady's maids, and nurses. Together, administrators and body servants rated as "upper servants," seldom performing manual labor and always receiving higher wages and enjoying more privileges than "lower servants." The latter group, which included everyone else, was expected to defer to them as part of a natural order. In households without such grand personages as butlers and housekeepers, the hierarchy was set in relation to the number of servants employed. Thus, in families with two or three workers, it was the cook (referred to as "cook" rather than "the cook," much as a doctor is "doctor" rather than "the doctor") who ran things.

The occupational hierarchy was governed further by an elaborate "servant-girl etiquette." An unwritten law, to which most servants adhered, made it taboo to perform tasks not strictly related to one's position. As one cook explained things, it was not her job to direct the chambermaid, but neither would she allow the chambermaid to interfere in the kitchen. It became especially important not to perform work below one's position. Anyone who did not "conform to the system" in this respect was sure to lose "caste." Likewise, the occupational ladder was arranged, rung by rung, in an acknowledged scale of promotion along which ambitious folk could climb to the top. Differences of rank were very real to servants. Elevation to a higher post was cause for celebration. Thus, a scullion, one of the lowest positions in the hierarchy, promoted to parlormaid was likely to become something of a snob, swaggering from the "intoxication" of her new position.[1] Increasing specialization among servants accelerated such divisions as the nineteenth century progressed. Servants grew ever more reluctant to enter families employing only one worker. People would

1. Lillian Pettengill, *Toilers of the Home: The Record of a College Woman's Experience as a Domestic Servant* (New York: Doubleday, Page, and Co., 1903), 131–32. James Dawson Burn, *Three Years Among the Working Classes in the United States During the War* (London: Smith, Elder and Company, 1865), 82; Mary Elizabeth Carter, *Millionaire Households and Their Domestic Economy* (New York: D. Appleton and Co., 1903), 157–59; Amelia Mandeville to Rebecca Mandeville, December 2, 1865, in Henry D. Mandeville and Family Papers, State Department of Archives and History, Louisiana State University. See also William Burns, *Life in New York: In Doors and Out of Doors*

be cooks or chambermaids but not both. Their reason was elementary. Specialists received higher wages and labored fewer hours than un-skilled or general workers. Viewed in this light, employer complaints about the servant shortage were often complaints about the shortage of people willing to work as general servants.

The second, unofficial ordering of servants ranked them by race, nativity, individual tastes, and employer status. Racial division was the most obvious because of the scorn white servants displayed for blacks. Many racially mixed staffs functioned smoothly, some of them with white lower servants working under the direction of black upper servants. Cases also arose where whites and blacks banded together against a common foe, as when Irish and Negro servants on the Pacific coast joined forces againt the Chinese with whom they competed for jobs. Many whites refused to work with blacks, however, and white servants generally remained aloof from blacks. Where the two races did work together, blacks were frequently and unmistakably reminded of their inferior position. White servants, for example, sometimes de-manded separate eating facilities from blacks, a segregation that lasted into the twentieth century. Further problems arose where blacks and whites had to live in the same establishment. It was often difficult to find white servants willing to share living quarters with Negroes. Con-sequently, black and white worked together less often in private house-holds than in hotels, where they could easily be segregated or permit-ted to live out.[2]

Ethnic divisions splintered the hierarchy even more, with native-white servants displaying their contempt for foreign help. Immigrants, remember, stigmatized service as an undesirable, un-American occu-pation. This alone would have obliged many workers to despise the foreign presence, but other, more practical, factors also shaped their

(New York: Bunce and Brothers, 1851), James Stuart, *Three Years in North America* (Edinburgh: Robert Cadell, 1833), I, 325, Mrs. A. J. [Margaret], Graves, *Woman in America* (New York: Harper and Brothers, 1843), 81.

2. William Fraser Rae, *Westward by Rail: The New Route to the East* (New York: D. Appleton and Co., 1871), 239; George Augustus Sala, *America Revisited* (2 vols.; Lon-don: Vizetelly and Co., 1882), II, 233–34; Philip S. Foner and Ronald L. Lewis (eds.), *The Black Worker to 1869* (Philadelphia: Temple University Press, 1978), Vol. I of Foner and Lewis (eds.), *The Black Worker: A Documentary History from Colonial Times to the Present*, 191–96; Warren A. Durant to Henry R. Slack, February 4, 1867, in Slack Family Papers, Southern Historical Collection, Library of the University of North Car-olina at Chapel Hill; Mary White Ovington, "The Colored Woman in Domestic Service in New York City," *Bulletin of Inter-Municipal Committee on Household Research*, I (May, 1905), 10.

prejudice. People accustomed to the "neatness and the refinement of a good house," for example, disliked working and living alongside such folk as the "common, uneducated Irish" for reasons of sanitation and compatibility. Moreover, native whites accused immigrants of lowering wages and, by working for starvation wages, of chasing respectable folks out of service entirely. These last two assertions were generally untrue. Immigrants inexperienced in housework were willing to labor for whatever pay they could get, but so were the least competent servants of all nationalities and races. Under normal conditions, all capable workers, regardless of birth, demanded fair wages. Native-white servants, however, thought differently.[3]

Quite aside from questions of race and nativity, educated servants and those from better material circumstances than most of their comrades were also repelled by the rabble in service. They resented being thrown into an occupation where they were socially stigmatized and forced to rub elbows with "all kinds" of unsavory characters. Such servants sounded very much like employers when speaking of the "vulgar familiarity" of ignorant and profane associates. An English girl, forced to work in a Boston home until she could find a teaching post, was very condescending towards her fellow servants. "My intimate relations with this section of the laboring class were worth all the mortification I endured," she recalled. "I was proud of every victory over my *own* class feelings." One employer exhibited an unusually clear understanding of this attitude when she wrote of her intelligent Irish-Protestant maid, "Her idea seemed to be mainly this 'I do not wish to be ranked as a servant always and counted in among all sorts of creatures just because for a while I choose to get my living by doing housework.'"[4]

Domestics serving in the wealthiest American families savored still another form of elitism. Aware of the power and prestige their employers held in society, these snobs proudly identified themselves with their employers' family names, lording it over people serving less prestigious families and over common folk who might be impressed by their intimacy with the rich. Some of these domestics were distinctly proud of the ladies and gentlemen they served and refused to live in

3. Florence Wilcox to Lucy M. Salmon, February 11 [1890], in Lucy Maynard Salmon Papers, Vassar College Library; *Report on Chinese Immigration, Senate Reports*, 44th Congress, 2nd sess., no. 689, pp. 572–73, 596, 621–23; Lucy M. Salmon, *Domestic Service* (New York: Macmillan, 1897), 91–92.

4. Georgiana Kirby, *Years of Experience: An Autobiographical Narrative* (New York: G. P. Putnam's Sons, 1887), 81; L. M. Gould to Lucy M. Salmon [1890], in Salmon Papers.

any but "respectable families." Even scrubwomen, who might occasionally be called upon to prepare a mansion for some special event, were envied by the other women in their tenements. A Danish girl listened spellbound to the tales of high society told to her by friends working in upper-class households. The girl repeated their gossip to her middle-class employer, speaking wistfully of how grand it would be to work for "de four hundert." She hastened to assure her mistress that she was not displeased with her own position and that she thought her employer's friends very nice people. Yet, she sighed, "dey ain't in society."[5]

Likewise, servants recognized qualitative differences between old and newly wealthy families. They preferred experienced, self-confident employers, those who did not feel compelled to browbeat servants in order to reassure themselves of their social positions. Servants ridiculed unsophisticated, inept, *nouveau riche* employers. "Society is made up of varieties," maintained a former lady's maid, "but it is easy for the *humble servant* to distinguish the well-born and highly-bred lady, under the plainest garb, from the *parvenu woman*, whose sudden good luck and well-filled purse dresses her in lace . . . and places her in circles where she is more *endured* than courted." Some immigrants expressed disappointment at the lack of gentility displayed by all of America's wealthy families, regardless of when or how those families had gained their fortunes, but more often it was the *nouveaux riches*, or "shoddyites," whom they singled out. Experienced foreign servants, trained to service in the oldest British and European families, were the most critical. A French butler ridiculed America's "new aristocrats" for their lack of social grace and ignorance of etiquette. They "live like pig in a palace," he scoffed, "not knowing what to do, so that the servants are laughing and saying . . . 'he is a farmer from Cincinnati.'"[6]

None of this is to say that servants always honored their class struc-

5. Eliza Potter, *A Hairdresser's Experience in High Life* (Cincinnati: n.p., 1859), 22, 104, 114; George P. Rawick (ed.), *The American Slave: A Composite Autobiography* (19 vols.; Westport, Conn.: Greenwood, 1972), II, Part 1, p. 328, XII, Part 2, p. 36, XIII, Part 3, p. 190, XV, 358; Ella Gertrude Thomas Diary (MS in Perkins Library, Duke University), June 1, 1869; Carter, *Millionaire Households*, 159–62, 232, 235. For similar distinctions in rural areas see Jeanne Hunnicutt Delgado (ed.), "Nellie Kedzie Jone's Advice to Farm Women: Letters from Wisconsin, 1912–1916," *Wisconsin Magazine of History*, LVII (1973), 3–27. Quoted in Elizabeth Jordan, "Mrs. Van Nostrand's Night of Triumph," *Harper's Weekly*, LII (March 7, 1908), 21.

6. Eliza Potter, *A Hairdresser's Experience in High Life*, 13, 53–55, 60–62; "A Butler's Life Story," *Independent*, LXIX (July 14, 1910), 82.

ture. Some servants were just as scornful of their own rules as they were of their employers' affectations. Regardless of recognized hierarchy and prescribed etiquette, servants frequently clashed. For example, backbiting and betrayal flourished where servants competed for their employers' favor. Most such battles were waged by calling names and telling tales behind one another's back. But open conflict was not uncommon. Some servants were schemers, plotting against fellow workers by drawing them into quarrels. Other fights were spontaneous outbursts for which no one was really to blame but in which neither contender would back down. In many such cases, dismissal of one of the combatants resulted. Some employers contributed to these affairs by allowing themselves to be intimidated by the more boisterous of the participants. They fired the meeker soul for the sake of domestic peace, even when no real cause for doing so existed. One such episode involved a New Yorker whose cook of five years was constantly at odds with his chambermaid of two and one-half years. Finally, there came a crisis, and the cook insisted that either she or the chambermaid must go. The employer had little choice. The cook, besides having more seniority, was more valuable and would have been harder to replace. The employer therefore fired the maid without ever learning the reason for the quarrel.[7]

The servant hierarchy illustrated a universal need for self-respect. It was reassuring for servants to know that someone, somewhere, was their social inferior. In this fancy, they imitated what they saw all around them in American life. Just as the upper classes looked down their noses at the lower classes, so butlers ignored chambermaids, native-white servants scorned immigrants, and immigrants despised Negroes. One foreign observer neatly summarized the pettiness of the whole system when he wrote, "You rarely meet [in the United States] with one of these aspirants to be considered on an equality with any one really superior to him in rank and position, but you may discover that he considers himself ineffably superior to the poor wight below him."[8] Servants, by their behavior, condoned and perpetuated the very class snobbery they so detested in their employers.

The second and perhaps most influential impersonal force shaping

7. Henry Dana Ward Diary, 1850–57 (MS in Manuscripts and Archives Division, New York Public Library, Astor, Lenox, and Tilden Foundations), April 8, 15, 1855. See also Ann T. Coleman, "Reminiscences" (MS in Ann Thomas Coleman Papers, Perkins Library, Duke University), VII, 15–16.
8. Charles Joseph Latrobe, *The Rambler in North America* (2 vols.; London: R. B. Seeley and W. Burnside, 1835), II, 140.

servants' lives was their duties. As seen, a servant's place in the class structure of service was based in large part upon his or her job. But duties were more than just a gauge of social standing. Servants, as employees, were required to perform certain tasks at specified times. These tasks formed the focal point of their lives and determined how they spent most of their waking hours. The number of different jobs and the varying number of servants in any given household makes generalization about particular duties difficult. In broad terms, however, most servants followed a similar routine. Each servant accepted responsibility for a number of daily assignments to be performed each morning. The afternoon was occupied by weekly assignments and special projects, such as preparing for an evening entertainment. Entire afternoons were devoted once a week to washing, ironing, baking, or thoroughly cleaning individual rooms. Sunday work was minimal, and part of that day was usually granted as time off.

Changes in these basic duties over the years could best be measured in the amount of sweat involved. As labor-saving devices and more efficient means of heating, lighting, plumbing, and sanitation were developed, work became easier. Many common duties of the early nineteenth century, such as spinning, weaving, candle making, and preparation of foods, were eliminated by factory produced goods. The more rapidly employers adopted these conveniences, the easier servants' work became. As specialization reached its peak in the twentieth century, servants became unwilling to perform more than a limited number of tasks. By the early 1920s, division of labor had so splintered the occupations of both male and female servants that nearly one hundred separately defined jobs and combinations of jobs existed. Still, in order to understand how servants spent their time and to appreciate the logic of the occupational hierarchy, the duties of individual service positions should be comprehended. In a large household at the turn of the twentieth century the complex hierarchy and schedule of duties became clearly delineated.[9]

The heads of the domestic hierarchy, the hired housekeeper and the butler, required years of experience and training in all phases of house-

9. The principal source for the following discussion is Carter, *Millionaire Households.* See also Mrs. William Parkes, *Domestic Duties; or, Instructions to Young Married Ladies* (New York: J. and J. Harper, 1828); Robert Roberts, *The House Servant's Directory* (Boston: Munroe and Francis, 1828); R. R. Bowker, "In *Re* Bridget—the Defence," *Old and New,* IV (October, 1871), 498–99; Mrs. S. W. Oakey, "Suggestions to Young Housekeepers," *Scribner's Monthly,* XVII (1878–79), contains a series of articles; Christine Terhune Herrick, *Housekeeping Made Easy* (New York: Harper and

hold labor and management. They were professionals, indispensable to the operation of large establishments requiring many servants. Even if they did not serve a single family all of their lives, housekeepers and butlers generally spent their lives in service. They, above all servants, showed the most deference to employers and betrayed the least dissatisfaction with their lot. Although they might occasionally have a "row" with employers, such spats usually concerned professional matters or points of etiquette.[10]

Actually, two types of hired housekeeper existed. One was only a glorified maid-of-all-work. She most often worked for a small family or a bachelor, sometimes being employed only a few days per week. She was responsible for light housekeeping and perhaps cooking, with heavy work, such as laundry, performed by outside help. The true housekeeper held an altogether different position. She worked in a large household with many subordinate servants. Hers was an administrative post. She acted as deputy for her employer and received the same deferential treatment from the other servants as was shown the family. She assumed responsibility for the smooth operation of the household and the performance and personal behavior of the lower servants. She managed household expenditures, including the purchase of cleaning supplies and payment of servants' wages. She regulated all stores and provisions and supervised the hiring, training, and firing of servants. Hers, in short, was a post of responsibility, requiring intelligence, housekeeping skill, and administrative ability.

Butlers worked jointly with hired housekeepers in heading a domestic staff, although they were slightly below housekeepers in status. If no housekeeper was employed, the butler assumed both jobs. Generally, the butler's duties included directing the footmen, who served as his assistants, and insuring that the visible part of the household machinery ran smoothly. His personal responsibilities included security of the house; care of china, silverware, and glassware stored in the butler's pantry; purchase, storage, and decanting of wines and liquors; and attendance to such miscellaneous tasks as placement of household

Brothers, 1888) and *The Expert Maid-Servant* (New York: Harper and Brothers, 1897, 1904); Lida Seely, *Mrs. Seely's Cook Book* (New York: Macmillan, 1902); Clara E. Laughlin (ed.), *The Complete Home* (New York: D. Appleton and Co., 1906, rpr. 1912); Virginia Terhune Van de Water, *From Kitchen to Garret* (New York: Sturgis and Walton, 1910). The fact that Oakey's articles include much material from the Parkes book indicates how slowly servants' duties changed over the years.

10. Cornelius Vanderbilt, Jr., *Queen of the Golden Age: The Fabulous Story of Grace Wilson Vanderbilt* (New York: McGraw-Hill, 1956), 261–62.

floral and fruit arrangements and preparation of menus and place cards for dinner parties.

Some of a butler's duties were nebulous, being more or less, as one employer phrased it, to "buttle." One of his least easily explained yet most important assignments was to maintain a dignified atmosphere in the household. The butler was indispensable to any household with "pretensions to fashion." He served as the establishment's fountainhead of dignity and its authority on questions of etiquette and decorum. He and his staff of footmen were immaculate in dress and as rigid in expression as military sentries. The butler's speech, countenance, and movements betokened ineffable calm. As described by a French butler serving in the United States, "The very essence of a butler's duty is, do the thing gently, without asking. You must know what they [employers] want all the time without interrupting the conversation. You must tell the other servants by the eye, by the lifting of a finger, so that all runs smooth as if there were no servants and yet wants are all supplied."[11]

To accomplish this, a butler required footmen. Indeed, he could not have existed, either theoretically or practically, without them. Because a true butler acted primarily as an administrator, a single male servant was undeserving of the title "butler." There were, of course, many one-man households, particularly before 1870, when male staffs were comparatively small. In those days, a single male servant might have served as butler, valet, footman, and coachman. He waited at table, greeted callers, attended to his male employer's wardrobe, did the marketing, and performed the heavier work of the household. But such a man, even though he may have been called a butler, did not rate the title. Only footmen performed manual labor in fully staffed establishments. Their number varied according to an employer's wealth and taste, but even at the end of the great age of servants, in about 1900, at least four footmen were required to give "an unmistakable air of ease" to a home.[12]

Footmen had many duties. Where a single footman was employed, he began his day by sweeping the front steps and walk. Next, he assisted the parlor maid with any heavy work she could not accomplish alone, such as moving and polishing furniture. He then cleaned the breakfast silverware and brushed and cleaned the clothes and shoes to

11. "A Butler's Life Story," 82.
12. Francis J. Grund, *The Americans in Their Moral, Social, and Political Relations* (New York: Johnson Reprint, 1968), 237; Carter, *Millionaire Households*, 188.

be worn by the gentlemen of the family. Finally, after washing and making himself presentable, he completed his morning duties by preparing the breakfast table—laying the cloth and setting the plate. He served as waiter at all meals and was responsible for cleaning the silverware, china, and glassware. He stood ready to answer the door at any time, to run family errands, and to attend the carriage when it was in use. In households with larger staffs, footmen had cleaning duties in individual rooms or hallways, but in all cases, their work was to be completed before breakfast so that they were out of the family's way. After breakfast, footmen changed into livery or dress clothes and entered into a hectic schedule of setting tables, serving meals, attending the personal needs of family and guests, greeting and announcing callers, and running errands. They were, indeed, *foot*men.

Another important male servant was the valet. At first glance, this seems an uncomplicated, leisurely, and easily defined job. The valet was responsible for his employer's appearance and comfort. He cared for his wardrobe, ran his errands, arranged his travels, aided in his toilet, and occasionally attended to his finances and correspondence. Yet the valet's position was a curious one. On the one hand, he served as a "gentleman's gentleman," his employer's "man." As such, he was closely identified with his employer and commanded the respect of merchants, hotel managers, and all others he came in contact with as his representative. It could be an easy life, especially if his employer was a man-about-town or someone who traveled extensively. On the other hand, probably no other servant was so aware of having a "master," and it was assumed that few industrious, self-respecting fellows would endure such a position for very long.

The lady's maid was the valet's counterpart in serving the mistress of the household. Insofar as the toilet of women was more complex and elaborate than that of men, she filled a more demanding position. She had to be a skilled hairdresser, seamstress, even dressmaker. She assumed responsibility for her employer's clothes and jewelry, as well as for her personal care. She accompanied her on all of her travels and, when not attending the lady at evening entertainments, usually remained awake until she returned home, regardless of the hour.

Parlormaids were responsible for cleaning main floor hallways and sitting rooms, such as parlors, libraries, dining rooms, and drawing rooms. They began each morning by airing rooms, removing ashes and cinders from fireplaces, cleaning grates and andirons, preparing new fires, and filling coal scuttles. Next they swept carpets with a good horsehair broom and, once weekly, with a coarse-bristled carpet broom. They then dusted furniture, as well as doors, window panels, skirting boards, and mantel, with a soft round brush or a linen duster. Picture frames, china ornaments, mirrors, and bric-a-brac were cleaned with a fine painter's brush or feather duster. Finally, they dusted window curtains with a feather broom. Once a week they washed windowsills and windows. Stairs, banisters, and hallways, if part of the parlor-maid's domain, were swept and dusted before the family came downstairs to breakfast.

Chambermaids were primarily responsible for sleeping and dressing quarters. They began their morning as soon as the family was up and dressed by opening bedroom windows and pulling back the bedding to air. Next, they emptied and cleaned chamber pots, cleaned and arranged fireplaces, emptied washbasins, and replenished washing and drinking pitchers. They then made the beds, after which they swept and dusted the dressing and bedrooms, following the same technique used by parlormaids. Bedroom carpets were taken up, shaken, and swept under twice weekly. In the evening, while the family was dining, chambermaids returned to resurrect dressing rooms from the disarray of the dressing hour and to prepare bedrooms for the family's retirement by turning down beds, drawing curtains, and setting lamps and fires.

Laundresses did the washing and ironing. Wealthy establishments had a full-time laundress, often with assistants. In smaller households, a laundress was employed once weekly, or a regular servant, most often the cook, was made responsible for the job. Laundering was hard work, requiring a sturdy back and strong arms. It became easier with the development of the washing machine and wringer, but the evolution of these work savers was a slow process. Most nineteenth-century servants never enjoyed such luxuries, and laundering remained the most physically demanding of all regular housekeeping tasks. It also required intelligence and skill. Proper treatment of different fabrics and stains was very nearly a science. Woolens, cottons, and linens all had to be washed in different types of water, at different temperatures, with different cleaning compounds, and with varying degrees of vigor. Without expert knowledge of these nuances, a wardrobe could be destroyed. For most of the period, laundresses also had to prepare their own starch, bleach, and cleaning compounds and boil their own water.

Cooks ruled the kitchen. When serving in large establishments, cooks (usually men) were known as chefs, and they had a number of assistants to perform the more menial culinary tasks. Chefs could thus devote their attention to marketing, keeping accounts, and practicing the "art" of cooking. "Cooks" (usually women) were found in middle-class households. Their duties were more arduous than the chef's, for in addition to ordering and preparing food, they also washed dishes, swept and scrubbed the kitchen and store room, and performed the innumerable chores of a chef's assistant, such as peeling potatoes and cleaning the stove. Some daily tasks were made easier as the century progressed by the use of mechanical gadgets and labor-saving inventions. Before the advent of the wood- or coal-burning stove, for example, cooks contended with smoking fireplaces, which required daily cleaning. Even with wood- and coal-burning stoves much work, such as the daily cleaning of the grate and the weekly cleaning of the flue, remained until the widespread use of gas ranges in the twentieth century.

A good nursemaid was indispensable in a household with children, yet this was one of the most difficult posts for employers satisfactorily to fill. A nurse had to be a perfect blend of intelligence, cleanliness, and morality. It was important that she be an early riser and light sleeper, and she ought not to be overly fond of night life. It was convenient if she found contentment in reading and sewing so that she might always be available to the children. She should have no speech impediment, and it was desirable that she be pretty and fair complexioned. Hers was a full-time job; she was to the children what the lady's maid was to their mother. She attended the children at all hours of the day, dressing them, playing with them, and sleeping near them. In some cases, she also fed the children and, with infants, performed the unpleasant task of changing diapers. Indeed, many upper-class children saw more of their nurse than of their parents. Yet nurses were often handicapped in their duties by mothers who forbade them to reprimand or to punish their darlings. With precocious or bratty children this was a severe trial, especially if the mother always took the child's side in arguments.

A variety of servants' servants were necessary for the efficient operation of households with large domestic staffs. Scullery maids, probably the lowest-ranked, hardest-worked, and worst-paid of all servants, were essential to chefs. They washed dishes, scrubbed pots, disposed of garbage, and swept, mopped, and scrubbed the kitchen. Kitchen maids also assisted chefs by peeling and slicing fruits and vegetables, preparing meats, and keeping utensils and cooking facilities spotlessly clean. The "useful" or dining-hall maid cleaned servants' living quarters in large establishments. She performed every imaginable housekeeping chore, including waiting at the servants' table, washing their dishes, sweeping and dusting their quarters, laundering their uniforms and linen—everything but cooking.

These were the usual occupations of indoor servants in private homes. Outdoor servants, such as gardeners, coachmen, chauffeurs, and handymen, will not be considered here. In households with enough servants to fill each position, the domestic machinery hummed with efficiency, and no one was overworked. But in smaller, less wealthy establishments, the same number of tasks, albeit on a smaller scale, had to be performed by fewer people. The first servants to be dispensed with were upper servants and footmen. They were extravagances not found in middle-class homes. Even upper-middle-class families often survived with only three or four servants. These were usually a cook, who also served as laundress; a housemaid, filling the functions of chambermaid and parlormaid; a "second girl," who assisted the cook and housemaid; and if possible, one male servant to do the heavy work, act as valet and waiter, and mark his employers as people of means. Even more common was the two servant household, in which duties were divided between a cook-laundress and a housemaid.

The most frequently encountered arrangement in American homes, however, was the single general housemaid, or "maid-of-all-work." Her duties included all that the name implied. Most Americans who employed servants had one girl who performed all household work, with the occasional exception of laundry. Laundry was either performed by a laundress brought in weekly or, after 1870, sent to a commercial laundry. If there were daughters in the family, they and their mother sometimes helped by doing light work—making beds, completing simple culinary tasks, and the like. Still, the maid-of-all-work's day was a long one. She usually began work at five-thirty or six in the morning, as did most servants, and within four or five hours had accomplished, on a modest scale, the morning duties of cook, chambermaid, parlormaid, and footman. Afternoons were varied by special weekly projects, all of which were scheduled around the time needed to prepare meals. It was hard work but not impossible. As one girl wrote of her hectic day, "I think I am getting along nicely. I have

A servant at work? This would certainly have been one of the maid-of-all-work's early morning chores.

Few maids-of-all-work enjoyed the opportunity to sit for even such an informal portrait as this one. Notice the fresh, neatly pressed apron that this Detroit girl has donned for the occasion.
Courtesy of the Burton Historical Collection of the Detroit Public Library.

learned all of my duties. I think sometimes I forget some of them but not very often."[13]

In rural areas, house servants also had outdoor chores. Maids-of-all-work on modest-sized farms, for instance, cooked, washed, ironed, and kept the house clean, but they also milked cows, fed chickens, tended gardens, and churned butter. During the harvest they might even be called upon to work in the fields if enough regular hands could not be secured. Likewise, a hired boy, although principally an agricultural worker, might be required to cut wood, carry water, help in the kitchen, and generally lend a hand with "every thing about the house."[14]

Hotel servants performed duties similar to those of private servants. Housekeepers directed hotel staffs; chambermaids cleaned and polished bedrooms; waiters, porters, and bellboys did the work of footmen; headwaiters acted as butlers; chefs and kitchen help carried on as everywhere; and after 1850 skilled laundry workers added lustre to the reputations of many first-class "houses." As hotel staffs increased in size, their organization became more complex than that of even the largest households. Housekeeping functions were divided into departments, each with its own staff and work schedules, until the personnel structures of the largest hotels seemed as bewildering as their mazes of passageways.[15]

The third element common to servants' lives was their working hours. Although varying in length, these were generally characterized by their inordinate length and irregularity. Whether working in city or country, many servants labored from sunrise to sunset, but this was not an unusual work schedule in the nineteenth century. Before contractual restrictions on hours in the 1820s and passage of legislation limiting the hours of industrial workers in the late 1840s, laborers in many occupations worked nearly equally long days. But as other workers organized and reduced their hours, servants failed to do so

13. Lydia to [Margaret Scott], April 20, 1886, in Adrian (Michigan) Girls' Training School Records, Michigan State Archives.

14. David E. Schob, *Hired Hands and Plowboys: Farm Labor in the Midwest, 1815–1860* (Urbana: University of Illinois Press, 1975), 189–90, 195–96, 199–202; Sarah C. Himes to Adam Himes, March 20, 1870, in Sarah Catherine Himes Letters, Perkins Library, Duke University; Patience Pennington [Elizabeth Waites (Allston) Pringle], *A Woman Rice Planter*, ed. Cornelius O. Cathey (Cambridge: Harvard University Press, 1961), 108.

15. "Waitress Work in Summer Hotels," *American Kitchen Magazine*, XIII (June, 1900), 85–86; "Trained Waitresses," *Hotel Monthly*, VII (November, 1899), 16–17, John B. Goins, "The American Colored Waiter," *Hotel Monthly*, IX (April, 1901), 27 is part of a series on the waiter's duties that continued to August, 1902.

and were left behind in successive agitations for the twelve-, ten-, and eight-hour days.

Of course, as in their duties, much diversity could be found in servants' hours. Geography, custom, size of staff, and type of job were all factors to consider. While a servant in Kansas worked only five hours a day, another in Georgia worked eighteen. The same range could be found within a single city. Before 1870 most servants worked well over twelve hours each day, six or seven days a week. The number of work hours tended to decline over the years, but this was such a slow process that few workers witnessed a significant change during their lifetimes. By the early 1900s, probably three-fourths still labored at least ten hours a day, and though less usual, a seven-day week was not unheard of. Agitation by reformers for the eight-hour day called attention to the servant's plight and helped to reduce hours somewhat, but more than a few servants continued to work twelve- to fourteen-hour days as late as 1917.[16]

Admittedly, not every hour represented unrelenting toil. Mealtimes, varying from one-half to one hour, two or three times daily, gave an opportunity to relax. Certain tasks, such as polishing silver, peeling vegetables, and sewing, were leisurely pursuits that permitted a sitting position. There were also unofficial breaks, which even the most conscientious servants indulged in. Pausing on an errand to gaze in shop windows and gossiping with a neighboring servant while hanging the laundry were popular ways of stealing a few moments. Also, nearly all servants enjoyed a few official hours off during the week, although the amount of time varied. Some servants had a free hour or two every day, while others might only be allowed a few hours off each week or month. Before 1870 a full day off was rare. Between 1870 and 1900, the average servant probably enjoyed at least one afternoon and one evening off per week. After that date, an increasing number enjoyed a couple of hours each day as well as several free evenings per week.[17]

Yet even time off was not completely free. Because the feudal contract dictated that all of a servant's time belonged to the "master," servants, even when off duty, remained "on call" for emergencies and to answer the door and later the telephone. A girl who had only five to

16. See Salmon, *Domestic Service*, 143–46, for examples.
17. Helen C. Callahan, "Upstairs-Downstairs in Chicago, 1870–1907: The Glessner Household," *Chicago History*, VI (1977–78), 202, identifies four specific categories of free time.

seven hours of actual daily work might be required to be on hand twelve to fourteen hours. Some servants were so overburdened with work that, in order to finish it, they had to forego their free time. Even if completing their regular chores and excused from standing watch against emergencies, servants generally had a curfew placed on them when venturing outside the house. Some workers hesitated to leave the house even then for fear that employers, in their absence, might attempt some household task for themselves, causing a servant "to work with extra labor to repair the damage." Small wonder that when inquiring about a job servants sometimes asked not how much free time they would be given but if any free time would be allowed.[18]

The hours of hotel servants were as varied and irregular as in private homes. Although hotels were better organized than most private homes, many servants worked seven-day weeks, their days splintered and complicated by broken shifts, overtime, and "on call" time. Small hotels, particularly before the 1840s, were usually informally operated, and the help enjoyed liberal free time. Yet, even in small hotels, work days were long. In large establishments, length and distribution of hours varied by department. By the 1920s the daily hours of hotel employees were restricted by law in some states, but weekly averages remained burdensome. A survey of New York hotels in 1921 showed that the hours of chambermaids in twelve hotels ranged from 49.5 to 70 hours per week during a seven-day week. On the other hand, kitchen help usually worked 8- or 9-hour days, six days weekly, although there, too, broken shifts sometimes boosted weekly averages to 60 hours, with 12- to 13-hour days preceding days off.[19]

Vacations were also unpredictable, ranging from a few legal holidays to several months each year. Nearly all servants enjoyed all or part of such holidays as Independence Day and Christmas to themselves. Actual vacations were also to be had, although, as in all else, there was no fixed custom as to time of year, length, or conditions. Some servants received paid vacations. Others lost their full wages or some part of them during the holiday period.

Servants complained more about long, indefinite hours than about any single aspect of their working conditions. The long hours and exacting demands of employers left many servants physically and men-

18. New York *Times*, March 9, 1879, p. 9; Flora to [Lucy M. Sickles], October 9, 1891, and Maria to Margaret Scott, June 3, 1886, both in Adrian Records.
19. Consumers' League of New York City, *Behind the Scenes in a Hotel* (New York: n.p., 1922), 16–27.

tally drained by day's end, with no ambition save to crawl into bed. A girl who worked in a boarding house of nineteen residents wrote, "I wate on them all at the table and wash all the dishes alone and besides outher worke which takes me all day. I have no time during the day for my self. If I do any thing for my self such as writing or sewing it must be 9, 10 or 11 o clock at night. I am so tired then." Bumps, bruises, housemaid's knee, and feet and legs weary, if not swollen, from climbing a hundred stairs took a daily toll. Sometimes a night's rest was not enough, so that even if recovering from the nervousness and confusion of the previous day, a servant's "first waking consciousness was an ache." Servants blamed their weariness on inconsiderate and indifferent employers, employers who, not knowing what a day's work was, appreciated neither their labors nor their problems, and who regarded them as "machines." Servants had to be on their feet constantly, complained one girl, or employers thought them lazy. If they finished their assigned tasks and paused to rest, they received more work; if they paced themselves to conserve energy, they were called slow. Most servants agreed that their actual work was not so burdensome as the constant demand of being on call, but it was difficult to separate the two. Everything ran together. Their time was never their own; very few hours could be enjoyed in total relaxation. "I have to work hard," moaned one woman, "not at hard work, but constant work. I cannot lay me down to rest when I am tired, there is so much for me to do."[20]

Even upper servants felt the strain of long hours and heavy responsibilities. A Mississippi girl, working as combination housekeeper and governess, complained in page after page of her diary about the mental and physical strain of her life. Many of her grumblings resembled those of employers, especially when she contemplated her problems in hiring good lower servants and in keeping the "insolent" ones under

20. Flora to [Lucy M. Sickles], October 9, 1891, in Adrian Records; Amy E. Tanner, "Glimpses at the Mind of a Waitress," *American Journal of Sociology*, XIII (July, 1907), 49–50; New York *Times*, December 5, 1872, p. 3; Edith J. R. Isaacs, "Why Maids Leave Home: Real Letters That Also Show How They Might Be Induced to Stay," *Delineator*, LXXXIV (January, 1914), 46; Ann T. Coleman to Niece, May 5, 1883, in Coleman Papers. See also Rawick (ed.), *The American Slave*, II, Part 2, p. 26; Anna B. Smith to Harriet B. Stowe, July 26, 1841, in Beecher-Stowe Collection of Family Papers, Schlesinger Library, Radcliffe College; Jannicke Saehle to Johannes Saehle, September 28, 1847, in Theodore C. Blegan (ed.), *Land of Their Choice: The Immigrants Write Home* (Minneapolis: University of Minnesota Press, 1955), 263; Thomas McCann to Mary McKeonn, October 18, 1884, in McCann Correspondence (T-1456), Public Records Office of Northern Ireland, Belfast; Maria to Margaret Scott, June 3, 1886, in Adrian Records.

control. Yet her managerial duties and her responsibility as governess reminded her that she was, after all, only a servant. She worked like "a galley slave" from morning to night. "I am rejoiced to come to my room & take off my hot clothes, dip a little in cold water, & seat myself to rest & write," she wrote on one particularly warm July evening. By December she conceded, "I am broken down mentally & physically." The housekeeper of the Veranda Hotel at New Orleans had similar problems. She recalled working from four o'clock in the morning to midnight, during which time she was constantly busy, her strength "often taxed to the utmost."[21]

Long work days and few leisure hours also meant that servants spent much of their lives isolated in their employers' households, denied what they considered their natural liberties. Servants yearned to escape the control of employers. Their lack of freedom, more than any other aspect of servants' lives, worsened the social stigma. It was the main reason given by factory, shop, and office workers for avoiding service as an occupation. Even after conditions in the early mills and factories began to deteriorate, factory work was still preferred.[22] In single-servant households, lack of freedom created a sense of loneliness and isolation that servants lamented through the years. "I had nobody to talk to," recalled one servant; "it seemed to me that there was nothing in my life but dirty dishes to wash and a kitchen to clean up." A young Michigan girl reacted the same way: "I do not care how much hard work I have to do if I only could have a little pleasure, but it is so lonesome hear." "Ladies wonder how their girls can complain of lonliness, in a house full of people," volunteered another girl, "but oh!

21. Mary Susan Ker Diary (MS in Southern Historical Collection, Library of the University of North Carolina at Chapel Hill), July 18, 29, September 30, November 4, December 1, 1888; Coleman, "Reminiscences," V, 5.

22. Nancy F. Cott, *The Bonds of Womanhood: "Woman's Sphere" in New England, 1780–1835* (New Haven: Yale University Press, 1977), 48–49; Lucy Larcom, *A New England Girlhood* (Boston: Houghton Mifflin, 1924), 199; Anna B. McMahan, "Something More About Domestic Service," *Forum,* I (June, 1886), 401; Ida Jackson, "The Factory Girl and Domestic Service," *Harper's Bazar,* XXXVII (October, 1903), 953–55; Women's Educational and Industrial Union Committee on Domestic Reform, *The Effort to Attract the Workers in Shops and Factories to Domestic Service,* Report No. 1 (Cambridge, Mass.: n.p., 1898), Table 1; Henrietta Roelofs, *The Road to Trained Service in the Household,* YWCA Commission on Household Employment, Bulletin No. 2 (New York: n.p. [1918]), 7–10; Leslie Woodcock Tentler, *Wage-Earning Women: Industrial Work and Family Life in the United States, 1900–1930* (New York: Oxford University Press, 1979), 143–44; Daniel J. Walkowitz, "Working-Class Women in the Gilded Age: Factory, Community, and Family Life Among the Cohoes, New York, Cotton Workers," *Journal of Social History,* V (1971–72), 464–90.

it is the worst kind of loneliness." Finally, from the South, came this lamentation: "My time will be up hear the eight of June I dont think I will stay any longer it is such a lonaly time about hare i never put over such times in all my life I have no one to speak to from morning till night."[23]

So ran a servant's day. It was dreary enough, to be sure. Not only were servants locked into a stigmatized stereotype by employers and the American public, they were programmed into a daily routine that was a strange mixture of monotony and exhaustion. This furthered the stigma on service. The relentlessness of their hours, if not the work, and their lack of leisure time spelled lack of "freedom," an intolerable state of affairs for laborers in America. Yet the situation was not hopeless. Had employers made this loss of freedom worthwhile, had they offered servants adequate compensation for the degradation they endured, all might have been well. The questions were what was offered, and what did servants consider adequate compensation.

23. Mary Anderson, *Woman at Work: The Autobiography of Mary Anderson* (Minneapolis: University of Minnesota Press, 1951), 13–14; Anna to Margaret Scott, August 25, January 1, 1886, both in Adrian Records; Salmon, *Domestic Service*, 151*n*; Jane Glenn to Hannah S. Wiley, May 29, 1869, in Calvin Henderson Wiley Papers, Southern Historical Collection, Library of the University of North Carolina at Chapel Hill.

CHAPTER SIX

THE FRUITS OF LABOR
Wages, Housing, and Diet

"Remuneration! O! that's the Latin word for three farthings." So said Shakespeare's Costard, and so agreed many servants. As they stumbled through their briar-infested lives, servants anticipated compensation for their scratches and fatigue. They labored not for glory and rarely for love, but for shelter, food, and coin. These were the most important parts of their lives. Predictably, the bountifulness of these fruits varied in time and place. While one girl worked fifteen hours a day for a family of ten, slept in the cold, dingy attic of a three-story house, and received a mere pittance in pay, another girl worked only nine hours in a three-person bungalow, slept in a pleasant, private bedroom, and earned twice the wages. But contented, comfortable servants were a minority. While most servants were well-off in comparison to much of the working class, they still grumbled that the net value of wages, lodging, and victuals was worth little more than three farthings.

Servants' wages, their most important means of compensation, varied widely. No fixed wage scale existed for servants, not even an average wage. At best, there were ranges of wages, controlled by an array of economic and noneconomic circumstances. Geography was one factor, involving not only regional variations but the local customs and economic conditions of individual communities and states. At the most basic level—within each household—sex, age, race, nationality, experience, duties, type and size of establishment, and employer personality became additional considerations.

In general terms, servants' wages increased nationwide between 1800 and 1920, but they did so very slowly and rather haphazardly. As wage rates inched forward, sudden increases were rare but so, too, were losses. Servants' wages seldom dropped very far, even during periods of national economic depression and unemployment. During the combined economic crisis and immigration flood of 1837–1850, servants' wages remained remarkably stable, even when those of other laborers declined. By the mid-1850s many servants earned wages equal to those paid skilled workers during the 1820s, although these rates leveled off and sometimes fell during the Civil War. Wages rose rapidly after the war, until slowed by the depression of the early 1870s. They then rebounded during the 1880s, stagnated during the depression of the 1890s, climbed steadily from 1900 to 1914, and finally dropped, once again, during World War I. This is as exact as one dares to be in describing a national pattern. In fact, in view of the variations in local and regional wages, it is best to ignore national trends altogether. Differing costs of living and per capita wealth caused wages to fluctuate wildly in different parts of the nation. Antebellum southern wages, especially in the large cities, often equaled wages paid elsewhere in the nation, but after Appomattox the wages of southern servants stagnated, remaining depressingly low for the next half century. Wages were generally lower in the postbellum South than in the North, lower in southern and midwestern cities than in northeastern and far western cities. Random examples could be selected to challenge all such generalizations. Indeed, since data on wages is scattered in letters, diaries, household account books, newspapers, and group surveys, it is difficult to generalize at all. Nevertheless, such evidence as exists, tends to support a few general statements about the ranges of wages paid. And there is no doubt that these wages resulted from regional and local economic and social conditions.[1]

1. George J. Stigler, *Domestic Servants in the United States, 1900–1940*, Occasional Paper No. 24 of the National Bureau of Economic Research (New York: National Bureau of Economic Research, 1946), 12; James D. B. DeBow, *Statistical View of the United States: Compendium of the Seventh U.S. Census* (Washington, D.C.: Government Printing Office, 1854), 164; U.S. Bureau of the Census, *Eighth United States Census: Statistics of the United States* (Washington, D.C.: Government Printing Office, 1866), IV, 512. For examples of the difficulties of comparing wages, see Lucy M. Salmon, *Domestic Service* (New York: Macmillan, 1897), 88–97; Alice C. Hanson and Paul H. Douglas, "The Wages of Domestic Labor in Chicago, 1890–1929," *Journal of American Statistical Association*, XXV (1930), 47–50.

Extreme and sudden variations in wages were checked by several factors. Wages survived depressions because employers tended to fire servants—although always as a last resort—rather than reduce wages. Those who tried to lower wages frequently lost their servants. Wages increased slowly during boom periods because of new demand for servants, but they rarely skyrocketed, even in good times, since, after a certain point, employers preferred hiring slightly less efficient servants at more moderate prices. Wages also remained free of the influence of collective bargaining and legislation. Attempts to unionize servants were short-lived, and surviving organizations seldom concerned themselves with wages, though in instances where strikes or lockouts were ordered, wages often sparked the revolt. A few state governments enacted minimum wage laws for hotel workers after 1900, but these only served to maintain a living wage.

A frequently encountered geographic influence was the city-country division, wages in the former generally exceeding those in the latter. This appears illogical at first glance, for competition within the larger urban work force should have driven city wages down. However, employer competition for the best servants kept wages at honest levels, causing employers to complain about the high price of even poor-quality help. Also, in the cities there were more specialists, who commanded higher wages than did the general household workers who dominated rural regions. Rural and small-town wages were not to be scoffed at, though. They were maintained at respectable levels and, especially before the Civil War, occasionally equaled or surpassed those of nearby cities. Rural employers had to offer competitive wages in order to retain young women who would otherwise be lured to the city. Still, rural employers lacked the resources of urbanites, and so rural rates generally ranked below the urban scale.[2]

Wages in individual communities were ruled to a large extent by local custom, each community having recognized "going rates" for servants. Intelligence offices often controlled these rates in large cities, but elsewhere employers paid what their neighbors paid. Thus, when a certain New Englander hired a servant from a nearby town, neither

2. David E. Schob, *Hired Hands and Plowboys: Farm Labor in the Midwest, 1815–1860* (Urbana: University of Illinois Press, 1975), 192–93; David M. Katzman, *Seven Days a Week: Women and Domestic Service in Industrializing America* (New York: Oxford University Press, 1978), 308–309; Jeanne Hunnicutt Delgado (ed.), "Nellie Kedzie Jone's Advice to Farm Women: Letters from Wisconsin, 1912–1916," *Wisconsin Magazine of History,* LVII (1973), 22.

she nor the servant inquired as to what wages would be paid. "I presume," explained the woman, "it will be two dollars pr week as that is the regular price here." Employers who were especially desperate for servants sometimes broke local rules in order to attract reliable help, even though such behavior was frowned upon in most communities as "bad business." Both the New York *Times* and the Chicago *Tribune* conducted animated public debates in the 1870s through their letter columns concerning the "servant problem" and the high wages being paid for poor help. Employers would seize any legitimate opportunity to lower wages. Whenever a sudden oversupply of servants occurred, wages temporarily dropped. One employer rejoiced at the closing of two large factories employing many of her community's females since it created an abundance of unemployed workers available "at any price."[3] Other employers were laws unto themselves. Regardless of local wage increases, they paid the same rates for years and decades on end. This explains, in part, why some employers experienced so much trouble finding good servants. By ignoring accepted wage levels, they could frequently hire none but inferior workers.

Additional factors appeared within individual households. For instance, men received higher wages than women even when the sexes performed similar work. Quite aside from the fact that higher wages were necessary to entice men into service because it was considered more degrading for men than for women, male servants, far more than female servants, enhanced an employer's social position. Servants realized this, employers admitted it, and male servants were therefore able to demand and receive good wages. Furthermore, because employers placed male servants in highly visible jobs meant to exploit their value as status symbols, men had to be selected as much for their stately appearance as for their abilities, a consideration that appreciably increased their monetary value. One hired housekeeper complained bitterly about this state of affairs. She insisted that male servants did less and were paid more (usually two to four times more)

3. Fanny H. Boltwood to [Hannah S. Terry] [October 18, 1851], in Boltwood Family Papers, Burton Historical Collection, Detroit Public Library; *Bulletin of the Domestic Reform League*, I (February, 1907), n.p.; Mehetable M. Goddard to Lucretia Davis, February 21, 1830, in May-Goddard Papers, Schlesinger Library, Radcliffe College; Mary Elizabeth Carter, *Millionaire Households and Their Domestic Economy* (New York: D. Appleton and Co., 1903), 70. See also Griffith A. Nicholas [Elizabeth Strong Worthington], *The Biddy Club* (Chicago: A. C. McClurg and Co., 1888), 135. See too New York *Times*, October 29, 1873, p. 6, November 16, 1873, p. 4, May 5, 1875, p. 6, February 23, 1879, p. 9 for suggestions that employers band together to limit wages.

than female servants (excepting housekeepers) and that sex repre-sented the "unique and fundamental cause" for differences in wages. She exaggerated the situation, but her accusation had some validity. A government report for the same period during which this woman wrote verified that male servants' wages were 76 percent above those of the ladies.[4]

Despite the racial and ethnic prejudices many employers displayed in hiring, wages remained relatively free of these influences. All other factors being equal, skin color or accent did not automatically lower wages. A gap developed between the wages of blacks and whites in the twentieth century, but even then the difference occurred among men rather than women, and it was due not so much to racial prejudice as to the fact that black servants were momentarily out of fashion. The same was true with immigrants. Xenophobia forced many foreigners to work for low wages in whatever jobs they could find. But this was not always so, and immigrants in service often received wages equal-ing or exceeding those of native whites. Even when non-English-speaking immigrants received lower starting wages than other ser-vants because of the language barrier, progress in English proficiency was usually rewarded by increased pay.[5]

Servants' duties also influenced wages. The higher a servant's posi-tion in the domestic hierarchy, the higher his or her wages, but the degree of skill displayed in performing duties also counted. Servants were categorized according to skill as "good," "average," and "raw" or

4. Carter, *Millionaire Households*, 119, 133; Gail Laughlin, "Domestic Service," in *Report of the United States Industrial Commission on the Relations and Conditions of Capital and Labor* (19 vols.; Washington, D.C.: Government Printing Office, 1901), XIV, 747.

5. James Bogert, Jr., Account Book with Hired Servants (MS in Museum of the City of New York), 1821–57; Mary J. Owen to Jennet S. Tavenner, April 7, July 22, 1857, both in Cabell Tavenner and Alexander Scott Withers Papers, Perkins Library, Duke University; Karl J. R. Ardnt (ed.), "A Bavarian's Journey to New Orleans and Nacog-doches in 1853–1854," *Louisiana Historical Quarterly*, XXIII (1940), 495; John W. Blassingame, *Black New Orleans, 1860–1880* (Chicago: University of Chicago Press, 1973), 65–66; Isabel Eaton, "Special Report on Negro Domestic Service in the Seventh Ward Philadelphia," in W. E. B. DuBois, *The Philadelphia Negro: A Social Study* (New York: Benjamin Blom, 1899), 449–52; Mary V. Robinson, *Domestic Workers and Their Employment Relations*, Bulletin of the Women's Bureau No. 39 (Washington, D.C.: Government Printing Office, 1924), 52; Ole Munch Raeder, *America in the Forties*, trans. and ed. Gunnar J. Malmin (Minneapolis: University of Minnesota Press, 1929), 38–39; Salmon, *Domestic Service*, 91–92; Inter-Municipal Household Research Commit-tee, "Immigrant Women and Girls in Boston" (Typescript in Women's Educational and Industrial Union Records, Schlesinger Library, Radcliffe College), 14–15; Bertha H. Smith, "A Club for Maids," *Ladies' Home Journal*, XXXIII (February, 1916), 64.

"green," their wages falling proportionately. The high wages paid by wealthy employers offer the best example of this. Millionaires insisted on having the best available servants, some people going so far as to recruit trained servants directly from Europe and Britain. But the wealthy had to pay for good servants, as much as double the wages for the same worker in a middle-class home. Likewise, first-class hotels paid higher wages than second-rate competitors, supposedly because their workers were more efficient. Exceptions to the wage-skill relationship were very young and very old servants. They normally received the lowest wages in their job classification, regardless of skill.[6]

With so many factors to consider, evaluating the wages of servants is difficult. When compared to the pay scale in other unskilled and semiskilled jobs in which they might have worked, servants' wages seem to have been fair and competitive. Yet systematic comparisons are virtually impossible, both because the types of skills necessary in service differed from other occupations and because servants commonly received room and board in addition to money wages.

Comparison is especially hard with male servants. In the first place, male servants represented only 1 percent of the nation's male laborers. Moreover, few male occupations were comparable to service. Although generally categorized as unskilled or semiskilled, servants were often very skilled. Male servants needed a finesse, a composure, a state of mind not associated with common laborers and factory workers. In this respect, they were better suited to be store clerks, office workers, and salesmen. Yet these occupations, in turn, required skills commanded by only the best butlers, valets, and footmen. If it is assumed that most servants, being largely unskilled, would have earned wages outside of service equivalent to those of common laborers and factory hands, then service comes out ahead. With the advantages of room and board and freedom from the seasonal unemployment and layoffs suffered by many laborers, male servants enjoyed a financially secure position.[7]

6. Willard Phillips Accounts of Servants and Domestics for 1818–1819 (MS in Willard Phillips Papers, Massachusetts Historical Society); "The New York Labor Market: Female House Servants," *Harper's Weekly*, I (July 4, 1857), 418–19; Sarah W. Dana Account Book for Domestics (MS in Schlesinger Library, Radcliffe College), 1871; Mary Haskell Account Books (MS in Minis Family Papers, Southern Historical Collection, Library of the University of North Carolina at Chapel Hill), XII (1899–1913); "Scarcity of Female Help," *Hotel Monthly*, VI (July, 1898), 19; "A Wage Scale for Cooks," *Hotel Monthly*, VII (June, 1899), 10; *Hotel Bulletin*, II (1907–1908), 209.

7. See, for example, Henry B. Fearon, *Sketches of America* (London: Longman, Hurst, Rees, Orme, and Brown, 1819), 160, Thomas C. Gratten, *Civilized America* (2 vols.; London: Bradbury and Evans, 1859), I, 266, DeBow, *Statistical View of the United*

The wages of female servants may be evaluated with more assurance. It is easier to compare female servants to other occupations because so few alternative jobs were open to women. Most gainfully employed women worked as servants, needleworkers, shop girls, and factory operatives. Servants equaled or surpassed all of these in earning power. Factory girls probably enjoyed an edge over most other female laborers in the early days of factory employment when employers offered high wages and attractive working and living conditions. But by the mid-1830s, conditions were less appealing, and the wage gap between factory and service closed. Many factory girls continued to earn superior money wages, and if living at home or otherwise provided with board and lodging, they enjoyed an edge in total earning power. But girls who paid for at least part of their own room and board—and many did—stood, at best, on a par with servants. Servants were certainly better off than the thousands of needleworkers who crowded the female labor market. These women, often living in city slums, became "prisoners of poverty," the most "helpless and degraded" laborers in the United States. Needleworkers sometimes earned the same cash wages as servants, but they lacked the benefits of room and board and earned their living only by long hours of relentless work. As more skilled occupations became available to women after 1870, servants' wages suffered in comparison, but female servants retained a high economic position among unskilled and semiskilled workers. Women who otherwise objected to service as a livelihood admitted that this was true.[8]

States, 164, U.S. Bureau of the Census, Eighth United States Census, IV, 512, Stuart Blumin, "Mobility and Change in Ante-Bellum Philadelphia," in Stephan Thernstrom and Richard Sennett (eds.), Nineteenth-Century Cities: Essays in the New Urban History (New Haven: Yale University Press, 1969), 168–69; Salmon, Domestic Service, 94–97.

8. Caroline F. Ware, The Early New England Cotton Manufacture: A Study in Industrial Beginnings (New York: Russell and Russell, 1966), 238–39, 240–42, 251–69; Helen L. Sumner, History of Women in Industry in the United States, in Report on Conditions of Women and Child Wage-Earners in the United States, Senate Documents, 61st Cong., 2nd Sess., No. 645, IX, 47, 145; "Conditions in Domestic Service—Wages," Bulletin of the Domestic Reform League, III (January, 1909), n.p.; Norman Ware, The Industrial Worker, 1840–1860 (Boston: Houghton Mifflin, 1924), 48–49, 111–12, 119; Helen Campbell, Prisoners of Poverty: Woman Wage-Earners, Their Trades and Their Lives (Boston: Robert Brothers, 1887), 11–12, 124; Blaine Edward McKinley, "'Strangers in the Gates': Employer Reactions Towards Domestic Servants in America, 1825–1875" (Ph.D. dissertation, Michigan State University, 1969), 24–26; Women's Educational and Industrial Union Committee on Domestic Reform, The Effort to Attract the Workers in Shops and Factories to Domestic Service, Report No. 1 (Cambridge, Mass.: n.p., 1898), 11–12; YWCA Commission on Household Employment, First Report to the Fifth National Convention (n.p., 1915), 8, 14–15, 21, 26–27.

Servants' wages were high enough for the thrifty to save respectable sums of money. Although most servants did not accumulate the hundreds of dollars saved by some of their band, many did gain reputations as savers. They maintained small bank accounts, made cautious investments, granted donations to needy relatives, and stowed precious dollars under mattresses. Immigrants helped to finance the voyages of parents and siblings to America by sending home part of their wages. A Charleston, South Carolina, nurse offers another example of this propensity to save. Working for monthly wages of $6.00 to $7.00 in the early 1830s, by the mid-1840s, Mary had accumulated $256.96. Three years later she had $500.00, enough to quit service, marry, and become housekeeper in her own home.[9]

Perhaps surprisingly, most servants were not discontented with their wages. They sometimes grumbled, in the tradition of all workers, about the tight-fisted descendants of Scrooge for whom they labored, but unmarried servants with no family responsibilities admitted to receiving satisfactory to good pay. Normally, wage-connected complaints were aimed at two targets: employers who refused to pay "local wages" and the lack of promotional opportunity in middle-class households. The latter grievance, one verified by factory and shop workers who scorned service, was voiced by servants who continued to receive the wages they originally hired at, regardless of how much skill and experience they later acquired. Unlike workers outside service or even servants in large establishments the only way for most domestics to win wage increases was to change employers.[10] Still, most servants were satisfied with their wages, or at least not so dissatisfied with wages as with other conditions of service and with employer systems of paying wages.

This latter annoyance, unpaid and sporadically paid wages, was an intense source of friction. Servants were sometimes cheated out of their full wages or not paid at all. Hard times, for example, may not automatically have lowered wages, but they often meant delayed payment when financially distraught employers gave servants' wages low

9. John Berkley Grimball Diaries (MS in Southern Historical Collection, Library of the University of North Carolina at Chapel Hill), October 10, 1832, May 7, 9, 1834, May 3, 1837.

10. See Note 8 above; Lizzie F. Camp to [Jacob A. Camp], April 15, July 25, 1862, both in Camp Family Papers, Collection of Regional History, Cornell University; Christina Goodwin, "An Appeal to Housekeepers," *Forum*, XIX (August, 1895), 757; Mrs. S. T. Rorer, "How to Treat and Keep a Servant," *Ladies' Home Journal*, XVII (May, 1900), 26; Ida Jackson, "The Factory Girl and Domestic Service," *Harper's Bazar*, XXXVII (October, 1903), 955–56.

priority on their lists of pressing debts. Other employers, rather than giving servants their promised wages, paid only what they estimated their services to be worth. Many employers also diluted wages by making deductions. They levied fines for breakage of household articles or for insubordination. They withheld wages in compensation for money that servants had supposedly stolen or for time lost because of unauthorized absence. Consequently, some servants ended their scheduled pay period (which could be weekly or monthly) with very little if any cash wages due them. What cash remained was sometimes allowed to accumulate and later paid at intervals of one to four months or longer. This system was convenient for employers since it required only occasional outlays of cash and provided a disciplinary control against carelessness, insubordination, and threats of sudden departure. It could also serve as a moral lever against wasteful expenditures of wages by servants. Uneducated servants, unaccustomed to handling even modest amounts of money, could benefit or lose by this system, depending on the honesty of their employers. One girl who was refused her wages after being accused of stealing a dollar from her employer did not know what to do. She claimed innocence to the charge and wanted to leave her position for fear that she would be accused of stealing all missing items in the house thereafter. Grown women were also taken advantage of, sometimes leaving their places after weeks of hard work without a penny's compensation.[11]

The tip was an important adjunct to the cash wages of hotel servants during most of the period. Tipping was not a common practice in the early days of the Republic, supposedly because landlords paid their staffs sufficient wages and because American servants, especially native whites, were too proud to prostrate themselves as mendicants.

11. Elizabeth E. Stuart to William Baker, May 22, 1854, in Helen Stuart Mackay-Smith Marlett (ed.), *Stuart Letters of Robert and Elizabeth Stuart and Their Children, 1819–1864* (2 vols.; New York: Harbor Press, 1961), II, 160; John F. Marszalek (ed.), *The Diary of Miss Emma Holmes, 1861–1866* (Baton Rouge: Louisiana State University Press, 1979), 457; New York *Times*, March 26, 1875, p. 5; Samuel Andrew Agnew Diary (MS in Southern Historical Collection, Library of the University of North Carolina at Chapel Hill), March 27, 1866; Flora to [Lucy M. Sickles], October 9, 1891, in Adrian (Michigan) Girls' Training School Records, Michigan State Archives; Ann T. Coleman, "Reminiscences" (MS in Ann Thomas Coleman Papers, Perkins Library, Duke University), VI, 11. See also the Phillips, Dana, Haskell, and Bogert account books as well as John Stanford Household Expense Book (MS in New York Historical Society), 1825–58; Watkins Domestic Account Book (MS in Abiathar and Emily L. Watkins Papers, Manuscripts and Archives Division, New York Public Library, Astor, Lenox, and Tilden Foundations); Octavia A. Otey Diaries (MS in Wyche and Otey Family Papers, Southern Historical Collection, Library of the University of North Carolina at Chapel Hill), last twenty pages, unnumbered.

Some travelers continued to praise this most excellent American custom into the 1880s, but by at least the mid-1840s, tipping had become a standard practice in urban areas and at resort hotels. The rapid growth of tipping was blamed by some Americans on the increasing number of European immigrants working as servants. Europeans, it was said, were raised in an environment where tipping was customary and where servants were not ashamed to grovel for gratuities. Also, because hotel employers apparently allowed cash wages to decline as the century progressed, gradually integrating tips into their estimates of fair wages, tips became necessary for survival. Whatever the reason, the "universal panacea of a dollar" became a permanent feature of American life, and few servants, regardless of nativity, rejected a tip when it was offered.[12]

This is not to say that many servants did not prefer a straight cash wage. These people realized that tipping was unpopular with the public and that the custom marked them as "grafters," further reducing the respectability of their occupation. Nor did they care to rely on fickle customers for their livelihood. "Suppose every waiter here got a regular salary with no chance for extras," summarized one hotel waiter, "do you suppose he'd be jumping hurdles for a lot of fussy people? . . . Do you think he'd present the glad smile to those he'd like to choke, break his neck making everybody comfortable, and then listen to their hard-luck stories or more painful jokes? No, sir; he'd serve the stuff just as he got it from the kitchen."[13] Servants were very much divided on the issue of tipping by the twentieth century, though most seemed to favor abolishing tips *if* they could be assured of respectable salaries.

Most servants received compensation in addition to or in lieu of cash wages. Clothing frequently contributed to wages, even though it was often the worn or unwanted apparel of employers. Some servants were furnished new clothes, but the cost was sometimes subtracted from their money wages. Another form of payment was produce. This might be expected in rural areas, but city servants also received such payments in the first few decades of the nineteenth century. A Negro

12. Mrs. M. C. J. F. Houstoun, *Hesperos; or, Travels in the West* (2 vols.; London: John W. Parker, 1850), II, 7–8, 219–20.
13. Robert Sloss, "The Way of the Waiter," *Harper's Weekly*, LII (January 11, 1908), 20–22. See James Samuel Stemons, "Tipping—the Other Side," *Independent*, LV (March 26, 1903), 726; Theodore Waters, "Shall We Give Tips?" *Everybody's Magazine*, XVI (February, 1907), 211–12; "Editor's Easy Chair," *Harper's Monthly*, CXXVII (July, 1913), 313.

waiter in New York City, Samuel Shepard by name, was hired in 1824 for one hundred dollars cash, ten bushels of potatoes, and ten bushels of corn on the cob.[14] Other servants demanded partial payment in such delicacies as butter, sugar, tea, and coffee.

Room and board were integral parts of servants' wages until the twentieth century, when the number of live-in domestics declined sharply. The exact savings on food and lodging afforded by living with the employer depended on the local cost of living, but for servants in lower income brackets, it could prove dramatic, often doubling cash wages and placing service on a level with more respectable trades. Servants not receiving food and lodging suffered a hardship. For example, a New Orleans widow supporting herself as a daily household worker was paid "so little for so hard work" that she had only enough money "to pay room rent and a little some thing to eat." Some employers, mostly hotelkeepers, gave extra wages in lieu of room and board, but such stipends seldom met the cost of living. Thus a New York waiter complained in 1883 that his twenty-four-dollar-per-month salary was not so grand as it seemed, for nearly a third of it went for lodging and laundry. Of seventy-five New York hotels in 1921 the difference in wages between those supplying room and board (twenty-nine) and those giving extra wages (forty-six) was only $4.77 to $6.00 weekly. Considering that the average weekly cost of room and board was $9.00, servants not living at their hotels were obviously being shortchanged.[15]

Food and lodging were not always unalloyed blessings. Neither the quality nor the quantity of food provided was predictable. Where only one to three servants were employed, the fare was usually the same as the family's, albeit sometimes less plentiful or eaten cold. Servants at hotels and large private households had plenty to eat, but it was of a lower quality than the family's food. Servants generally ate cheaper cuts of meat, fewer fresh fruits and vegetables, and fewer desserts. Stews and hash appeared regularly on their menu, as did bread, rice,

14. Bogert Account Book, April, 1824.
15. Emmett J. Scott, Jr. (comp.), "Additional Letters of Negro Migrants of 1916–1918," *Journal of Negro History*, IV (1919), 426; John Nolan to Parents, June 10, 1883, in John Nolan Letters, Public Records Office of Northern Ireland, Belfast; Consumers' League of New York City, *Behind the Scenes in a Hotel* (New York: n.p., 1922), 28–31, 35–38. See also Eaton, "Special Report," 453–54, Gail Laughlin, "Domestic Service," 747, Leslie Woodcock Tentler, *Wage-Earning Women: Industrial Work and Family Life in the United States, 1900–1930* (New York: Oxford University Press, 1979), 146–47, 170–71.

potatoes, and other filling starches. Kitchen workers, waiters, and waitresses often had the best food, or at least the best opportunity to secure good food. Where not legally entitled to leftover delicacies, these workers often supplemented their diet by caching part of the stores.[16]

Yet general consensus asserted that servants were as well if not better fed than most members of the working classes. Indeed, some servants looked "much better and fatter" than they had before entering service. Perhaps the best testimony to the generally good quality and plenitude of their rations is the failure of servants to consider diet an important servant problem.[17]

More varied and of poorer quality were servants' living and working quarters. The separation of these quarters from family sections of households often caused servants a good deal of inconvenience and discomfort. Living quarters, especially, were in remote corners and noticeably lacking in pleasantness and attractiveness. Such an environment did little to increase servants' morale or to improve their opinion of service. Both hotel and household servants suffered cramped, ill-lighted, poorly ventilated quarters, but a description of household conditions will suffice to characterize the situation.

Service areas were seldom as cheerful or as well planned as they might have been. Kitchens appeared most inadequate. Architectural fashions brought kitchens out of the basements of most city houses by 1870, but many older houses, slow to be renovated, still confined cooks and general servants to the dark, airless little grottoes of the past. Even when placed above ground, kitchens often remained unsatisfactory. Inadequate window space, poor exposure, and inadequate lighting and ventilation could be injurious to health and spirits. The absence of such elementary touches as curtains and brightly painted or whitewashed walls added to the dreariness. Kitchens were ill arranged, with no thought given to organization or convenience. Few architects or employers thought of saving servants time and energy by efficient placement of stoves, sinks, work spaces, and storage areas

16. New York *Times*, March 16, 1879, p. 9; Newman Palmer to Sarah Palmer, April 27, 1869, in Sarah L. Palmer Papers, Collection of Regional History, Cornell University; "Women in Culinary Trades," *Harper's Bazar*, XXXIV (February 16, 1901), 460; Katherine H. Bryan to Emily Hammond [February], 1899, in Hammond, Bryan, Cumming Families Papers, South Caroliniana Library, University of South Carolina.

17. Maggie Maher to Clarinda B. Boltwood, October 24, 1867, in Boltwood Family Papers. See, for example, YWCA Commission on Household Employment, *First Report*.

until well into the nineteenth century. The same dismal environment affected other service areas, such as laundry rooms.[18]

What made work areas—particularly kitchens—even more depressing was the habit of assigning these same rooms to servants as recreation areas. Those who worked in a sprawling mansion might be blessed with a servants' hall. Otherwise, the kitchen became the center of servants' social as well as working lives. Only a lucky few sat in family parlors or were provided their own sitting rooms. Most workers spent their evenings amusing themselves and entertaining friends in the same dreary environment in which they spent the larger part of the day. Thoughtful employers transformed kitchens into fairly comfortable parlors by furnishing one corner with a piece of carpet, a small table, a good reading lamp, and a cushioned chair. But this was not the norm.

The one advantage of kitchens as social centers was that they generally were less barren and cheerless than the gloomy, cramped quarters that served as servants' bedrooms. Neither architects nor employers seemed overly concerned with servants' comfort or convenience in this respect. So universally did attics and basements serve as bedrooms that architects seldom made any other provisions for servants. Only occasionally was a small room adjacent to the kitchen or in the rear of an upper floor provided. Where both men and women were employed, their quarters were separated, with men sleeping in the basement or in a divided portion of the servants' wing. There were two exceptions to these general rules. Hired housekeepers, where employed as administrators for lower servants, enjoyed the privilege of a private room. Butlers also reveled in this luxury, even if married and thus not required to live on the premises. The object in the latter case was to provide butlers with some privacy in which to change clothes, perform their toilet, and relax. Such a room also allowed them to remain overnight should they be required to supervise a late evening entertainment.

The depressing location of servants' quarters could have been remedied by making them more cheerful and comfortable, but most quarters were furnished with only the bare essentials: bed, washstand,

18. "The Stranger in the Gates," *Harper's Bazar*, VI (July 19, 1873), 450; Alice E. Moore, "From Kitchen to parlor," *American Kitchen Magazine*, VII (September, 1897), 232–36; Charles E. White, "The Servant in the Little House," *Ladies' Home Journal*, XXX (November, 1913), 54; Edith M. Jones, "The House That Will Keep Servants," *Country Life in America*, XXXVII (March, 1920), 50–51.

chair, and perhaps, chest of drawers. Rugs, curtains, and wallpaper were rare. Overcrowding frequently aggravated these dismal surroundings. Two to four girls working in an urban, middle-class household were sometimes squeezed into a tiny ten-by-ten-foot room, where they slept two to a bed, shared a single chair, and hung their clothes on a row of nails.[19] Employers generally considered the task of furnishing servants' rooms to be an irritation rather than their responsibility. Consequently, many servants' rooms resembled perpetual rummage sales for decrepit furniture and patched bed linen.

Heat, light, and ventilation tended to be equally inadequate in either the attic or the cellar. Windows, if not lacking entirely, were often only small dormers that provided little light or air. There were certainly no fans to aid ventilation, and the only light came from candles or kerosene lamps. Electricity and gas lighting, sometimes only grudgingly installed in family quarters, were rarely found in the farther reaches of American houses. When heat was required, servants again suffered, for few fireplaces graced attics and cellars. Even when stoves became common sources of heat after about 1840 servants were not always trusted with them, although they sometimes had small coal grates. Early furnaces did not benefit servants either since they were barely powerful enough to heat the first and second floors. Not until the 1870s did attics feel their welcome glow.[20]

Adequate plumbing and bathing facilities were likewise unknown to attic and cellar tenants, but in this regard, servants were on a more equal footing with employers. Washbasins and chamberpots were a way of life in all but the wealthiest American homes until the late nineteenth century. Even running water was not a common urban convenience before mid-century, and then it was confined largely to cellar and kitchen pumps. Very wealthy employers in large northeastern cities had bathrooms with tubs and toilets in the 1830s and 1840s, but these were far beyond the means of most employers. Bathtubs were not common in middle-class homes until the 1870s, and indoor toilets were luxuries for the middle classes until the 1890s. Attics enjoyed

19. Campbell, *Prisoners of Poverty*, 230; A. S. "Correspondence," *Nation*, XLIII (December 23, 1886), 521.
20. Frank R. and Marian Stockton, *The Home: Where It Should Be and What to Put in It* (New York: G. P. Putnam and Sons, 1873), 95; Charles Lockwood, *Bricks and Brownstones: The New Row House, 1783–1929. An Architectural and Social History* (New York: McGraw-Hill, 1972), 183; Bainbridge Bunting, *Houses of Boston's Back Bay* (Cambridge: Harvard University Press, 1967), 138–39, 278; Carter, *Millionaire Households*, 140–41.

none of these facilities. Servants continued descending to the kitchen to fill water pitchers, and down another flight of steps to bathe. Even when bathrooms became widespread in the twentieth century, servants were often denied use of family bathtubs, and only the well-to-do could afford additional tubs for servants.[21]

Perhaps most depressing, servants lacked privacy in their own rooms. Architects and employers insisted that separation of family and service areas insured servants of as much privacy as it did employers. This point of view contained some truth, for despite their isolated loneliness, servants could be as relieved as employers to occupy quarters out of sight and sound. Their concealed nooks provided servants with havens of welcome seclusion. Yet a servant's solitude was at the mercy of whim. Some employers felt no compunction about entering servants' quarters at any hour, infringing upon the privacy they so jealously guarded for themselves. One girl complained that even though well treated by her employer, she lacked privacy in her own room. Her quarters adjoined one of the family chambers, an arrangement that subjected her to intrusion at any hour. "I do not know what minute one or the other member of the family may pop in," she explained, "& the door between the rooms does not lock."[22]

Still, servants' quarters were not one of their major grievances. Perhaps, in comparison to their accustomed accommodations, even attics were an improvement. Squalid urban tenements were the alternative for many servants to what they experienced in middle-class households. At Savannah, where, as in the rest of the South, it was not customary for black servants to live in, one Negro scullery maid "begged" her employer for permission to sleep in the house. When given rooms other than in the garret or cellar, servants could be well content. One girl, for example, described her room as being very "pleasant," with "a large old fashioned bureau, and a little stove, a good bed, and two chairs." Then too, after 1870 employers and architects showed more concern with providing adequate quarters for servants. Thanks to a more vocal domestic reform movement and to improvements in heating, lighting, and plumbing, employers had fewer excuses for leaving even attic rooms uncomfortable and unattractive.

21. Siegfried Giedion, *Mechanization Takes Command: A Contribution to Anonymous History* (New York: Oxford University Press, 1948), 659, 682–86; Elizabeth Mickle Bacon, "The Growth of Household Conveniences in the United States from 1865 to 1900" (Ph.D. dissertation, Radcliffe College, 1944), 31–33, 231–33.
22. Libbie to Margaret Scott, May 14, 1887 in Adrian Records.

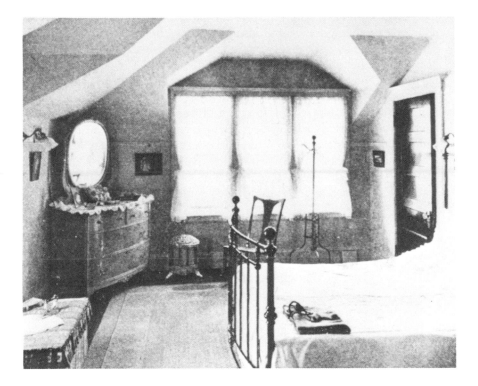

Rooms to make servants happy, these were far from the norm.

By 1901 the secretary of a Chicago servant girl's union confirmed that only a few girls still slept in damp laundry rooms or on cots, although complaints about overcrowding and lack of privacy could still be heard.[23]

Generally, then, servants could not single out any one source of their compensation—wages, room, or board—as being particularly paltry. Yet they clearly remained unimpressed by the overall benefits of ser-

23. Louisa Porter Minis Diaries (MS in Minis Family Papers, Southern Historical Collection, Library of the University of North Carolina at Chapel Hill), January 31, 1901; Alice to Margaret Scott, March 14, 1888, in Adrian Records; Chicago *Tribune*, August 25, 1901, p. 8. See also New York House of Refuge, *Twelfth Annual Report* (New York: n.p., 1836), 22; Jackson, "The Factory Girl and Domestic Service," 953–57.

vice. In cases where they enjoyed fair wages, good food, and comfortable lodgings, long hours and discipline could be endured. But not all servants were so generously rewarded. Some servants did not enjoy any of these benefits, and few enjoyed all of them. Consequently, people did not enter service unless forced to it, and many who became servants felt intimidated, ashamed, and defensive. No one wanted to labor in an occupation where so much of one's time was controlled by another person. This was what galled servants. No amount of money, good food, or pleasant living conditions, even if forthcoming, could compensate for their lost liberty or disguise their lowly position. Many servants rebelled against this situation not so much to improve the material advantages of servitude as to combat the social stigma.

CHAPTER SEVEN

WAR AND PEACE
Employer-Servant Relationships

Americans and their servants were not always on the best of terms.
Their relationship was oftentimes comparable to that of two war-
ring yet interdependent nations, with employers defending class lines
against insurgent servants, and servants taking courageous stands
against the mighty forces of middle-class convention. Yet, because so
much depended on personalities, bonds of peace and friendship also
existed. There were oppressive masters; there were understanding
employers. There were arrogant helps; there were obedient servants.
The ambiguous positions of masters and servants in a democracy confused matters. The traditional master-servant relationship, as it had
originated in slavery and serfdom, was archaic. Outside the antebellum South, no one in America was really a master, no one was a serf
or a slave. Yet servants, fearing that such conditions might develop,
felt trapped. They were betwixt and between, on the verge of being
employees but hauntingly close to serfdom. It was easy for servants to
react if they were treated as either employee or serf, but often they
were treated as both. This ill-defined position became a stumbling
block in harmonious relations between Americans and their servants.
Some people hurdled the hazard gracefully; others fell flat on their
faces.

Servants had good reason to rebel. It is a cliché that no man is a hero
to his valet, but as with many clichés, it sounds trite only because it is
so true. Employer pretensions, hypocrisy, thoughtlessness, and lack of

compassion embittered servants, turning them sour and cynical. Petty tyrannies sometimes forced servants to the breaking point. One girl "inwardly resented the petty assumptions" of employers less intelligent than herself, employers who, as she put it, were "constantly on the alert lest I should be moved to cross the line of demarcation."[1] Another girl was never so unhappy as when working for a woman who spoke to her and the other servants "just as if she thought we had no feelings."[2] More than one worker left service on account of such lack of respect.

Some people, including many servants, believed that female employers were the worst offenders. A stereotype developed by the mid-nineteenth century of the kindhearted, sensible male employer who was always pointing out his wife's errors and suggesting more humanitarian treatment of their servants. It was supposed that the "natural antagonism" between women made it impossible for female employers to control female servants. Many servants swore that husbands were not so exacting, tyrannical, or class conscious as their wives, and that they were infinitely better organizers and managers.[3] This impression, however, probably came from the fact that servants had little contact with the male members of a household. Except where hired housekeepers directed the service affairs of the household, wives hired, fired, and directed family servants. Consequently, they were the tyrants who bore the brunt of servants' contempt. Masters, because seldom seen, seldom engaged in combat and so appeared to be less odious.

Whatever the case, many servants fought back, the most obvious sign of their rebellion being an extremely independent, not to say haughty, bearing. Their arrogance was legitimized by a hint of modernism in America's employer-servant relationship that challenged its more feudal aspects. Alexis de Tocqueville was among the first to comment on this disturbing dichotomy. The United States, wrote the famous French observer of antebellum America, could boast of both aristocratic and democratic social traditions, a situation that left ser-

1. Georgiana Kirby, *Years of Experience: An Autobiographical Narrative* (New York: G. P. Putnam's Sons, 1887), 79.

2. Quoted in Catherine E. Beecher, *A Treatise on Domestic Economy* (New York: Harper and Brothers, 1847), 212–13. See also New York *Times*, December 5, 1871, p. 3.

3. Elizabeth McCracken, "The Problem of Domestic Service II—from the Standpoint of the Employee," *Outlook*, LXXXVIII (February 29, 1908), 494–95; Eliza Potter, *A Hairdresser's Experience in High Life* (Cincinnati: n.p., 1859), 61–62; Kirby, *Years of Experience*, 79–80; Chicago *Tribune*, August 25, 1901, p. 8.

vants unsure of their position. They were haunted by a "confused and imperfect phantom of equality," which promised perfect parity at one moment but then suddenly shouted a reminder that some people were more equal than others. No permanent class of servants existed in the United States, Tocqueville pointed out, for class lines were too mobile, American society too egalitarian for men and women to spend their lives as menials. This situation forced servants to rebel; failure to do so implied acquiescence in their position. "They consent to serve and they blush to obey," explained Tocqueville; "they are not sure that they ought not themselves to be masters, and they are inclined to consider him who orders them as an unjust usurper of their own rights."[4] The same attitude prevailed in 1920. The egalitarian posture of servants through the century remained largely a defensive maneuver, a device to outwit those who infringed upon their dignity. It was the arrogance of felt inferiority.

To combat this sense of inferiority, servants resorted to a variety of egalitarian poses. Their egalitarianism was generally expressed in personal revolts, including demands for respect by employers, adoption of middle-class dress and manners, and extreme mobility. Occasionally, however, servants joined in group protests. Both types of revolt deserve attention.

As a gesture of personal revolt, some servants demanded that employers address them with the same civility that employers expected of servants. An "imperious temper" did more harm than good with servants who were quick to distinguish between a request and a command. Servants actually intimidated some employers, who considered themselves perfect martyrs, "slaves" and "serfs" at the mercy of "masters" and "remorseless tyrants." Other employers hesitated to scold or discipline servants, even when justified, for fear of losing them, or because they abhorred a period of soured tempers during which housework would be poorly performed. Socially aware employers feared shattered reputations should spiteful servants perform unsatisfactorily or commit some outrage during an important entertainment. And all employers lived in trepidation of hearing the "wooden damn," as unplaced workers, announcing their departure, slammed the *front* door in leaving.[5]

4. Alexis de Tocqueville, *Democracy in America*, trans. and ed. Phillips Bradley (2 vols.; New York: Random House, 1945), II, 87, 191–95.
5. Mehetable May Goddard to Lucretia Dawes, January 26, 1829, July 8, 1831, both in May-Goddard Papers, Schlesinger Library, Radcliffe College; E. Elcourt, "The Per-

"Everybody wondered what Meekly wanted with a prize bull-dog, when his cook could scare any tramp that ever walked. The trouble was she scared Meekly too!" Some employers would have seen nothing funny in this cartoon. For them, it would have seemed only a slight exaggeration of harsh reality. *Harper's Bazar*, XXXIII (May 12, 1900).

Rebellion against the word *servant* became another well-known expression of domestic egalitarianism. "I fairly hate the word 'servant,' " fumed one girl in a succinct statement of this view.[6] Throughout the period 1800 to 1920, servants recoiled from the appellation, which linked them to medieval serfdom, indentured servitude, and Negro slavery. This revolt was restricted at first to native whites, but eventually the sensitivities of blacks and Americanized immigrants also demanded a more respectable title. As another girl said with emotion, "Servant, that means what 'slave' used to. 'Servant girl,' she is only a 'kitchen mechanic,' that's what people say."[7]

As a result, Americans adopted a number of euphemisms for servant, of which the best known was *help*. The word's origin is obscure, but it was already popular in colonial New England by the eighteenth century where it was used as a term for free, unskilled laborers of all types probably to distinguish them from indentured servants. *Help* acquired several new connotations during the early nineteenth century as the word became a means of discriminating native whites from blacks, rural helpers from city servants. By 1828 the word had gained broad acceptance in the northern United States, for Noah Webster defined it, in part, as "a hired man or woman; a servant."[8]

The small-town or rural connotation that attached itself most firmly to *help* implied several things. First, it suggested that rural and small-town Americans lived on terms of greater familiarity than city folk, and that, consequently, rural servants were treated with respect and enjoyed a singular degree of social equality. Second, it implied that the help's position was a temporary one, that she had no intention of spending her life in bondage. In time, this interpretation served to distinguish part-time help, such as laundresses and charwomen, from regular, full-time servants. Consequently, a third distinction followed. *Help* referred to a general, nonspecialized, nonprofessional servant. In her original, rural habitation, the help was responsible not only for the normal housekeeping duties of cooking, cleaning, and washing but

---

secuted Woman," *Lippincott's Magazine*, V (January, 1870), 27–28; "The Princess Biddy; or, 'Help' and 'Self-help,' " *Putnam's Magazine*, XIV (August, 1869), 247; Edwin P. Whipple, "Domestic Service," *Forum*, I (March, 1886), 25–26.

6. Quoted in Lucy M. Salmon, *Domestic Service* (New York: Macmillan, 1897), 155*n*.

7. Chicago *Tribune*, August 25, 1901, p. 8.

8. Albert Matthews, "Hired Man and Help," *Publications of the Colonial Society of Massachusetts*, V, *Transactions* (1897–98), 245–54; Noah Webster, *An American Dictionary of English Language* (2 vols.; New York: S. Converse, 1828).

for many outdoor chores. The true help was thus adaptable, a maid-of-all-work, the only servant in the house.[9]

But *help* soon outgrew its rural birthplace to become part of the urban vernacular, too. Moreover, city servants began making their own contributions to the language. Many people liked to be called by their occupational title of cook, maid, or butler. Others doted on more exotic terms, like *domestic tradeswoman*, while the most uncompromising insisted on *employee*. *Domestic* was also acceptable for house servants, and it became one of the most widely used of all terms. Some servants also rebelled against being called by their Christian names, a common practice among employers, but one which servants regarded as degrading. They preferred to be addressed by their family names, with the appropriate prefix of "Miss" or "Mister" added for good measure.

Employers, of course, declared this rewriting of the dictionary to be ridiculous, a mere "alteration of *names*, while *things*" remained the same. Yet many of them, middle-class employers especially, accepted the affectations of servants, if somewhat grudgingly, because they too found *servant* distasteful. They, like their domestics, associated *servants* (*masters* too, for that matter, a word they shied away from and against which independent-minded servants actively rebelled) with slavery and were self-conscious about the connotations of such words in a democracy. Some employers were so undecided about what to call servants that they used several terms interchangeably. By the mid-nineteenth century, most Americans accepted popular substitutes for servant. Perhaps most frequently, servants in middle-class households became "girls." There were "kitchen girls," "upstairs girls," "trustworthy girls," "Protestant girls," "hired girls," a never-ending cavalcade of girls. "They are all girls," noted one commentator, "even if seventy years old and grandmothers." By the twentieth century, some people, instead of speaking of the "servant problem," referred to the "girl problem."[10]

9. David E. Schob, *Hired Hands and Plowboys: Farm Labor in the Midwest, 1815–1860* (Urbana: University of Illinois Press, 1975), 195; Nancy F. Cott, *The Bonds of Womanhood: "Woman's Sphere" in New England, 1780–1835* (New Haven: Yale University Press, 1977), 28–29; Marion, "Editorial Correspondence," *Arthur's Home Magazine*, XXI (March, 1863), 198–99; Georgie H. Cook to Lucy M. Salmon, February 12, 1889, in Lucy Maynard Salmon Papers, Vassar College Library; Filson Young, "Servants," *Living Age*, CCXXVII (December, 1911), 759.
10. Henry B. Fearon, *Sketches of America* (London: Longman, Hurst, Rees, Orme, and Brown, 1819), 81. See also James Fenimore Cooper, *The American Democrat*

Copying upper- and middle-class modes of dress was yet another form of personal rebellion. Working-class girls in all occupations never doubted that to be fashionably dressed was to be genteel, nor that it considerably enhanced one's chances of catching the eye of some hand-some—and preferably wealthy—beau. American ladies' magazines and daily newspapers abounded with illustrations and descriptions of the latest fashions. Servant girls, like everyone else, read these maga-zines and dreamed over the pictures. They imagined that cheap repro-ductions of fashionable clothes obscured the humbleness of their social position. By wearing these reproductions and their accompanying ac-cessories—including shawls, bonnets (topping the latest hairstyle), satin and lace trim, jewelry, parasols, gloves, and other "flounces, fringes, and feathers" of fashion—female servants tried to resemble "ladies."[11] Girls not only knew the cost of the latest styles, they recog-nized their value.

It should be stressed, however, that servants were not as well dressed as they appeared to be. Although servants sometimes bor-rowed employers' clothes or were bequeathed castoff articles, their garments were usually inexpensive imitations of current fashions. As ready-made clothing became cheaper and more readily available, a chambermaid might look as elegant as an Astor when seen at a dis-tance, but when viewed at closer range, her apparently expensive dress turned out to be printed calico. Also, servants' undergarments were often no match for their outer ones. Wages spent on hats and dresses left little money to replace tattered and patched, if not abso-lutely soiled, underclothes. Moreover, servants' ideas of current fash-ions were sometimes several years out of date, especially in rural areas and small towns. Employers did not know whether to laugh or be horrified by servants' gaudy clothes and mismatched color combina-

(Cooperstown, N.Y.: H. & E. Phinney, 1838), 112–15. I. M. Rubinow, "The Problem of Domestic Service," *Journal of Political Economy*, XIV (1906), 512; Izola Forrester, "The 'Girl' Problem," *Good Housekeeping*, LV (September, 1912), 375–82. See Elizabeth E. Dana Diaries (MS in Dana Family Papers, Schlesinger Library, Radcliffe College), May 3, 4, 18, 1869, Mrs. E. A. Williams to Master Lucius Boltwood, February 10, 1871, in Boltwood Family Papers, Burton Historical Collection, Detroit Public Library, Mary Coburn to Lucy M. Salmon, April 24, 1890, in Salmon Papers.
    11. H. E. Scudder (ed.), *Recollections of Samuel Breck* (Philadelphia: Porter and Coates, 1877), 298–99; Mrs. Henry Ward Beecher, *All Around the House; or, How to Make Homes Happy* (New York: D. Appleton and Co., 1879), 275; Griffith A. Nicholas [Elizabeth Strong Worthington], *The Biddy Club* (Chicago: A. C. McClurg and Co., 1888), 71–72.

tions. Many people believed servants were positively vulgar in their tastes; less brutal commentators described them as quaint.[12]

On the other hand, some girls were able to indulge their fashionable impulses without going to extremes. They owned very limited social wardrobes, boasting only a plain Sunday dress, shawl, and attractive but modestly priced bonnet. These they wore year after year with little thought or inclination to change them. Other people, while occasionally buying new clothes, did not devote their lives to amassing collections of stylish garments. Some servants practiced frugality. One girl bought what she considered to be a somewhat expensive dress but then, rather than buying a new cloak to match it, was content in cutting her old cloak in a more fashionable style. Another girl spent most of her clothing money on work dresses and kept her underclothes serviceable by neatly patching them. Probably most often, girls purchased both useful and fashionable items. Thus, the purchases of one girl, while consisting mostly of shoes, calico aprons, and woolen hose, also included a variety of bonnets and a pair of silk gloves.[13] Such simple items, however, gave servants a sense of equality.

More to the point was servants' repugnance for livery. Brass buttons and satin pants were rarely worn by male servants before the Civil War. Immigrants and blacks seemed more willing than native whites to don such outfits, but everywhere livery was considered "a badge of menial service," akin to wearing "a halter" around one's neck. Consequently, antebellum American livery was strikingly conservative compared to the glittering gold and braid of European styles. A dark frock coat, usually with tails, and white gloves and tie was the usual uniform. American servants refused to wear anything more gaudy. Some observers attributed the absence of knee breeches and silk coats

12. Patrick Shirreff, *A Tour Through North America* (Edinburgh: Oliver and Boyd, 1835), 28; [Robert Tomes], *The Bazar Book of Decorum* (New York: Harper and Brothers, 1876), 162; Mary Grove Smith, "Immigration as a Source of Supply for Domestic Workers," *Bulletin of Inter-Municipal Committee on Household Research*, II (May, 1906), 8; Patience Pennington [Elizabeth Waites (Allston) Pringle], *A Woman Rice Planter*, ed. Cornelius O. Cathey (Cambridge: Harvard University Press, 1961), 86; Edith J. R. Isaacs, "My Servant and Yours," *Delineator*, LXXVIII (November, 1911), 380.

13. Mattie to Margaret Scott, August 17, 1886, Lillie to Margaret Scott, November, 1887, both in Adrian (Michigan) Girls' Training School Records, Michigan State Archives; Watkins Domestic Account Book (MS in Abiathar and Emily L. Watkins Papers, Manuscripts and Archives Division, New York Public Library, Astor, Lenox, and Tilden Foundations), 1852–53. See also New York *Times*, March 9, 1879, p. 9, March 16, 1879, p. 9.

as much to public opinion as to the prejudices of servants. Most antebellum Americans, including servants, associated livery, it was said,
with aristocratic decadence and foppery. Liveried servants and the
people who employed them were the butt of jokes and satires, which
undoubtedly stiffened servants' resolute stand.[14]

But as the number of very wealthy families, and thus the number of
male servants, increased between 1870 and 1900, livery became more
noticeable. During the Gilded Age, especially, liveried servants became one of the most visible and most valued signs of social arrival.
Grand balls and other sumptuous entertainments required dozens of
uniformed attendants. The very rich even adopted family liveries to
distinguish their retainers from those of other millionaires. Thus male
servants in the "House of Astor" wore specially designed blue livery,
while those serving the "House of Vanderbilt" donned maroon. The
butler was the only male servant never to wear livery since his position forbade him to dress as a lackey. Butlers wore tailored suits.
After 1880 this meant a blue morning suit during the day and evening
dress for dinner and evening entertainments. For the rest of the male
staff, the plain antebellum ensemble had evolved to consist of knee
breeches, silk tailcoat, white stockings, and black pumps with buckles.
Servants were no less humiliated by such uniforms, but fashion had
changed. American hotels had also begun putting their servants in
livery by the 1880s.

Livery had a similar history among female servants, although wom-
en's uniforms were plain affairs, consisting of neat, dark-colored dress,
white apron, cuffs, and hat. But many women rebelled against even
this modest attire, especially against the wearing of caps. The innovation of caps in the 1820s was viewed with horror by servants, who considered them a gross infringement upon "natural liberty." Women in
both city and country resented any interference with their dress, and
usually only those people working in wealthy households acquiesced.
Most middle-class servants continued to boycott uniforms throughout
the nineteenth century, especially where caps were concerned. As late
as 1901, Miss Mary Murphy, president of a Chicago servant girl union,
voiced the "prevailing sentiment" of her three hundred members when
reassuring one woman of the union's position on uniforms: "Wear uni-

14. William Cobbett, *A Year's Residence in the United States of America* (London: J.
M. Cobbett, 1822), 191. For a marvelously funny yet poignantly revealing satirical look
at American attitudes towards liveried servants, see George W. Curtis, *The Potiphar
Papers* (New York: G. P. Putnam and Co., 1853), 74–77, 82–88.

forms? Nay, nay, Pauline; nay, nay." [15] By that time, however, an increasing number of women seem to have relaxed their resistance. In very wealthy households, each of the female servants—chambermaid, waitress, parlormaid, and lady's maid—wore an assortment of uniforms on different occasions and at various times of the day. Large department stores held annual sales on caps and aprons, and some servants, in order to make themselves more marketable, specified when applying for jobs that they were willing to wear caps.

Perhaps the most annoying aspect of servants' independent spirit, insofar as employers were concerned, was their habit of perpetual motion. Employers could have tolerated a little arrogance or affected dress, but servants were constantly reaffirming their independence by changing their places, taking "French leave." Servants were like comets, "erratic" in their courses, shooting through households "in a fiery kind of way, both as to temper and range," and leaving catastrophe in their wake. Also like comets, they first appeared as "heavenly bodies," but soon exploded and disintegrated "in the sootiest darkness." Most employers were not so unfortunate as the San Francisco woman who replaced eighteen servants in one month, but the frequency with which employers complained of this problem testifies to its dimensions. Until newly hired servants actually arrived, employers could not be sure they would ever appear. Many servants failed to report to new employers on time. Usually they were only a few hours or days late, but quite often they seemingly disappeared from the hemisphere. Once servants arrived, the question became how long would they stay. "My girl still continues here—and seems satisfied," revealed an Ohio housekeeper, "but I wont feel sure about her until she has been here six weeks have had too many slips between the cup and the lip." [16]

Considering circumstances, this situation is understandable. It took a few weeks for employers and servants to know one another, to learn one another's "ways." Employer belief in this doctrine has been explained. Would the stranger entering their home be compatible with them in habits, personality, and ideas about housekeeping? Only time

15. Isaac Candler, *A Summary View of America* (London: T. Codell, 1824), 468, 487–88; Chicago *Tribune*, September 27, 1901, p. 1.

16. Elcourt, "The Persecuted Woman," 28; Henry B. Lucy, *East by West* (2 vols.; London: Richard Bentley and Son, 1885), I, 140; Elizabeth F. Camp to Jacob A. Camp, June 20, 1883, in Camp Family Papers (Additional), Collection of Regional History, Cornell University. See, for example, Scudder (ed.), *Recollections of Samuel Breck*, 299, James Bogert, Jr., Account Book With Hired Servants (MS in Museum of the City of New York), Sarah W. Dana Account Book for Domestics (MS in Dana Family Papers).

could tell. Servants, however, faced the same problems. They entered a household often knowing little about their employers. They did not know how they would be treated or if they would be able to please. As one girl complained in a neat reversal of the employer position, "I know nothing about the family they are strangers to me." Servants took a place and worked for awhile, but if they foresaw a rough road ahead, they would have been fools to remain. "May not this circumstance alone," one commentator asked rhetorically, "be sufficient explanation of the extreme mobility and inconstancy of domestic service?"[17]

It was the suddenness with which servants left that was most disconcerting. Admittedly, employers often encouraged this movement. Some employers were notorious for dismissing servants for trivial reasons and with scant pity or compunction. Urban employers during most of the nineteenth century reduced staffs when closing their households for the summer. Unless wealthy enough either to take their domestics with them to summer resorts and cottages or to maintain their households while away, servants had to be let go. Then, when employers returned in the autumn, servants rushed to find new places for the coming year. Many servants took their cue from this ritual. They felt little loyalty to employers, and they seldom hesitated to leave a place if a better opportunity offered itself. Workers hired in September, even though they vowed to stay until spring, might be gone by January. Servants were supposed to give at least a week's notice before leaving, but a few days' or no notice at all was more likely. Most exasperating was the tendency of servants to leave not only on short notice but at critical moments. Just before a large party or holiday celebration or upon the arrival of guests was a favorite time for servants either to quit or temporarily to abandon their posts. Desertions always seemed to come in batches, too. Things would go smoothly for awhile, but then employers were suddenly required to spend several weeks or months filling vacancies.[18]

Reasons for leaving were usually undramatic. Some servants had personal or family-related motives. In rural areas special problems arose, for servants returned to their homes at planting and harvesting

17. Carrie to Margaret Scott, March 16, 1887, in Adrian Records; I. M. Rubinow, "Household Service as a Labor Problem," *Journal of Home Economics*, III (1911), 135.
18. For various estimates of the turnover rate among servants, see Salmon, *Domestic Service*, 109–110; Mary Pattison, *The Business of Home Management* (New York: Robert M. McBride & Co., 1918), 52–53; Mary V. Robinson, *Domestic Workers and Their Employment Relations*, Bulletin of the Women's Bureau No. 39 (Washington, D.C.: Government Printing Office, 1924), 16.

time. Boredom and restlessness were added spurs to departure. Most servants, being young and unmarried, sought the excitement of life. Easily bored with monotonous jobs, they were always optimistic about finding work elsewhere. For some, this meant leaving service entirely. Then too, giving notice was the only threat of work stoppage that an individual had at her command.[19] Although tenure of service varied so widely that averages have little meaning, the careers of most servants were notable only for their brevity, and the majority of people probably remained in service not over five years.[20] Servants saw service as an expedient, a stepping-stone to something higher. Young women, for example—and this was a frequent complaint of employers—labored only until some Prince Charming carried them off to be mistresses of their own homes. Even if taking another job in service, workers hoped to find better paying, less exacting places than those they left.

Personal rebellion, of which all of the foregoing episodes are examples, remained the principal means of protest for servants dissatisfied with hours, employers, or some other aspect of their lives. Yet organized revolts occurred also, inspired by servant unions. Most unions were little more than social clubs or benevolent societies that served mainly as sources of companionship and relaxation. But others had a militant purpose, agitating for higher wages, shorter hours, better working conditions, and more privileges. Hotel workers, beginning in the 1850s, organized the most successful unions, most notably the Hotel and Restaurant Employees Union, founded in the 1890s. Although it is difficult to estimate its influence, HREU lobbying probably helped to pass laws limiting hours and increasing wages for hotel workers in several states. Likewise, strikes by hotel workers became effective means of improving conditions by the mid-1880s.[21] Still, the mass of servants, those working in private residences, remained largely untouched by unions, strikes, and legislation. Household ser-

19. Helen C. Callahan, "Upstairs-Downstairs in Chicago, 1870–1907; The Glessner Household," *Chicago History*, VI (1977–78), 208.

20. See, for example, Massachusetts Bureau of Statistics of Labor, "Social Conditions in Domestic Service," *Massachusetts Labor Bulletin*, No. 13 (February, 1900), 6.

21. Philip S. Foner and Ronald L. Lewis (eds.), *The Black Worker to 1869* (Philadelphia: Temple University Press, 1978), Vol. I of Foner and Lewis (eds.), *The Black Worker: A Documentary History from Colonial Times to the Present*, 191–96; New York *Times*, June 3, 1869, p. 1; "Women in Culinary Trades," *Harper's Bazar*, XXXIV (February 16, 1901), 460; "Chicago Waiters' Association," *Hotel Bulletin*, II (1907–1908), 296; Howard N. Rabinowitz, *Race Relations in the Urban South, 1865–1890* (New York: Oxford University Press, 1978), 73; Matthew Josephson, *Union House, Union Bar: The History of the Hotel and Restaurant Employees and Bartenders Inter-*

vants were too isolated from one another to form strong unions. Jane Addams maintained that house servants failed to organize because they belonged to "a class composed of the unprogressive elements of the community," but this fails to explain why hotel workers, who came from the same social and economic background as domestics, were much more successful. The fact is, a community's domestics, scattered in dozens of households, did not work together in large numbers or associate as readily when off duty as did hotel workers. Domestics lacked the sense of unity and purpose shared by people who struggled side by side in the same place under the same living and working conditions. Solitary domestics could not even define common complaints, so varied were the conditions of household service. Their isolation also made servants timid and doubtful of success. Single servants, like sheep separated from their flock, were defenseless, and they knew it. They feared the wrath of employers, who were known to fire union members for conspiratorial activities. Add to this the obstacles facing all workers—especially female workers—organizing at this time, and their prospects were not good.[22]

This is not to say household workers had no unions. Many domestics enjoyed the benefits of social and benevolent societies by the late nineteenth century. These clubs, some of them aided by concerned employers and reformers, aimed at providing workers with companionship and a social life free from employer restraints. The Progressive Household Club, for example, founded and operated by Los Angeles servants in 1904, offered a variety of services to its five hundred members. Workers owned a spacious clubhouse, containing kitchen, laundry room, and recreational facilities. Here the club sponsored social and cultural activities, operated an employment service, provided low-rent rooms to unemployed members, and offered storage space for members' personal effects. Activities and facilities were financed by dues, member loans, and fees from club services.[23]

national Union AFL-CIO (New York: Random House, 1956), 3–17; U.S. Bureau of Labor, Third Annual Report of the Commissioner: Strikes and Lockouts (Washington, D.C.: Government Printing Office, 1887), 794–97, Tenth Annual Report of the Commissioner: Strikes and Lockouts (2 vols.; Washington, D.C.: Government Printing Office, 1895), I, 874–77, Sixteenth Annual Report of the Commissioner: Strikes and Lockouts (Washington, D.C.: Government Printing Office, 1901), 288–91.

22. Jane Addams, "A Belated Industry," American Journal of Sociology, I (1895–96), 538–40; Ida M. Tarbell, The Business of Being a Woman (New York: Macmillan, 1912), 146–47, 162–63; Rubinow, "Household Service as a Labor Problem," 137.

23. Bertha H. Smith, "A Club for Maids," Ladies' Home Journal, XXXIII (February, 1916), 64; "A Servant's Union," Harper's Bazar, XXXIII (June 2, 1900), 319.

Some unions even displayed a streak of militancy. Day washerwomen in New York City, for example, organized and went on strike for higher wages as early as 1835. Shortly after the Civil War, female servants at Newark, New Jersey, banded together to demand a ten-dollar-per-month minimum wage. Other groups, such as the American Servant Girls' Association, in Kansas City; the Domestic Servants' Union, in New York City; the Household Union, in Holyoke, Massachusetts; and the Servant Girls' Union, in Toledo, Ohio, were organized during the late 1890s and early 1900s for the purpose of confronting local employers. Large staffs in individual households also attempted coercion. In 1891 the entire staff of a wealthy Chicagoan walked off the job, and in 1902 some eighty servants at a Newport summer cottage shocked eastern society by walking out over excessive hours.[24]

Such efforts, however, seldom succeeded, particularly where servants sought to reform working conditions through force of numbers. An example of the obstacles to successful unionism among household workers may be seen in one of the earliest large-scale displays of servant militancy. In April, 1901, an eighteen-year-old Chicago housemaid, Miss Wendt by name, convinced several friends that working conditions in service could be improved only through mass protest. Aided by the Women's International Union Label League and assorted Chicago social workers, including Jane Addams, these dedicated few formed the Working Women's Association of America. By the end of July, the WWAA had enlisted three hundred members, elected officers, and made plans to join the American Federation of Labor. By August it had prepared a manifesto in behalf of Chicago domestics, demanding shorter work days, more free time, the right to a "club life," the right to entertain friends—especially male followers—in employers' kitchens, and the right to have a "business agent" represent them in disputes with employers. Members also hoped to set minimum and maximum wages, a step, they insisted, that would protect both employers and employees from unfair demands. Organizers hoped, too,

24. Stanley Lebergott, *Manpower in Economic Growth: The American Record Since 1800* (New York: McGraw-Hill, 1964), 282–83; Helen L. Sumner, *History of Women in Industry in the United States*, in *Report on Conditions of Women and Child Wage-Earners in the United States*, Senate Documents, 61st Cong., 2nd Sess., No. 645, IX, 184; Rabinowitz, *Race Relations in the Urban South*, 73–74; David Macrae, *The Americans at Home* (New York: E. P. Dutton and Co., 1952), 57; Philip S. Foner, *Women and the American Labor Movement: From Colonial Times to the Eve of World War I* (New York: The Free Press, 1979), 241–42; Callahan, "Upstairs-Downstairs in Chicago," 208; "The Appeal to Women," *Harper's Weekly*, XLVI (October 18, 1902), 1506–507.

that once these initial goals were secured, the union might broaden its range of activities to include "training and educational advantages" for members.[25]

Despite this concrete program, servants joined the union with widely differing views of what should be accomplished. "We'll have our nights off when we want them," spoke up one girl, "and we'll have something to say about washing day too." "We'll show them," was the rank-and-file consensus expressed by another. An equally passionate Irish woman believed the union was needed to protect girls from employers who, showing no regard for physical or mental health, treated servants like machines. "I must join that union," she vowed, "and I will be the first one to start a strike."[26] This was a common attitude, but decidedly opposed to that of union leaders.

Leaders had more moderate plans. Miss Wendt, the originator and elected secretary of the union, was representative of this faction. "We are going to put servant girls on a new basis," she told a reporter; "the untrained ones will have to learn their trade." She believed employers would see the benefits of this view and urge girls to join the WWAA. Nor were leaders as ready to strike as their followers seemed to be. Leaders assumed an academic perspective of their problems. For example, they planned to reduce hours, their principal grievance, by means of moral suasion. They hoped that the united pressure of their members plus the backing of organized labor and Chicago's women's clubs would convince employers of the inordinate length of the servant's day.[27]

But after an initial burst of enthusiastic support and activity, the union gained little headway. Its hundreds of members seemed to testify to the union's popularity, yet they represented only a tiny part of Chicago's 35,000 female domestics. Many servants were unaware of the union's existence for several months, and even when informed of it, they showed little interest in joining. While one girl was wildly excited about the organization and the possibility of a strike, another girl working in the same household was bored by the whole affair. A native-born woman was suspicious of the union, attributing its origin to foreign-born servants with radical ideas. Another girl simply doubted that the union could succeed. Women, this second-generation Irish girl explained, could only complain about their problems; they

25. Chicago *Tribune*, July 27, 1901, p. 1, July 28, 1901, p. 1, August 25, 1901, p. 8.
26. *Ibid.*, July 27, 1901, p. 1, August 25, 1901, p. 8.
27. *Ibid.*

had no talent for organizing. She admitted that she would like a ten-hour day, but she did not believe the union could obtain it. "It's the rich in the parlor and the poor in the kitchen," she matter-of-factly explained, "and that's the way it's goin' to stay."[28]

In any event, control of the union soon slipped from the grasp of servants into the hands of professional reformers and "club women." From the very beginning, the International Union Label League advisors had been the ones articulating union demands. It was their photographs that appeared in the newspapers, and it was they who were described as the "Women Who Led in Organizing the Union of the Housemaids." The girls and their officers were largely ignored. In issuing the union's demands, reformers spoke of what *they* wanted for the girls. They were well meaning, to be sure, and they unquestionably expressed what "the girls" wanted to say. But the movement was really their own.[29]

Even more disheartening was the infiltration of employers. This danger became apparent at the union's first "open meeting," in August. The girls, "dressed in all the finery of the season," were accompanied by friends and followers, in what was probably the best-attended meeting in the union's history. A prestigious array of local labor and women's club leaders and several nationally known social reformers addressed the enthusiastic audience. The speakers delivered inspiring orations, emphasizing the need for making service a respectable "trade" and for organizing it on a more efficient basis—both sacred tenets of post-1870 domestic service reform catechism. They praised the union as an important step in this "revolutionizing" process. One speaker, however, an important women's club leader, took the audience by surprise. While approving the union's demands for reform, she also advocated formation of an employer's union, one that could "meet and talk over the problems with the girls, discuss their needs, and the housewives' needs."[30] One can imagine the buzz that passed through the assembly. This was not at all what the girls had in mind, and such sentiments, expressed so openly and so seriously by one of

28. *Ibid.*
29. See Nancy Schrom Dye, "Creating a Feminist Alliance: Sisterhood and Class Conflict in the New York Women's Trade Union League, 1903–1914," *Feminist Studies*, II (1975), 25, for another example of reformer domination in a female union, although Dye believes that the primary problem in this case was a "conflict between feminism and unionism" among union leaders.
30. Chicago *Tribune*, August 23, 1901, p. 7.

their supposed counselors, undoubtedly contributed to the rapid and drastic decline in union membership that followed this meeting.

Divisions within the membership, domination of the union by outsiders, and dwindling enthusiasm among the rank and file soon took its toll. By the end of October, the union was "on the point of disintegration." The number of members attending meetings had dropped steadily for three months. No new members had been recruited; the treasury was empty. The constitution had not been ratified, and efforts to do so were shuffled aside by discussion of the approaching Christmas dance. No more than a dozen girls attended any of the October meetings, and when only eight women appeared for the October 24 conclave, no further gatherings were scheduled.

Given the history of domestic service in the United States, all of these problems were predictable. The girls could not agree on a unified program because their problems and suggested solutions were so diverse. Once the union had lost its novelty, once reformers and leaders had established the union's moderate tone, and once it became clear that fulfillment of union goals required slow, patient change rather than revolution, the rank and file lost interest. Similar situations occurred time and again. During the first twenty years of the twentieth century, a rash of local domestic unions in the Midwest, South, and Far West obtained charters from such bastions of organized labor as the American Federation of Labor and the National Women's Trades Union. But by the early 1920s, all had dissolved their affiliations. The Industrial Workers of the World also failed in its attempt to organize domestics, though here, government suppression played a role.[31]

The battle between discontented servants and unhappy employers was too loud to be ignored or to be represented as atypical. But isolated cases of employer oppression and servant impudence were often blown out of proportion. Obnoxious employers and servants were too often allowed to tarnish the reputations of the conscientious ones. Nearly all servants and employers squabbled, but the majority man-

31. Elizabeth Ross Haynes, "Negroes in Domestic Service in the United States," *Journal of Negro History*, VIII (1923), 435–36; Benjamin R. Andrews, *Economics of the Household* (New York: Macmillan, 1924), 467–68; "Plans for Improvement of Domestic Service," *Monthly Labor Review*, X (May, 1920), 116. For examples of a variety of efforts to organize household workers, see *Life and Labor*, first published in 1911, the official journal of the National Women's Trade Union. See also Foner, *Women and the American Labor Movement*, 407–411. Although quoted extensively by Foner, see also Daniel T. Hobby (ed.), " 'We Have Got Results': A Document on the Organization of Domestics in the Progressive Era," *Labor History*, XVII (1976), 103–108.

aged to resolve their differences and to live together peacefully, if not harmoniously.

Some employers learned the art of compromise. Admittedly, they often attained their enlightened view of the servant problems only upon discovering that it aided in retaining needed servitors, but results, after all, are more important than motives. Wise housekeepers, whether from self-interest or sympathy, did what they could to ease the less agreeable aspects of their servants' lives. A few employers, finding it best to accept servants for what they were, became philosophers on this subject. They discovered that if one ignored occasional "eccentricities of manner and dress," most servants performed quite satisfactorily. "My things move smoothly if I overlook a thousand things that I could not endure if I looked at them," wrote an Albany housekeeper. She believed servants were often unfairly criticized and that there were "about as many bad mistresses as servants." The secret to a peaceful household, she maintained, was to withstand intermittent trials as cheerfully as possible.[32]

Some employers felt a keen sense of responsibility for their servants' physical and moral well-being. Conscientious employers instructed servants in personal cleanliness and taught them to read and write. They warned them against evil influences and bad company and guaranteed their physical welfare by providing good clothing, food, and shelter. Admittedly, such good deeds also contributed to protecting their homes and families, but this was not the only motivation. Consider the conditions under which a Buffalo, New York, housekeeper accepted "a poor little fatherless and motherless" girl as maid. The waif, sent to the woman's home by an orphanage, appeared at her door "in a cold, dripping state" one rainy March night. "I had not the heart to turn her off," the woman later explained, "although she looked so ill I did not know but I was taking fever, or small pox, into the bosom of my family." As it turned out, the girl was only tired and hungry, and after a good night's sleep and a warm meal, she proved to be "an angel."[33] Yet this housekeeper's sense of responsibility had led her to take a sizable risk.

32. Harriet Martineau, *Society in America* (3 vols.; London: Saunders and Otley, 1837), III, 135, 144; Martha Chauncey to Mary Williams, November 22, 1851, August 13, 1852, December 20, 1855, all in Josiah Butler Williams Family Papers, Collection of Regional History, Cornell University.

33. Anna L. Williams to Elizabeth F. Camp, March 25, 1864, in Camp Family Papers (Additional).

Some employers fused this sense of responsibility with an abiding appreciation and fondness for their servants. They were not afraid to praise servants, and they placed implicit trust in their servants' abilities and characters. Something beyond moral duty moved these employers to show compassion for sick, injured, grieving, and aged servants; to aid servants in need of money or a job; and to counsel servants with personal problems. Female servants about to be married could convert employers into mother hens. Was the prospective bridegroom an alcoholic? Did he have a steady job? Was he a fortune hunter? A bigamist? Such questions had to be asked, and appreciative employers assumed responsibility for doing so.[34]

The spirit of the golden age survived to such an extent in some instances that servants were treated as members of the family. This was most often the case where a single girl worked in a small, middle-class household. There she might be "treated more like a daughter than a hired girl," joining family amusements and practical jokes, accompanying the family on social outings, enjoying liberal time to herself, and escaping the degradation of caps and the title "servant." The acme of comradeship was attained when mistresses helped with the housework. Girls were delighted that they and the lady of the house should actually "work *together*." Servants working in such households became so attached to their employers that when finally leaving, as leave most did, heart-rending farewell scenes were enacted amidst many tears and sniffles.[35]

Such treatment could not have been won by undeserving servants. Many workers combined the virtues of loyalty, honesty, efficiency, and chastity with an admirable regard for their duties and place. Despite

34. See, for example, Mehetable M. Goddard to Samuel Goddard, February 3, 1833, in May-Goddard Papers, Lucius M. Boltwood to Clarinda B. Boltwood, September 9, 1864, August 18, 1887, both in Boltwood Family Papers, Cornelia P. Spencer to Mrs. Swain, March 3, 1869, Cornelia P. Spencer to Friend, August 7, 1882, and Cornelia P. Spencer to June Love, December 29, 1890, all in Cornelia Phillips Spencer Papers, Southern Historical Collection, Library of the University of North Carolina at Chapel Hill, Allan Nevins and Milton Halsey Thomas (eds.), *The Diary of George Templeton Strong* (4 vols.; New York: Macmillan, 1952), II, 187.

35. Essie to Margaret Scott, January 16, 1887, Carrie to Margaret Scott, January 15, 1888, both in Adrian Records; Thomas McCann to Mary McKeonn, September 8, 1883, in McCann Correspondence (T-1456), Public Records Office of Northern Ireland, Belfast; Caroline Dunstan Diaries 1856–70 (MS in Manuscripts and Archives Division, New York Public Library, Astor, Lenox, and Tilden Foundations), July 4, 1856; Kate Bond to Ellen, December 1, 1870, in Bond and Grayston Immigrant Letters, Collection of Regional History, Cornell University.

their celebrated arrogance, despite their bold demands for equality, servants were not the thoroughgoing rebels they sometimes seemed to be. They did not want to haul down the American class system; they simply did not want to be at its bottom. They longed to cross the line between lower-class anonymity and middle-class respectability. They tried to be good servants and sought employers' advice on how to rid themselves of "Bad habits." When well fed, sheltered, and appreciated, orphans, immigrants, and other "misfits" who may never have known the affection and security of a real home could be transformed into steadfast servants. This is what sociologists call successful acculturation. Only when their loyalty and talents were taken for granted, only when they believed themselves bullied or exploited did they become resentful. As one young girl so succinctly put it, "I think if a girl is treated kindly she will stay longer than when she is not." [36]

Many servants were obedient, even docile. They were thankful for their jobs and frightened of losing them. Some were shy and timid by nature. Others, if failing to give satisfactory service, were "mortified and ashamed." Some domestics, especially older, more experienced ones, became upset only when employers attempted to interfere in their work. They considered housework their "business," and resented employers who tried to make servants' business "their'in." Then too, servants accused of impudence were more often naïve than ill-mannered, cynical, or arrogant. Raised without proper training in the laws of etiquette, servants could be blissfully unaware of their "audacity." As one girl wrote, "I run over to Mrs. Buck for a few minutes and write back again with out permission and Mrs Stone calls this disobedience." The girl could not understand why she was forbidden to come and go as she pleased, especially when her work was finished, for she "did not slack it as some girls would." Even good servants occasionally exploded when they felt slighted or insulted, but the "domestic tempest" eventually passed, and "smiling faces" reappeared. [37]

    36. Maggie Maher to Clarinda B. Boltwood, October 6, 1868 and [March or April], 1869, both in Boltwood Family Papers; Carrie to Margaret Scott, March 5, 1886, in Adrian Records. See also New York *Times*, December 5, 1871, p. 3. For the comments of historians on domestic service as a vehicle of acculturation, see Theresa M. McBride, *The Domestic Revolution: The Modernisation of Household Service in England and France, 1820–1920* (New York: Holmes and Meier, 1976), 83–86, 111–21; David M. Katzman, *Seven Days a Week: Women and Domestic Service in Industrializing America* (New York: Oxford University Press, 1978), 171–73, 274–77.
    37. Dunstan Diaries, October 14, 1856; Mary B. H. to Lucy M. Salmon, April 24, 1889, in Salmon Papers; Mary Alden Hopkins, " 'Living in': A Glimpse Behind the

Some servants knew their place and kept it. They respected the ladies and gentlemen they worked for and spoke lightly of their "servitude." They knew how servants were supposed to behave, and they acquiesced. "When the cold, unsmiling Mrs. G. demanded my given name," recalled one girl, "I was afraid it would make appearances worse to say 'Georgiana.' That would sound ridiculously fine for the station; so, to save myself, while blushing at the untruth, I replied: 'Ann.' " Other servants were more calculating. They curried favor with employers by playing the humble mendicant. "If there is anything more classy than a lady," philosophized one schemer, "it is her servant, who chooses her mistress with a fine cunning." Such servants, though with less honest intentions, always behaved in an ingratiating manner. They addressed employers as "sir" and "madam" and affected a pleasingly respectful "air," all of which led employers to overlook more disagreeable behavior.[38]

When the right blending of temperaments was achieved, servants and employers remained together for many years. Some servants insisted, contrary to public opinion, that most domestics disliked constant change and were thankful for good places. Pathetic testimony to this opinion came in an elderly servant's summary of her life: "I will soon have to leave and find a home with a stranger. This has been my lot for the last thirty years. The Savior said the foxes have holes, and the birds of the air have nests, but I have nowhere to lay my head." Devoted servants sometimes served more than one generation of a single family, working in a home for twenty, thirty, even forty years. Admittedly, these were exceptional cases, and most people found it extraordinary if servants stayed five to ten years in one place. Still,

Scenes in a Hotel," *Collier's Magazine*, XXXXVI (November 26, 1910), 20; McCracken, "The Problem of Domestic Service II," 494–95; New York *Times*, May 5, 1875, p. 6; Susan Hale to Lucretia P. Hale, June 8, 1889, in Caroline P. Atkinson (ed.), *Letters of Susan Hale* (Boston: Marshall Jones, 1921), 226; Mary Elizabeth Carter, *Millionaire Households and Their Domestic Economy* (New York: D. Appleton and Co., 1903), 46–48; Flora to Lucy M. Sickles, October 16, 1891, Anna to [Margaret Scott], June 20, 1886, both in Adrian Records; Clarinda B. Boltwood to Lucius M. Boltwood, August 11, 1863, in Boltwood Family Papers.

38. Kirby, *Years of Experience*, 78; Anne Forsyth, "Seven Times a Servant," *Delineator*, LXXVI (October, 1910), 252, 342, and "Seven Times a Servant," *Delineator*, LXXVI (December, 1910), 469. See also Eliza Potter, *A Hairdresser's Experience in High Life*, 22, 104, 223, Thomas Affleck to Wife, December 19, 1865, in Thomas Affleck Papers, State Department of Archives and History, Louisiana State University, Judy Jackson to Mary Griffin, June 17, 1867, and Judy Jackson to Son, November 21, 1868, both in Williams Family Papers, New York *Times*, March 30, 1879, p. 9.

The southern mammy was the symbol of the perfect nursemaid and the model of faithful service throughout the nineteenth century.

long, faithful service could be commanded by good conditions and kind treatment.[39]

Some servants, even after leaving an employer, kept in touch and maintained a sense of devotion. They and their employers exchanged letters and Christmas greetings, informing one another of their fortunes and failures. A North Carolina servant and her employers corresponded after the latter had moved to Tennessee. Jane, the servant, had been unable to accompany the family when it migrated, but when her former employer journeyed to North Carolina shortly thereafter on a business trip, he persuaded Jane to return with him to Tennessee. There she spent several more years in the family's service. An Irish maid in Massachusetts corresponded frequently with her former employers. On one occasion she sent a birthday gift to one of the family's children and instructed the boy to obey and love his "dear and good parents." She apologized to her former mistress in the same letter for not writing more often. "I have the hart to do any thing for you," she revealed, "and I love you as a mother and my best friend and will always think of you and the good home I had with you."[40]

Strong personal attachment in the homes of millionaires was less likely. The atmosphere was too sterile, employers too aloof for personal attachments to thrive. The wealthy could sometimes retain servants for respectable lengths of time, but this was because of the relatively high wages and good living conditions they offered, not the homey atmosphere of their austere households. More often, the servant "grown gray in the service of one household" was an "almost unheard of character in American homes of wealth."[41] This is not to say that servants in wealthy homes took no pride in the family name, but, as mentioned, they cared more about the personal status thus accrued than for their employers as people.

39. Ann T. Coleman, "Reminiscences" (MS in Ann Thomas Coleman Papers, Perkins Library, Duke University), VII, 14; Note dated January 13, 1800 (MS in May-Goddard Papers, Box 1, Folder 7A); Nicholas B. Wainwright (ed.), A Philadelphia Perspective: The Diary of Sidney George Fisher Covering the Years 1834–1871 (Philadelphia: Historical Society of Pennsylvania, 1967), 61, 527; Chicago Tribune, January 5, 1902, p. 42; "A Vanishing Relation," Independent, LXVI (August 23, 1906), 466.

40. Jane Glenn to Hannah S. Wiley, May 29, 1869, Hannah S. Wiley to Calvin H. Wiley, February 7, 1870, May 16, 1873, all in Calvin Henderson Wiley Papers, Southern Historical Collection, Library of the University of North Carolina at Chapel Hill; Maggie Maher to Clarinda B. Boltwood [March or April], 1869, in Boltwood Family Papers; Bridget Scully to Mrs. James B. DeBow, May 25, 1865, in James D. B. DeBow Papers, Perkins Library, Duke University. See also Anna Smith letters to Harriet Beecher Stowe, in Beecher-Stowe Collection of Family Papers, Schlesinger Library, Radcliffe College.

41. Carter, Millionaire Households, 136–37, 213, 280–83.

Still, service was not all it should have been. North, South, East, and West, in city, village, and countryside, at all times between the first inaugural of Thomas Jefferson and the close of the Great War, the servant problems remained a miserable constant in American life. Servants were unhappy; employers were unhappy. The many good guys could neither disguise nor compensate for the troublemakers. An arbiter was required, someone to sift, analyze, and correct the legitimate complaints of employers and servants. A champion was needed, someone to fearlessly engage the national *bête noire* in mortal combat. Answering the challenge and charging headlong into the fray came the American reformer.

CHAPTER EIGHT

ONWARD CHRISTIAN SOLDIERS
Servant Reform Before 1870

Throughout American history, a vanguard of conscientious crusaders has been ever ready to keep American democracy on its predestined course by righting the nation's social wrongs. Moralists and humanitarians, some of them cranks but most of them well meaning, have eagerly attacked the sins and confronted the dilemmas of their fellow citizens. One of the most widespread and least successful reform movements in the American experience occurred in domestic service. For a century Americans lectured, petitioned, published, organized, and legislated, in a vain attempt to solve their servant problems. Solutions and methods sometimes changed, but the results remained the same. Servants and employers continued at odds, and the servant "problem" remained "one of the burning questions of the day."[1]

The purpose of servant reformers throughout the period 1800 to 1920 was very straightforward: they wanted to increase the supply of good servants. Reformers had both practical and idealistic reasons for pursuing this goal. Most reformers were clearly "pro-employer." They bore no malice towards servants; they wanted to make them happy, productive members of society. But they were determined to accomplish this on their own terms, by converting servants to the manners and morals of America's upper and middle classes. Themselves members of these classes, the servant-employing classes, the chief concern

1. Anne L. Vrooman, "The Servant Question in Social Evolution," *Arena*, XXV (June, 1901), 645.

of reformers was to protect the sanctity of the American home. This required "good" servants, that is, faithful, Christian (Protestant), obedient, humble, chaste, honest, cleanly, and if possible, efficient servants. Most reformers were women, the people most often plagued by the trials of housekeeping. These two points made reformers very practical—some would say self-serving—in their outlook, but reformers were also idealistic. Seeking to restore those mythical golden age days of benevolent masters and faithful servants, reformers saw their efforts as part of a national scheme for moral and humanitarian improvement.

Regardless of motive, reformers produced two different plans for increasing the supply of good servants. At first, they sought to change the attitudes of servants towards service. They encouraged servants, in an extensive campaign of moral suasion, to take pride in their work and to be loyal to their employers. Later, after about 1870, reformers changed their tack. They began trying to attract a better caliber of worker to service by lessening tensions between hirer and hired and improving the working and living conditions of servants. In other words, they began challenging employers to accept responsibility for the failure of earlier reforms, thus turning "servant reform" into the reform of domestic service. Each of these epochs merits analysis of its rationale, methods, leaders, and consequences. This chapter will describe the earlier period.

Before 1870 hopes for reform depended on individual, religiously motivated employers pursuing reform within their own homes. This approach, patterned after British reforms dating from the fifteenth century, was adapted to American conditions early in the nineteenth century. Its moral thrust, already securely fixed in the British heritage, was further invigorated by the religious emotionalism of the Second Great Awakening, that giant cauldron of vitality in which so many other antebellum reform movements bubbled and brewed. The best way to revive the golden age, said reformers, was for employers to administer the Golden Rule with missionary zeal. Employers were to elevate servants morally and intellectually by molding them to fit the image of the good servant. To most reformers and employers this meant treating servants fairly and courteously. Their approach was tainted, however, by a paternalism that assumed that employers were morally and intellectually superior to servants. Reform of working and living conditions was ignored. The social stigma on service was acknowledged but, in the main, thought to be well deserved and, in any case, irrelevant to the problems at hand. Reform would come when servants learned to accept existing conditions.

Several means were at hand for instilling the spirit of reform in both servants and employers. Instructional booklets and moral tracts for the former and household manuals and etiquette books for the latter were among the earliest tools. Later, benevolent organizations, formed by employers and philanthropic citizens' groups, also demanded reform. Each of these agents had a specific objective and different means of accomplishing it. Some methods were more successful than others, but each was designed to reform the American servant.

The most direct method of reform was the tract or manual instructing servants in their moral duties. Such manuals dated from at least the fifteenth century, when they were popular in England.[2] The earliest American manuals were imported from England, and as Americans began writing their own handbooks, they copied, sometimes verbatim, the dictates of British reformers.[3] The tracts were condescending in tone, emphasizing that deference from servants would be rewarded with kindness by benevolent masters. Servants were cautioned against all the vices employers traditionally abhorred. "General rules" of conduct, sanctioned by appropriate verses of Scripture, bade them to be religious, obedient, pure of thought and deed, and disciples of the Protestant work ethic. Their place in life, servants were told, was determined by Providence. Earthly trials were tests of faith, designed to identify those people worthy of God's final glory.

Fine advice, this, but the manuals offered servants no practical information or counsel. Such topics as how to negotiate for wages and working conditions, how to find a good place, and how to protect legal rights were ignored. Seldom were housekeeping duties explained. Likewise, little mention was made of the obligations of employers to servants. Fair wages paid on time, sufficient food, adequate lodging, and perhaps clothing were all that employers were obliged to supply. Anything else—friendly, courteous treatment, or even a cheerful "good morning"—depended on servants' behavior. The best general advice that could be given was for servants to "put up with many in-

---

2. See, for example, R. E. Chambers (ed.), *A Fifteenth Century Courtesy Book* (London: Early English Text Society, 1914); *A Present for a Servant-Maid; or, The Sure Means of Gaining Love and Esteem* (London: n.p., 1749); *The Servant's Friend; or, The Master and Mistresses Best Gift to Their Servants, Apprentices, and Workmen* (n.p. [17—]); Jonathan Swift, *Directions to Servants* (New York: Pantheon Books, 1964).

3. For example, compare *The Servant's Friend*, 7–8 to *A Friendly Gift for Servants and Apprentices* (New York: Samuel Woods and Sons, 1821), 14.

conveniences, even hardships," rather than foolishly lose a good place or jeopardize a good reference. The only times servants might legitimately disobey masters, said reformers, was when ordered to break God's law, and even then, servants must excuse their audacity "in a decent, and modest, though resolute manner."[4]

Reformers tried to reconcile servants to their social position by assuring them that service was neither menial nor degrading. Girls were told that a lady's true qualities were measured by her goodness of heart and purity of soul, not by the capricious standards of fashionable society. Strict obedience to their mistresses was the best way for girls to prove that they possessed these admirable qualities. "True delicacy, true refinement," vowed reformers, "is in the heart, and does not in the least depend on the whiteness of the hand or the fineness and fashion of a gown. She can never feel in a degraded state who, amidst the labors of the kitchen, can look beyond this life and see in another world the crown that is laid up for those who fear God." Nor should servants forget that, regardless of appearances, mistresses were never idle. American wives, mothers, and housekeepers had complex responsibilities that were far more arduous than the limited, clear-cut tasks of servants.[5]

Etiquette books and household manuals for employers appeared after the same pattern as servant manuals, originating in the colonial period and copied from British prototypes. Household manuals were the more important of the two. Although early manuals might better be termed cookbooks, in time they constituted an amazing compilation of advice on all phases of housekeeping from the daily activities of cooking and cleaning to more delicate assignments, like caring for the sick and managing servants. In discussing servants, most pre-1870 household manuals pursued the same themes as servant manuals. Servants were generally portrayed as vexatious creatures who lacked any sense of loyalty. Employers were urged to be tolerant, to pay wages promptly, and to avoid scolding unless provoked beyond endurance. Typical advice from an 1821 manual warned against the "vicious habits" of the servant class. "It is better for servants to have too much

4. *A Friendly Gift*, 13, 16. An exception to the format of most early servant manuals is Robert Roberts, *The House Servant's Directory* (Boston: Munroe and Francis, 1828), supposedly written by a manservant in one of Boston's "most respectable families." Although Roberts dwells on the same subjects as other reformers, he also gives advice on servants' working responsibilities and devotes more space than was usual to the moral and humanitarian duties of employers.

5. *A Friendly Gift*, 29–30.

employment than too little," the author declared, "because, for want of resources, and the inclination to employ themselves usefully and innocently, much leisure assists in corrupting them."[6]

Etiquette books began to rival household manuals in popularity by the eighteenth century as middle-class women became as concerned with their manners and social image as with housewifery.[7] During the nineteenth century, etiquette books became invaluable social bibles that taught Americans how to be ladies and gentlemen and gave them advice on how to treat servants. Since bad servants threatened an employer's composure and aura of gentility—and thus their social reputation—etiquette books told employers how to curb their tempers and maintain a respectable social distance between themselves and servants. A typical manual, written in 1836, advised that, first and most importantly, employers must never betray their dependency on servants by appearing helpless or ignorant of housekeeping. Nearly as important was to resist provocation. Ladies and gentlemen were to be patient and mannerly with servants, no matter how exasperating the latter became. One's demeanor and voice must remain "composed" yet contain no hint of "familiarity or sympathy." Servants were to be taught their place, and employers were to avoid at all costs "the dangerous and common error of exercising too great humanity in action." If unable to follow these simple rules, employers had better be prepared to dig in, "to take the most decent creature who applies, trust in Providence, and lock every thing up."[8]

The common element in all of this reform literature was its condescending tone, which became most evident when reformers equated servants with children. The association seemed natural for several reasons. The image of the docile servant, as defined by the golden age, invited such a comparison. So, too, did the large number of children and young persons employed as servants. The even larger number of immigrants and unsophisticated adults in service tempted reformers

6. Mrs. William Parkes, *Domestic Duties; or, Instructions to Young Married Ladies* (New York: J. and J. Harper, 1828), 110. For a general introduction to these repositories of wisdom, see Russell Lynes, *The Domesticated Americans* (New York: Harper and Row, 1963), 57–64.

7. Julia Cherry Spruill, *Women's Life and Work in the Southern Colonies* (Chapel Hill: University of North Carolina Press, 1938), 212.

8. A Gentleman, *The Laws of Etiquette; or, Short Rules and Reflections for Conduct in Society* (Philadelphia: Carey, Lea, and Blanchard, 1836), 199–225. See Arthur M. Schlesinger, *Learning How to Behave: A Historical Study of American Etiquette Books* (New York: Macmillan, 1946), and Dixon Wecter, *The Saga of American Society* (New York: Charles Scribner's Sons, 1937), 157–95.

and employers to accuse servants of childlike simplicity. Consequently, ideas about child raising and the care of servants appeared strikingly similar through much of the nineteenth century.[9]

Interestingly enough, the authors of these pre-1870 servant manuals, household guides, and etiquette books could claim no special expertise in servant reform. Most of them were professional crusaders, each with a favorite cause, but few counted servant reform as their major interest. Their solutions for reform were personal remedies, based on their own experiences and frustrations with household servants. Most of these writers were literary women, authors of morality tales and sentimental novels. They included Lydia Maria Child, June C. Croly, Eliza W. Farrar, Sarah J. Hale, Catherine Sedgwick, Lydia Sigourney, Harriet Beecher Stowe, Sarah P. Willis, and a flock of lesser knowns. A few men flourished among the reformers. Timothy Shay Arthur and William Alcott were the most notable, but they were easily outnumbered by what Nathaniel Hawthorne described as that "damned mob of scribbling women."[10]

But manuals, tracts, and essays were not enough. Reform had become such an urgent concern by the 1820s that Americans started banding together in reform societies. The most important organizations were initiated by urban northeasterners. First to appear was the New York Society for the Encouragement of Faithful Domestic Servants, founded in 1825. It spawned imitators at Philadelphia, Boston, and Albany by the 1830s but remained the largest and best organized of the early societies. Once again British precedent was being followed. The Society for the Encouragement of Faithful Servants had been founded at London in 1789, and a similar group was formed at Dublin ten years later.[11]

9. Catherine E. Beecher, *A Treatise on Domestic Economy* (New York: Harper and Brothers, 1847), 154, 211; Griffith A. Nicholas [Elizabeth Strong Worthington], *The Biddy Club* (Chicago: A. C. McClurg and Co., 1888), 54–55. See also Bernard Wishey, *The Child and the Republic: The Dawn of Modern American Child Nurture* (Philadelphia: University of Pennsylvania Press, 1968).

10. For comments on the motives of female reformers as novelists, see Helen Waite Papashvily, *All the Happy Endings: A Study of the Domestic Novel in America, the Women Who Wrote It, the Women Who Read It, in the Nineteenth Century* (New York: Harper and Brothers, 1956), xvii, and Ann D. Wood, "The 'Scribbling Women' and Fanny Fern: Why Women Wrote," *American Quarterly*, XXIII (1971), 3–24. Neither Papashvily nor Wood, however, addresses herself to the nonfictional writings of these novelists.

11. Managers of the Society for the Encouragement of Faithful Domestic Servants in New York, *Fifth Annual Report* (New York: D. Fanshaw, 1830), 13–14; Managers of the Society for the Encouragement of Faithful Domestics, *First Annual Report* (Phila-

The founders and supporters of the American societies were the up-per- and middle-class men and women who normally lead such benev-olent organizations. Their officers and managers were associated with many other reform movements of the period. Typical leaders included Moses Allen, Matthew Carey, John Griscom, John Pintard, and Arthur Tappen. These same men and their wives directed the major moral re-form societies of antebellum America: the American Bible Society, American Tract Society, American Home Missionary Society, Ameri-can Sunday School Union, American Education Society, and a host of other groups dedicated to such worthy causes as immigrant protec-tion, care of orphans, elimination of pauperism, prison reform, public health, and abolition of slavery. They were philanthropists and altru-ists, but they were also employers of domestic servants and, as such, were dissatisfied with the morals and ethics of these people. Likewise, many patrons of the societies, though among the nation's wealthiest and most influential people, were seeking relief from their servant problems.

The purpose of these societies was inherent in their titles: to locate and make available a supply of "faithful" household servants. In order to accomplish this feat, societies undertook the "difficult and doubtful experiment" of promoting the "moral and religious improvement of Domestic Servants" and inspiring "mutual good will and friendship be-tween them and their employers." The most formidable barrier to achieving this goal was the mobility of the servant population. Even when found, capable servants were difficult to retain. Their *"love of incessant change"* corrupted "many who would otherwise be ac-counted good servants."[12] The societies wanted to correct this fault by encouraging long-time service.

Societies attacked the problems in two ways, the first being the es-tablishment of registry offices. Reform or replacement of commercial intelligence offices became an object inseparable from moral improve-

---

delphia: Mifflin & Perry, 1830), 3–4; J. Gray, "Society for the Encouragement of Ser-vants," *Gentleman's Magazine and Historical Chronicle*, LIX (1789), Part 1, iv; Irish Society for the Encouragement of Servants, *Rules and Orders* (Dublin: n.p., 1799). Blaine Edward McKinley, " 'Strangers in the Gates': Employer Reactions Towards Do-mestic Servants in America, 1825–1875" (Ph.D. dissertation, Michigan State Univer-sity, 1969), 99–118, gives a good description of the founding and activities of the Ameri-can societies.

12. Managers of the Society for the Encouragement of Faithful Domestic Servants in New York, *First Annual Report* (New York: D. Fanshaw, 1826), 3–7, and *Fifth Annual Report*, 3.

ment of servants. By establishing their own employment bureaus, thus controlling their own supply of hand-picked servants, societies hoped to eliminate the imposition of commercial suppliers on both employers and servants. Society registry offices differed from commercial offices in several ways. Servants were charged no fee when registering, but they were required to produce verifiable character references. Any attempt at forgery was punishable by having one's name published in local newspapers—a form of public blacklisting. Employers, for a five dollar annual fee, were entitled to an unlimited number of servants. However, employers could be turned out of the society for giving false or inaccurate descriptions of servants to either the society or to fellow subscribers and for *"enticing or inveigling away a servant from any other person."* Harsh or unjust treatment of servants was also grounds for expulsion.[13]

The societies' second means of obtaining faithful servants was materially to reward "good behavior and longevity." Hoping to convince servants that faithfulness and stability were virtues and that restlessness and mobility were symptoms of immorality, societies bestowed cash premiums and other rewards on servants who rendered long and faithful service. The New York society, for example, gradually perfected a system for granting cash bonuses to domestics who served an employer for at least one year. Each subscribing employer could nominate one servant free of charge and additional servants at five dollars apiece. If registered servants remained with their employers for one year after enrollment, they received either a Bible or a cash reward of two dollars. Cash premiums were then given for each subsequent year of continuous service with that employer, the value of the premiums increasing yearly. Similar benefits included payment of ten dollar annuities to domestics who, after serving a single employer for at least five years, became "incapacitated" or "indigent" at any future date. The same sum was due female servants who married after five years of faithful service. Societies also operated savings programs whereby servants who held accounts for at least five years could earn an interest rate of 1 percent per annum.[14]

13. Managers of the Society for the Encouragement of Faithful Domestic Servants in New York, *Fifth Annual Report*, 19–20; Managers of the Society for the Encouragement of Faithful Domestics, *Constitution* (Philadelphia: Mifflin & Perry, 1829), 2.

14. Managers of the Society for the Encouragement of Faithful Domestic Servants in New York, *First Annual Report*, 12–17, and *Fifth Annual Report*, 8–9, 20–21; Managers of the Society for the Encouragement of Faithful Domestics, *First Annual Report*, 2, 5.

Much of this activity was motivated by a strong religious impulse. Some society officers were ministers or lay ministers, and all professed to be devout. They referred to themselves as "Christian philanthropists" and maintained close working relationships with such organizations as the American Sunday School Union. Thus, such acts as the awarding of Bibles for loyal service had a double significance. The Bibles served as symbols of gratitude and achievement, but they also represented important means of reform. Recipients were to read their Bibles regularly, to use them as guides to moral lives and humble service. "If our servants were christians in sincerity," reasoned managers of the New York society, "we should have little cause of complaint, and every scheme for their improvement must be radically defective which does not *directly* aim to make them wise unto salvation." [15]

Societies sponsored other activities aimed at strengthening the moral and religious fiber of servants. For example, the New York society presented an annual thirty-dollar award to the author of the best tract on the subject of a servant's "moral and religious duties." These tracts, which bore such titles as *Sarah; or, The Victim of Pride* and *A Father's Advice to His Daughter on Going Out to Service*, endorsed the societies' most sacred precepts. Winning entries were printed and distributed free of charge to servants and sold to subscribing employers and the public. The same was done with a variety of other religious tracts, hymnals, and related material. Benjamin Franklin's *Poor Richard*, for instance, was reprinted and distributed as an antidote to "that extravagance in dress, and general improvidence" that were "too common among servants." Tracts and books were loaned to "deserving servants" by the societies' offices, and employers were encouraged to form "kitchen" libraries, filled with "entertaining, but religious and instructive books." Servants, it was hoped, would spend their leisure hours memorizing these oracles, thus forsaking "less innocent enjoyments." [16]

Societies reminded "masters" of their responsibilities to servants, but did so within the feudal-religious framework. This implied that servants had more responsibilities than did employers and that, if servants failed in their duties, employers were exempt from theirs. It

15. Managers of the Society for the Encouragement of Faithful Domestic Servants in New York, *Fifth Annual Report*, 14.

16. Managers of the Society for the Encouragement of Faithful Domestic Servants in New York, *First Annual Report*, 14–15, 18–19, 31–32, *Second Annual Report* (New York: D. Fanshaw, 1827), 9–10, and *Third Annual Report* (New York: D. Fanshaw, 1828), 10. Associated societies published similar tracts. See, for example, American Sunday School Union, *Ann Connover* (Philadelphia: n.p., 1835).

also required that employers maintain a respectable social distance from servants, always impressing the latter with the disparity in their stations. Thus employers were criticized for neglecting the Golden Rule, but they were equally at fault if, indulging in a "mistaken benevolence," they were overly kind and forgiving to unworthy servants. Employers must make servants "better men and women" by indoctrinating them in their obligations of loyalty and respect and by shaping their behavior through the *"influence of conscience."* Societies believed it was the "insuperable pride" of servants, causing them to revolt against the "very *name* of servant," that was the greatest obstacle to faithful service. Their arrogance and apparently selfish motives left the societies open to criticism.[17]

In view of this attitude, the limited success of early reform societies is understandable. They all claimed modest gains in the number of loyal servants and satisfied employers. They all published annual reports showing increases in the number of subscribers, subscriber requests for servants, servants enrolled, and known engagements. Yet never did the number of successfully contracted engagements come close to equaling the number of requests for servants, and never did the societies handle more than a fraction of a city's servants and employers.[18] Societies also failed to reform commercial intelligence offices. No statistical measure exists of success or failure in this area, only the fact that society offices folded while commercial agents continued to thrive and practice the same abuses. Society offices probably had some tempering effect while in operation. Some commercial suppliers, for instance, eliminated fees for servants in order to compete with society offices.[19] Nonetheless, by 1836 all of the major societies had folded, and any reforms they may have inspired while in operation quickly eroded. The societies would not be revived for nearly a half century.

Benevolent institutions offered another and in some ways more helpful and practical approach to organized reform. These institutions were active primarily in northeastern cities. Their objective was to protect the morals of unemployed female servants by giving them a place to live. Organizations maintained dormitories and boarding

17. Managers of the Society for the Encouragement of Faithful Domestic Servants in New York, *First Annual Report*, 7, 9, 16; Philanthropos, "On the Society for the Improvement of Faithful Domestic Servants," *Working Man's Advocate*, January 8, 1830.
18. See McKinley, "'Strangers in the Gates,'" Table 4 for a convenient tabulation of available statistics for the New York and Philadelphia societies.
19. Parkes, *Domestic Duties*, 119n.

houses that offered lodging and meals at modest prices, thus sparing girls not only starvation and exposure but the moral evils of commercial boarding houses. Benevolent "homes" provided "boarders" with spiritual nourishment, too, in the form of daily religious instruction. The American Female Guardian Society was the first and longest lived of these organizations, founded in 1837 and continuing into the 1880s. This society aided working girls in all occupations, but others, such as the Christian Home for Female Servants, founded at New York in 1853, and the Saint Joseph Home for Sick and Destitute Servant Girls, founded at Boston in 1866, accepted only servants.[20]

A few institutions went so far as to operate vocational training programs that prepared girls for service, but these were limited in scope. An example is the Girls' Lodging House, founded by Charles Loring Brace as an appendage of the Children's Aid Society. In most ways, the GLH was like other homes. Its purpose was "to teach them [the girls] to work, to be clean, and to understand the virtue of order and punctuality; to lay the foundations of a housekeeper or servant; to bring the influence of discipline, of kindness, and religion to bear on these wild and ungoverned creatures." Unlike other homes, however, the GLH provided on-the-job training in scrubbing, cleaning, bedmaking, sewing, and plain cooking. Unfortunately, this training was rudimentary, no more useful than that given in orphan asylums. The hope of the GLH was that its girls would soon be placed in "some good home or respectable family," where patience and understanding would "do the rest." A more formal training school was attempted by the GLH in about 1870, but girls were in such demand that there was little time for thorough instruction.[21]

No matter. Reform, by 1870, was taking a new direction. Emphasis on religious benevolence was ebbing. Religious organizations, such as the YWCA, home missionary societies, and church charities, would continue to sponsor working-class boarding houses and to play a notable role in reform, but they would largely be supplanted by new, more secular groups motivated less by God and more by science. Their philosophies would also be different. More attention would be paid to the

20. McKinley, "'Strangers in the Gates,'"118–20; New York *Times,* January 14, 1869, p. 8, January 27, 1871, p. 8.
21. Charles Loring Brace, *The Dangerous Classes of New York and Twenty Years' Work Among Them* (New York: Wynkoop and Hallenbeck, 1880), 305–306, 309–10, 315; Joseph M. Hawes, *Children in Urban Society: Juvenile Delinquency in Nineteenth Century America* (New York: Oxford University Press, 1971), 97; McKinley, "'Strangers in the Gates,'"132–33.

working and living conditions of servants and less to the state of their souls. The religious-moral-ethical aspect of the servant problems, although still important, would be overshadowed by economic, sociological, psychological, and technological considerations.

A trace of this new tone was already creeping into reform literature by 1840. A few reformers, including William Alcott, Timothy Shay Arthur, Elizabeth Ellet, and Sarah J. Hale, began hinting, by that year, that employers were at least partly to blame for the servant problems. They suggested that ungenerous behavior towards servants was unworthy of ladies and gentlemen and retarded the smooth functioning of households. Reformers were no less condescending to servants nor any less insistent on the need to maintain class lines, but they now began to appreciate the complexity of their dilemma.

One harbinger of this new, sympathetic view was novelist Catherine M. Sedgwick. In 1837 Sedgwick wrote a fictional account of the trials of a young servant girl in *Live and Let Live; or, Domestic Service Illustrated*, a book designed to shock employers into recognizing the pitiable condition of American servants. Sedgwick was among the first to state that reform required more than subservient servants. Reform, she insisted, must begin with employers resolving to treat servants fairly. This was the way to transform arrogant, disloyal domestics into pleasant, dedicated friends. Sedgwick was as condescending as earlier reformers, but her perspective was new. She was aware of the trials uneducated, unskilled, and unfaithful servants posed for housekeepers, but she insisted that housekeepers could inspire better service more readily by training servants and sympathizing with them than by coercion. Sedgwick suggested that the best way to control servants was to earn their respect, that is, for housekeepers to become heroes worth imitating by demonstrating their own expertise in housework. Her objects were to make housekeepers "feel their duties and obligations to their 'inferiors in position' " and to incite them "to a zealous devotion to 'home missions.' "[22]

Sedgwick used every known stereotype of service to enliven and drive home these points in *Live and Let Live*. The questionable character of intelligence offices, the sexual exploitation of young girls, the lack of training among both servants and housekeepers, the division of labor in service, and the differences between city "servants" and coun-

22. Catherine M. Sedgwick, *Live and Let Live; or, Domestic Service Illustrated* (New York: Harper and Brothers, 1837), v–vi.

try "helps" are all portrayed. Lucy, the heroine of this morality tale, is forced by "the stern coercion of necessity" to go out to service. She is an intelligent, sensitive, dutiful native-white girl—Sedgwick's vision of the perfect servant and the symbol of what service could be. During her many adventures, Lucy encounters all types of inept and deceiving servants as well as the whole range of employers, from kindly to pompous, all of them acting to magnify Lucy's angelic qualities. Most employers, as portrayed by Sedgwick, are well meaning but thoughtless, failing to consider "the feelings and rights" of their domestics. Through Lucy's experiences, Sedgwick illustrates this thoughtlessness at work in creating the servant problems.[23]

Even more outspoken was William Alcott, cousin of that grand eccentric, Bronson Alcott. William Alcott was the first American reformer to insist that all previously suggested reforms were useless. He believed that neither submissive servants nor benevolent employers could solve America's servant problems. The root of the problems, as Alcott saw it, was the American system of housekeeping. Americans, by allowing European customs and aristocratic pretensions to invade and corrupt their households, had grown too lavish. This aristocratic cancer had even diseased the lower classes of America's once frugal and contented rural communities. Those in "middling and even low circumstances" now employed a laundress once weekly. Americans, charged Alcott, had betrayed their democratic heritage. They had strayed from the days when mothers and daughters had performed housework without the aid of hired strangers. Of course, Alcott realized that Americans could not dispense completely with servants. It was too late for that; the decadence had corroded too deeply. Still, he maintained, servants should be eliminated "as much as possible" from American homes. Americans would abolish their servant problems only to the extent that they could do without servants.[24]

Alcott's solution was not a comforting one; few Americans were ready for his extreme measures. Yet an answer to the servant problems very similar to his would soon be offered by the nineteenth century's foremost authority on the servant problems, Catherine Esther Beecher. In most ways, Catherine Beecher resembled other servant reformers of her time. She believed that the uneducated lower classes posed a threat to social order and that the "laws of virtue and Heaven"

23. *Ibid.*, 15–17, 21, 70–71.
24. William Alcott, *The Young Wife; or, Duties of Women in the Marriage Relation* (New York: J. C. Derby, 1837, 1855), 153–68.

had to be defended against "insubordination, anarchy, and crime." She also believed that the traditional master-servant relationship, as well as the relationships among American social classes, were worsening because of increasing wealth and leisure and decreasing adherence to the old Puritan values of thrift and hard work.[25]

Beecher had a new solution for these evils, though. She believed that previous reformers had emphasized servants' moral duties at the expense of their rights and freedom. Reformers had been preoccupied with nurturing servants on religious sanctionings of faithfulness and obedience, with frightening or coercing them into good behavior. This, declared Beecher, was superficial reform. It created change in the quickest possible way without guaranteeing the permanency of reform. American housekeepers, she continued, using the home as the focus of a new moral authority, must seek to develop the "character" of servants, that is, to ingrain lasting behavior. Character development became, according to Beecher's biographer, the "key both to individual success and to social interdependence. . . . This theme dominated antebellum attitudes towards child-raising and education, and by 1860 'character formation' had effectively replaced religion as the primary basis for learned moral behavior in both school and home."[26]

Beecher presented her solution in two path-making works on servant reform. First came *A Treatise on Domestic Economy*, which appeared in 1841 and was reprinted with occasional additions and under various titles for the next thirty years. Beecher's purpose in writing *Treatise* was to ease the "deplorable sufferings of multitudes of young wives and mothers" caused by the "combined influence of poor health, poor domestics, and a defective domestic education."[27] Stressing the necessity of better training for both mistress and maid, *Treatise* was the most comprehensive household manual published to that date. It contained information on all phases of housekeeping, including child raising, health, diet, cooking, furnishings, marketing, manners, gardening, even architecture and plumbing. It announced a new conception of what was important in household education. It offered women, far too many of whom were as ignorant of their duties as servants were of theirs, a wider and more thorough preparation in housekeeping than they had ever received.

25. Kathryn Kish Sklar, *Catherine Beecher: A Study in American Domesticity* (New Haven: Yale University Press, 1973), 113–14, 125–27.
26. Sklar, *Catherine Beecher*, 129.
27. Beecher, *Treatise on Domestic Economy*, 5, 151.

Employers heard even more revolutionary advice in *Treatise*. Yes, Beecher admitted, servants were a constant source of irritation and misery for Americans, but employers should rejoice that their servants were not the "cringing, submissive" menials of less democratic countries. If American servants were "incompetent, unstable, and unconformed to their station," it was "Perfect Wisdom" that assigned those trials to employers as means of instilling them with "patience, fortitude, and self-control." Beecher went on to explain that the way to insure servants' loyalty was to manage them with respect and courtesy. More importantly, if servants became overbearing, rude, or dissatisfied with their "condition," the remedy was to educate them. Servants should be convinced with rational arguments, not simply told or cajoled into believing that labor was honorable and that "grades of subordination" were part of the natural order.[28]

Beecher's second contribution to reform was *Letters to Persons Who Are Engaged in Domestic Service*, published in 1842. Here Beecher described for servants their household duties and moral responsibilities, becoming the first person to write separate manuals for employers and servants. In *Letters* Beecher was unabashedly proemployer, admittedly writing the book at the urging of "benevolent ladies" who believed that servants needed a manual to instruct them in the "peculiar duties" of their "station." But instead of denying as libelous the notion that service was degrading, Beecher tried to instill servants with pride in their occupation by showing that service need not be degrading and that, indeed, it could be made an honorable trade. She explained that servants had unimaginable "power to do good." In caring for the sacred home and its occupants, she explained, servants enabled fathers to follow their professions and relieved mothers of many burdens. "Let any one select the class of persons that can be dispensed with *last of all*," Beecher challenged, "and it would be found that lawyers, merchants, doctors, and ministers would all be given up, before every family would agree to give up all aid from cooks, washers, nurses, and every kind of hired service in the family."[29]

Then she went even further. Abandoning four centuries of reform philosophy, Beecher presented servants with reasoned arguments showing why certain modes of behavior were more desirable than others. For example, she explained why it was unreasonable for servants

28. *Ibid.*, 204–210.
29. Catherine E. Beecher, *Letters to Persons Who Are Engaged in Domestic Service* (New York: Leavitt and Trow, 1842), 5–6, 62–68.

to expect to eat with employers, a popular demand in the servant rebellion. Many servants, she pointed out to her "friends," were untidy,
coarse, and ignorant of the social graces required on such occasions.
Exclusion of servants from family tables was good, she insisted, because it spared servants much embarrassment and encouraged them
to seek self-improvement. Then too, she continued, it was "inconve-
nient" to have servants at the dining table because they were needed
in the kitchen and to serve the family. Their presence at the table only
bred "disorder and confusion." Servants would learn the truth of this
analysis, she said, through education and contemplation. "The more
you read and study," she promised servants, "the more your character,
manners, and habits will be likely to improve." True happiness, she
assured them, did not depend on wealth, social position, or outward
appearance "but rather in such a character as enables you to meet the
duties and trials of your lot with patient cheerfulness, and faithful diligence."[30] Much of her counsel smacked of bad employer propaganda,
but the importance of *Letters* is that Beecher spent many pages explaining in a sympathetic tone. No one else had done that.

Beecher expanded her ideas on servant reform still further in 1865.
In a series of articles for *Harper's Monthly*, she formulated her ultimate vision of the completely self-sufficient, servantless "Christian
home." Beecher here legitimized William Alcott's plea, which had been
largely ignored for thirty years.[31] By presenting a model household,
systematically designed and scientifically organized, she proved that
domestic servants were unnecessary in middle-class American homes,
save for an occasional "assistant" to help with washing and ironing.
In 1869 these articles were integrated in a new, expanded edition of
Treatise, The American Woman's Home. This work, the consummate
expression of her ideas, which had developed during the previous
three decades, established Beecher as the leader not only of servant
reform but of total reform of the American household and housekeeping. Many of the ideas she popularized would be abandoned or modi-
fied in later years, yet Beecher had permanently changed the emphasis and direction of servant reform.

30. *Ibid.*, 85, 87–89, 150, 155, 180–227.

31. Exceptions to this general rejection of Alcott are Mrs. A. J. [Margaret] Graves,
Woman in America (New York: Harper and Brothers, 1843), 75–78, and Louise Palmer
Smith, "Biddy Dethroned," *Putnam's Magazine*, XV (January, 1870), 114–17, and "Dinner Versus Ruffles and Tucks," *Putnam's Magazine*, XV (June, 1870), 708–711, though
neither Graves nor Smith views servants in as kindly a light as does Beecher.

Catherine Beecher stands as a transitional figure not only in time but between two images of the American home, two images of the American housekeeper, and two images of the servant reformer. Publication of *The American Woman's Home* divides the period 1800–1920 nearly in half. Beecher looked back on the practitioners of "housewifery" and forward to an era of "home economics." She formed a link between household advisors who were moonlighting novelists and people of fashion and those who were "professional" educators with college degrees in household science. Not all Americans were so confident as Beecher that the golden age was in sight, but most people did acknowledge the birth of a new reform philosophy.

CHAPTER NINE

UNSUCCESSFUL SALVATION
Reform of Domestic Service After 1870

Both the inspiration for reform and the means of achieving it changed in the fifty years following publication of the *American Woman's Home*. Seeing that neither moral indignation nor the voice of appeasement could persuade workers to love and obey unworthy employers, reformers sought new solutions to the servant problems. Their end remained the same, namely, creation of a large, reliable servant force, but the means for attaining it changed subtly. The operation of households and the behavior of employers, rather than the character of servants, became their principal concerns. Reform of domestic service, rather than servant reform, became the answer. In the end, this phase of the reform movement would also fail. Despite an army of experts and a long list of proposed remedies, the "world riddle" of domestic service would continue to befuddle the wisest reformers. Few people would argue with the woman who wrote in 1905, "The average woman, to-day, is at sea on the servant question, and knows it."[1] The servant problems would survive, and reformers, employers, and servants could all, in varying degrees, be held responsible. No one in 1870, however, was willing to give up yet.

The new reform philosophy reflected the influence of a new scientific age. Between 1870 and 1900, a rising middle class devoted to specialization and professionalization made the United States a "scientific-

1. Priscilla Leonard, "Boston's Housework Experiment," *Harper's Bazar*, XXXIX (March, 1905), 225.

industrial" society. Americans thought in terms of efficiency. How could a factory be organized and operated for optimum production? What measurements and analyses would reveal weaknesses in an industry's organization and business practices? These questions were asked in every occupation and profession. Domestic service reformers were inspired by the new spirit, influenced especially by techniques of organization and measurement used by social workers and social scientists, two new professional groups produced by the age. By the 1890s most reformers thought of the servant problems "in terms of political economy instead of original sin." *System, business principles,* and *standardization* became important words in the new reform vocabulary. These ideas had received scattered praise in earlier decades, but only after 1870 were they popularized by a national penchant for such things. Reformers realized that if households were to compete successfully with shops, factories, and offices for the best workers, housework had to be organized according to "the best principles of modern industry."[2]

God had very little to do with all this. If the Almighty were to aid in reformation, most people now conceded that he would do so armed with timetables, organization charts, and efficiency studies. Substitution of an impersonal business relationship for the old paternalistic master-servant bond was hailed as the new solution to reform. The Golden Rule, though still important, could not, in itself, solve the problems. Likewise, moral suasion, appeals to reason, even character building seemed touchingly naïve. Shorter hours were pronounced more effective than Bible reading in eliminating problems not just because shorter hours would pacify servants but because modern business methods demanded them. The social stigma was to be eliminated by "standardizing" work and working conditions, thus dissolving "psychological reasons" for the abhorrence of service. Reformers showed less concern with saving servants' souls. God, instead of being a moral force, had resumed his eighteenth-century role as master mechanic of the universe.

This new spirit—some called it heresy—required new leaders. Although reform societies, which now reappeared in professionalized form, tended to camouflage individual reformers, many nationally

2. Simeon Strunsky, "Help Wanted, Female," *Harper's Monthly*, CXXXVIII (February, 1919), 402; Robert H. Wiebe, *The Search for Order, 1877–1920* (New York: Hill and Wang, 1967), especially 111–32, 151–54; Daniel T. Rogers, *The Work Ethic in Industrial America, 1850–1920* (Chicago: University of Chicago Press, 1978), 200–201.

prominent leaders did emerge. None of these people seemed to dominate as had Catherine Beecher, but adequate heirs to her crown stepped forward to direct reform efforts. Among the lesser known claimants were Isabel Bevier, Henrietta Roelofs, Mrs. Elihu Root, Jr., and Mary Roberts Smith, names seldom heard outside the cadre of servant and household reformers. Nationally known social and household reformers, such as Jane Addams, Helen Campbell, Christine Frederick, Charlotte Gilman, Christine Herrick, and Ida Tarbell, were also active, but not being associated exclusively with servant reform, they seldom served as a focus for reform activities.

The new reformers were not the literary ladies of the antebellum years; they were pressed in the mold of Catherine Beecher. Part of the new college-trained middle class themselves, they were sometimes college professors of household science, and they were prepared to make reform a "legitimate" profession. The University of Illinois instituted a four-year course in domestic science in 1875. Other schools gradually added such courses to their curriculums, and by the early twentieth century, as a national home economics movement hit full stride, domestic science was being studied at state universities in Nebraska, Missouri, Minnesota, Ohio, and Wisconsin, and at Stanford University, the University of Chicago, and Columbia University. Smaller colleges and academies also recognized home economics as a legitimate field of study, as did technical schools like the Pratt, Drexel, Hampton, and Armour institutes. By 1906 the "most conservative colleges for women" were adopting courses in home economics to provide in-depth study of the "statistical, economic, and sociological basis of domestic service."[3] Graduates of these courses were in great demand as teachers in colleges, normal schools, and vocational schools and as advisors to reform associations, philanthropic institutions, hospitals, reformatories, and settlement houses.

Probably the best-known servant reformer after 1880 was Lucy Maynard Salmon. Graduated from the University of Michigan with a doctorate in history, Miss Salmon taught at a number of schools before arriving in 1887 at Vassar College, where she remained for several decades as a popular professor of history and economics. It was at Vas-

3. Lucy M. Salmon, *Domestic Service* (New York: Macmillan, 1897), 259–61, 269; Isabel Bevier and Susannah Usher, *The Home Economics Movement* (Boston: Whitcomb and Barrows, 1906), 15; Gail Laughlin, "Domestic Service," in *Report of the United States Industrial Commission on the Relations and Conditions of Capital and Labor* (19 vols.; Washington, D.C.: Government Printing Office, 1901), XIV, 764–66.

sar, while in the midst of her professional research, that Salmon began studying the historical aspects of domestic service. She began delivering public lectures on the subject, writing articles for both popular magazines and scholarly journals, and supporting, both financially and as an advisor, reform organizations and training schools. Although fellow historians generally looked askance at her inquiries, believing the topic beneath the dignity of their profession, Salmon succeeded in winning the respect of servant and labor reformers.[4]

In 1897 Salmon published the results of her decade of research in a landmark monograph entitled, *Domestic Service*. The book's purpose was to suggest new reforms in domestic service, based on a nationwide survey of employers and servants conducted by Salmon in 1889–1890. One reviewer admitted that the book's "immediate popularity" would probably be limited by its academic tone, but he predicted that it would be considered "authoritative by students of economic questions fifty years hence." "It is the first attempt, in this or any other country," he continued, "to bring the problems which perplex the household *per se* into the great rushing stream of social and industrial overflow, organize them as part of the greater movement and then treat the subject in the historical and scientific spirit."[5]

In *Domestic Service*, Salmon suggested that service had been governed for too long by the "principle of isolation": isolation of servants from one another, isolation of employers from one another, and isolation of service from the realm of national economic, social, and labor reform. The servant problems had to be attacked from this perspective, as concrete national and even international economic and social issues. Also, added Salmon, the problems were ancient and complex, far beyond the ability of isolated individuals to control or abolish. She stressed this point in the first third of the book, where she gave a brief history of domestic service in the United States. From there, she went on to discuss the problems of service and the types of reforms necessary to remedy them.

While cautioning that no single answer could provide instantaneous

4. Louise Fargo Brown, *Apostle of Democracy: The Life of Lucy Maynard Salmon* (New York: Harper and Brothers, 1943), 120–22. This is the only biography of Salmon, and although Brown does not deal extensively with the genesis of Salmon's reform ideas, she does give a complete bibliography of Salmon's writings. The Lucy Maynard Salmon Papers, Vassar College Library contain notices, reviews, and programs of many of Salmon's lectures.

5. L. E. Rector, "New Views of Domestic Service," *Gunton's Magazine*, XIV (March, 1898), 180.

change, she presented four avenues by which advances might commence. The social status of servants had to be improved first. So long as "drudgery, menial servitude, and social degradation" were the most distinctive characteristics of service, men and women would choose other vocations. Reformers and employers, said Salmon, must end the social isolation of servants with domestic clubs; eliminate the degradation of service by abandoning the terms *servant* and *master* and the use of Christian names when addressing servants; and limit the severity of the social stigma—the most difficult obstacle to reform—by showing respect for servants and domestic labor. Such changes, Salmon assured the public, would attract "intelligent and capable" workers away from shops and factories and into service.[6]

Specialization of household labor was another solution. Salmon pointed out that recent technological advances were simplifying housework and even, in some cases, permitting removal of tasks from the home. The latter phenomenon was most desirable, Salmon believed, because it reduced the need for servants. Moreover, she noted, this trend was already under way, as seen by the growing popularity of commercially canned fruits and vegetables, prepared meats, commercial bakeries, ready-made clothing, and commercial laundries. Salmon admitted that such services as yet represented only a "transitional stage" of reform. The high cost and poor quality of many of these services had to be remedied before they could conveniently relieve housekeepers and servants of their tasks. But this only required time.[7]

Profit sharing was a third answer. Give servants a financial interest in their work, Salmon reasoned, and they would be more attentive and efficient in their duties. This idea assumed that servants were paid for a certain number of hours of work per day. To inspire good work during those hours, servants could be offered a number of cash incentives. For example, housekeepers might make a monthly estimate of household operating costs. If servants destroyed or wasted property or materials beyond this estimate, the cost could be deducted from their wages. But if servants saved money by conserving materials and avoiding accidents, the savings could be divided equally between employer and worker. Servants might also hire part-time assistants to perform the most disagreeable portions of their work, paying them out of their own wages. Another possibility was for servants to be paid for overtime. Salmon admitted that profit sharing was the most theoreti-

6. Salmon, *Domestic Service*, 204–211.
7. *Ibid.*, 212–34.

cal aspect of her program, and that it would probably work better in hotels and boarding houses than in private households. Nevertheless, she believed the suggestion worthy of consideration.[8]

Salmon's final proposal, and the means to attaining the first three, was public education in household affairs. Going a bit beyond Beecher, Salmon insisted that employers, servants, and the general public were all woefully ignorant of household economics. There was a dismal tendency, she noted, for household education to be conducted on a personal level, with mothers bequeathing the same antiquated housekeeping knowledge to daughters generation after generation. Aside from popular household manuals, no comprehensive body of scientifically gathered information existed. Such information must be assembled, said Salmon. Nor should the definition of "useful" household data be restricted to cooking and cleaning. Progress in the household, she insisted, must take advantage of progress in other fields, including economics, physiology, psychology, and history. All data relating to household reform must then be interpreted and distributed to employers, servants, and the public. Salmons' solution was to establish "a great professional school" dedicated to the investigation "of all matters pertaining to the household." Such a school could share its findings with the nation.[9]

The end result of these reforms, Salmon hoped, would be the professionalization of service and a lower number of live-in servants. Once operated on a business basis, she predicted, with laborers who were proud of their vocation, service could not fail to improve. Weekly, daily, and hourly workers, living outside their employers' homes and working under modern contractual agreements concerning wages, hours, and duties, would be natural results. It was, of course, as difficult for Salmon as for her contemporaries to visualize a totally servantless society. But she was confident that the number of servants could be diminished and that those who remained could be converted into part-time employees. Such a system, she believed, meant "a simpler and better manner of life for both employer and employee."[10]

Apart from her specific suggestions, which set the pattern for post-1900 reform, Salmon's most significant contribution to reform was to enhance the respectability of a scientific approach to the servant problems. Salmon oversimplified the historical background of service, but

8. *Ibid.*, 235–50.
9. *Ibid.*, 251–60.
10. *Ibid.*, 273.

she provided the servant problems with long overdue recognition as serious and complex social issues. Even though, like most other reformers, her sympathies rested more with employers than with servants, she did center attention on reform of servants' working conditions as a necessary step towards lasting change. Salmon erected standards for other reformers and, most importantly, gave hope that a fresh approach to reform might reveal previously overlooked solutions.

But however advanced their solutions, Salmon and other reformers still faced the monumental task of implementing them. As post-1870 reform forces massed for the attack, their arsenal dwarfed that of earlier reformers. Many of the old weapons were retained. Servant manuals, household handbooks, and etiquette books, for instance, were published in profusion. But relatively new vehicles of reform also gained prominence.

Magazine articles and monographs were used more often than previously, and magazines, especially, became a principal means of reform after the Civil War. As early as the colonial period, women's magazines had included occasional stories and essays on the servant problems, interspaced among more regular features on courtship, marriage, religion, cooking, needlework, and fashions. This traditional format continued in antebellum women's magazines, as they and more general popular journals expressed only mild interest in the servant problems. Then, during the 1870s, an avalanche of "Biddy essays" began. Comments on the servant problems appeared regularly in a plethora of weekly and monthly magazines founded during the fifty years after Appomattox partly because of a new and very large middle-class reading audience. Publishers began catering to this growing middle-class market, as evidenced by a drop in prices from an aristocratic thirty-five cents per issue to a mere ten cents, and formerly esoteric and "fashionable" magazines gave more attention to the popular issues of the day. No issue was more popular than household reform, and no element of household reform caused more excited debate than the servant problems.[11]

The new mass audience welcomed all suggestions for reform. Re-

11. Frank Luther Mott, *A History of American Magazines* (5 vols.; Cambridge: Harvard University Press, 1930–68), I, 349, 483–84, 587, 589, II, 4, III, 6–7, IV, 2–4, 8, 10–11, 16; Louise Palmer Smith, "Dinner versus Ruffles and Tucks," *Putnam's Magazine*, XV (June, 1870), 708–709. For the efforts of one popular women's magazine to reach this market, see Salme Harju Steinberg, *Reformer in the Marketplace: Edward W. Bok and* The Ladies' Home Journal (Baton Rouge: Louisiana State University Press, 1979).

formers, housekeepers, intellectuals, journalists, even servants contributed to the reform bibliography. Their opinions were printed in
every type of magazine and journal. Women's magazines, including
such standards as *Good Housekeeping, Harper's Bazar*, and *Ladies'
Home Journal*, were prolific contributors. Equally productive were
news and topical magazines, such as *Delineator, Forum, Independent*,
and *Lippincott's Magazine*; reform journals, such as *Arena* and *Charities*; and professional journals, like *Journal of Home Economics* and
American Journal of Sociology. Even such unlikely sources as *Popular Science* and *Scientific American* published articles on household
problems, and at least one successful magazine, *American Kitchen
Magazine*, was entirely dedicated to household reform. As one commentator insisted, "One can hardly take up a social journal without
reading the wail of the housekeeper." Moreover, many housekeepers
took this advice to heart, recording helpful hints in diaries and pasting
useful articles in scrapbooks.[12] Hotel trade journals, such as *Hotel
Mail, Hotel Monthly*, and *Hotel Bulletin*, also carried articles and editorials commenting on the servant problems in their field.

Magazines competed for reform-conscious readers by presenting
novel points of view. One innovation was the personal experience article, written by reformers who had worked as servants. These reformers, usually women, entered service for a few weeks or months in
order to gather first-hand information on conditions in service—a very
scientific method. They then recounted their experiences, which varied widely, in sympathetic portrayals of servant life. Such reformers
became notorious, and employers eyed them with suspicion. Servants
after 1900 told their own tales in published articles and letters to editors. Their contributions fluctuated in believability. Some accounts
were obviously embellished by ghost writers, and a few were probably
created by imaginative novelists. But other stories had the ring of
truth and told episodes in the lives of real men and women working as
servants in both private households and hotels.[13]

12. Goldwin Smith, "The Passing of the Household," *Independent*, LIX (August 24,
1905), 423. See Mary Williams' collection of 1879 *Scribner's* articles in Box V, Folder 19,
Josiah Butler Williams Family Papers, Collection of Regional History, Cornell University; E. L. Camp to Anna G. Edwards, September 22, 1908, in Camp Family Papers
(Additional), Collection of Regional History, Cornell University; Mary Haskell Account
Books (MS in Minis Family Papers, Southern Historical Collection, Library of the University of North Carolina at Chapel Hill), XII.
13. See the Bibliographical Essay for a sampling of these articles. See also Elizabeth
Meserole Rhodes, "When the Bixby's Were Investigated," *Good Housekeeping*, XLVI
(March, 1908), 235–41.

Whatever its form, whoever its author, such literature merely whetted an insatiable public appetite. Americans devoured any and all information concerning management of households and servants. Even newspapers joined the act. One reformer observed as early as 1873, "There is scarcely a weekly newspaper that has not a household department, and even the daily papers gladly make room among politics and news for a good household article."[14] In 1900 the New York State Library issued a bibliography of the most important writings on household and servant reform written since 1850. The list, which excluded newspaper articles, many pamphlets, and magazine articles from all but the most current periodicals, was over one hundred pages long.

Another important means of reform, revived in the age of organization, was the reform society. Societies grew in number, size, and activity after 1870, infiltrating all parts of the country. Many organizations were interested in the problems of domestic economy generally, but few were without their committee on servant reform. Societies, leagues, clubs, alliances, and unions were especially active after 1885 and dominated the reform movement during the next two decades. Some of these organizations—the Ladies' Protective Union and Directory and the German Housewives Society of New York, for example—differed little from the earlier societies for the encouragement of faithful domestic servants. In terms of national organizations, the founding at Boston in 1871 of the Women's Educational Association, later reorganized as the Women's Educational and Industrial Union, was the first step. It was followed by the Columbian Association of Housekeepers in 1891 and the National Household Economics Association in 1892. During the next decade, reformers banded together in cities across the nation. The Inter-Municipal Committee on Household Research, perhaps the single most active organization, was founded in 1904 when the WEIU joined forces with the household reform associations of New York City and Philadelphia and several interested national groups, including the College Settlements Association and the Association of Collegiate Alumnae. In 1909 the American Home Economics Association was founded at Washington, D.C.[15]

14. Frank R. and Marian Stockton, *The Home: Where It Should Be and What to Put In It* (New York: G. P. Putnam and Sons, 1873), 119. See also New York *Times*, April 6, 1879, p. 6.
15. The Women's Educational and Industrial Union Records, Schlesinger Library, Radcliffe College and the Salmon Papers supply information on many of these organizations. See also Robert B. Jennings, "A History of the Educational Activities of the Women's Educational and Industrial Union from 1877–1927" (Ph.D. dissertation, Boston College, 1978); Laura Starr Wilkison, "Household Economics," in Mary Kavanaugh

By the early twentieth century the activities of a large organization, such as the Inter-Municipal Committee, might include the collection of information pertaining to domestic servants and household economics through interviews and surveys, the establishment of employment bureaus, the certification of reliable commercial intelligence offices, and the distribution of reliable information via lectures, seminars, special reports, and monthly or quarterly bulletins. Bulletins kept members posted on the latest reform developments with essays, bibliographies, and summaries of the activities of societies around the country. Topics of inquiry in these publications included immigration, training schools, lodging houses for unemployed servants, working and living conditions of servants, personal experiences of servants and employers, legal rights of servants, experiments with day workers, and scientific evaluation of all "experiments and solutions—past and present." Organizations hoped, by distributing reliable information, to correct misconceptions about the servant problems that had been perpetuated by popular journals. Their objects were to study "existing phases of housework, to aid in securing fair conditions for employer and employee, and to place their relations on a sound business basis." [16]

Less scientific but no less important contributors to the domestic debate were the nation's women's clubs. These organizations had been centers of female "self-culture" and philanthropic activity since before the Civil War, but they entered their most active years only after 1870. With the founding of the General Federation of Women's Clubs in 1889, the popularity of such clubs spread to places as geographically and socially diverse as Chicago, Boston, and New Orleans. From its original fifty-club membership, the GFWC grew to one hundred clubs by 1892, and by 1902 there were over three thousand clubs boasting a quarter million members. When the independent clubs are added to this total, the number of women participating in such organizations probably exceeds half a million. [17]

Oldham Eagle (ed.), *The Congress of Women* (Chicago: American Publishing House, 1894), 233–36; New York *Times*, September 23, 1874, p. 8, September 28, 1874, p. 4, February 21, 1875, p. 5; "Concerning Women," *Harper's Bazar*, XXXIV (February 23, 1901), 525.

16. *Bulletin of Inter-Municipal Committee on Household Research*, II (March, 1906), 3; Lucy M. Salmon, *Progress in the Household* (Boston: Houghton Mifflin, 1906), 21.

17. Olive Thorne Miller, *The Woman's Club: A Practical Guide and Handbook* (n.p., 1891), 12–13; Jane C. Croly, *The History of the Woman's Club Movement in America* (New York: Henry G. Allen and Co., 1898), 8–9; Estelle M. H. Merrill, "Household Economics in Women's Clubs," *New England Kitchen Magazine*, III (June, 1895), 119–21.

Contemporaries divided in their judgment of the women's clubs' contribution to reform. Some observers praised the clubs for adding dignity to reform debate and a new dimension to reform efforts. They applauded the clubs for cooperating with more professional agencies in conducting surveys and experiments and for filtering down reliable, scientific data to housekeepers. Other observers considered them meddlers—incompetent meddlers at that. Because the clubs misunderstood economic forces, critics contended, they introduced disastrous reforms, repeated reforms that had long since proved worthless, perpetuated old wives' tales, and dismissed genuinely innovative plans as radical. The fact that many "professional" reformers were guilty of the same crimes was overlooked.

To be sure, the contributions of these clubs varied. Most women's club members, rather than discussing domestic service, continued to talk about their servants, becoming bogged down in such worn issues as the extravagance of servants' dress, the relative merits of Negro versus Irish servants, the effect of Catholic servants on Protestant homes, and the lack of loyalty and obedience among servants. But the best clubs did more. Prolonged study of the servant problems brought enlightenment for many club women. They began to sympathize with servants, to appreciate their problems, and to realize that employers had no right to control servants' private lives. They debated meaningful reform issues: the benefits of servant clubs, the place of servant reform in general social reform, the future of Negroes in the United States, the eight-hour day in housework, servant training schools, abolition of live-in service, cooperative housekeeping, "psychological" and "philosophical" aspects of the social stigma, and ways of putting service on a "more efficient basis." The best clubs kept abreast of national reform activities and invited national leaders to address their memberships. Some clubs even conducted surveys of their neighborhoods, recording the opinions of servants on local working and living conditions.[18]

Many reformers were highly enthusiastic about the potential benefits of formal training for servants. They were certain that this single reform would remove the stigma from service, put housekeeping on a

18. Mothers' Club of Cambridge, Massachusetts, "Minutes" [December], 1881, May 7, 1883, May 5, 1897, May 16, 1899, and January 12, 1912, and "Program Committee Minutes," 1889–91, (both MSS in Mothers' Club of Cambridge Papers, Schlesinger Library, Radcliffe College); "Program of Connecticut Consumers' League Conference on the 'Domestic Service Problem,' " February 16, 1916; and Mrs. Alfrieda M. Mosher to Mrs. Martin Wells, February 8, 1916, both in Consumers' League of Connecticut Papers, Schlesinger Library, Radcliffe College.

business basis, and make service not only a respectable profession but an art. The only training schools in operation before the Civil War had been cooking schools for housekeepers. These, however, did not offer the comprehensive courses in housekeeping that were needed. After 1870 practical training schools for servants, schools where workers would be taught housekeeping by women trained in domestic science at the nation's best colleges, became the goal. Such schools, it was hoped, would produce a "new class" of servants by weeding out incompetents and attracting native whites to service. This, in turn, would raise the moral and social tone of service. Servants would be judged and paid according to their level of skill, and impartial standards could be established for distinguishing good from mediocre workers. A few reformers went so far as to predict that uniform training and standards of efficiency would even reduce racial prejudices, since employers would eventually prefer well-trained black servants (not everyone could have native whites) to ill-trained whites.[19]

Slowly, the call of these "noble pioneers" for servant schools was heard. The first schools, patterned on early cooking schools and still devoting considerable attention to the culinary arts, appeared shortly after the Civil War. Many schools were privately operated commercial enterprises, but professional reform societies, women's clubs, church groups, and the YWCA also sponsored courses. Instruction soon went beyond cooking to include all phases of housework and new teaching techniques were also introduced. In some cases, "trainers" visited homes to instruct servants and housekeepers in the theory and practice of housekeeping. Also, as the popularity of housekeeping courses increased, vocational schools entered the field, training servants as well as domestic scientists. In 1915 a home economics specialist was appointed to the United States Bureau of Education, and in 1917 the Smith-Hughes Act bestowed official recognition on housekeeping as a valid form of vocational training.[20]

19. Harriet Prescott Spofford, *The Servant Girl Question* (Boston: Houghton Mifflin, 1881), 140–48; Mrs. C. H. Stone, *The Problem of Domestic Service* (St. Louis: Nelson Printing, 1892), 7, 10, 18–20; G. Vrooman, "Manual Training for Women and the Problem of Domestic Service," *Arena*, XIV (October, 1895), 313–14; M. V. Shailer, "The Practical Solution of the Domestic Service Problem," *American Kitchen Magazine*, VIII (February, 1898), 176–77; Carroll D. Wright, "Why We Have Trouble with Our Servants," *Ladies' Home Journal*, XXI (March, 1904), 22.

20. F. E. Fryatt, "The New York Cooking School," *Harper's Monthly*, LX (December, 1879), 22–29; New York *Times*, December 2, 1881, p. 4; Helen L. Sumner, *History of Women in Industry in the United States*, in *Report on Conditions of Woman and Child Wage-Earners in the United States*, *Senate Documents*, 61st Cong., 2nd Sess.,

One of the best housekeeping courses for servants was sponsored by the WEIU. Its School of Housekeeping, which opened in 1897, accepted students between the ages of sixteen and thirty of average intelligence and good moral character, who intended to make service their "trade." Girls were lodged, boarded, and instructed free of charge, but they were required to live at the school and, as part of their practical training, perform its housekeeping chores. They received instruction in all aspects of housekeeping, including cooking, laundering, and hygiene. Certificates were issued upon completion of a basic twelve-week course, although additional instruction was available to those who hoped to work in specialized areas. Even after being certified, however, students were not considered fully trained until they had served a three-month probationary period working in a private household. This requirement reflected the WEIU's belief that formal training must be tested by practical experience. Only then were students allowed to take their final examination and receive their diplomas. In 1902 the school was incorporated into the home economics department of Simmons College.[21]

So stood the reform movement in 1920. The drive for reform had been intense, with a dedication so fervent that reform efforts acquired an aspect of pilgrimage, of a search for salvation. The search, by 1920, had taken many forms, but all had failed. The problems remained unsolved. Individual reformers proposed various remedies, and organizations mobilized an army of resources, but to no avail. Something had gone wrong. Either employers and servants had not listened, or reformers had given them the wrong answers. The reasons for this failure must be explained.

Disputes concerning methods, goals, and general principles of reform were the most devastating obstacles. Solutions for reform remained as varied and complex as the problems to be corrected. Some suggestions were simply old-fashioned ideas that had been proposed and rejected decades earlier. Even progressive reformers often clashed over priorities. In judging their progress, reformers could not agree on where they had been, where they were going, how they would get

No. 645, IX, 30–31; Frances A. Kellor, "Southern Colored Girls in the North," *Bulletin of Inter-Municipal Committee on Household Research*, I (May, 1905), 6–8; Orra Langhorne, "Domestic Service in the South," *Journal of Social Science*, XXXIX (1901), 173–75.

21. Mary Morton Kehew, "The Domestic Reform League," *American Kitchen Magazine*, VIII (November, 1897), 52; Women's Educational and Industrial Union, *The School of Housekeeping* (Boston: n.p., 1902).

there, or what they would do once they arrived. Their confusion only compounded the problems of those employers who depended upon reformers to clarify the issues and to suggest viable answers to their dilemma.

A related problem was the increasingly technical nature of reform solutions. By 1900 some reformers had become too scientific for the average employer. Lucy Salmon, for example, admitted that her book, *Domestic Service*, was disappointing to many people who had "hoped to find in it a sovereign remedy for all domestic ills. Instead of that they found only rather repellent footnotes, statistical tables, appendices, and bibliographies." Other reformers, even though approving Salmon's work, also noted this flaw. Ida M. Tarbell, then editor of *American Magazine*, told Salmon in 1911 that she would like to publish a paper recently delivered by the Vassar professor. Tarbell was afraid, however, that the paper would require rewriting since its original form was "too scientific" for public consumption.[22]

Some housekeepers simply resisted change, preferring to cling to their ancient prejudices. They were traditionalists, proud of being "old-time housekeepers," no matter how inefficient their methods. They feared that, if housework were "systematized into a trade," it would "revolutionize home life," leaving them "worse off than before."[23] These people refused to relinquish traditional views regarding the feeblemindedness, immorality, and incompetence of servants. They scorned such innovations as servant training schools, cooperative housekeeping, and shorter work days as social quackery.

Employers would have had even less faith in modern reform had they known the problems many reformers experienced with their own servants. So-called authorities sometimes found their theories woefully inadequate when applied to their household problems. For example, as a housekeeper Lucy Salmon was plagued by an endless history of servant problems. She treated her domestics with kindness and patience in accordance with all of her carefully formulated principles. Yet something always went awry. Whether because her methods were unsatisfactory or because her servants were unreceptive, nothing could halt the procession of workers parading through her kitchen.[24]

22. Salmon, *Progress in the Household*, v–viii; Ida M. Tarbell to Lucy M. Salmon, June 8, 1911, in Salmon Papers.
23. Chicago *Tribune*, August 3, 1901, p. 16. See also Salmon, *Domestic Service*, 264–65.
24. Brown, *Apostle of Democracy*, 197–202.

Many employers, after years of false hope, finally abandoned reformers. They had treated servants generously and been taken advantage of. They had hired hourly workers and found them lacking. They had tried or observed scientific methods of housekeeping and were disillusioned. Small wonder employers began dismissing reformers as being long on theory and short on logic. "Cannot we remember," asked one exasperated dissenter, "that we may sometimes be as nearly right as those who talk more loudly and strongly than we upon domestic economy, laying down rules we never thought of suggesting; splitting into ninths a hair our short-sighted eyes cannot make out when whole, and annihilating our timid objections with a lordly 'I always do so,' which is equal to a decree of infallibility?" "Cannot we make up our minds," she implored further, "to be a law unto ourselves in all matters pertaining to our households?"[25]

And a law unto themselves they were. Whatever the reason, be it reformer-bred confusion, hostility, despair, or their own cantankerousness, employers disagreed as much as did reformers on the issues of reform. Different temperaments, expectations, and experiences resulted in different philosophies, grievances, and solutions. Popular positions could be determined on many issues, but not on all, and seldom was the majority opinion overwhelming. In 1906, for instance, 142 (54.6 percent) of the Massachusetts employers polled in one survey were unwilling to pay higher wages for better service, but 88 were willing to do so, and another 30 were undecided. While 114 (43.9 percent) of these· same employers were unwilling to give their servants more free time or shorter hours, 146 were either so willing or undecided. Questions requiring more than a simple "yes" or "no" answer revealed an even wider variety of opinion.[26]

Servants were themselves an obstacle to reform. Servants victimized by unpleasant employers and unscrupulous intelligence offices generally distrusted all reforms. They ridiculed schemes reformers and employers thought perfectly marvelous. Few servants read the reform material written for their edification, and even fewer participated in reform surveys. Some servants were afraid to cooperate with reformers; others were simply belligerent. Only 719 servants returned

25. Marion Harland [Mary Virginia Terhune], *Common Sense in the Household: A Manual of Practical Housewifery* (New York: Charles Scribner's Sons, 1890), 366.
26. Massachusetts Bureau of Statistics of Labor, *Trained and Supplemental Employees for Domestic Service*, Part II of *Annual Report for 1906* (Boston: n.p., 1906), 93–99, 104–107, 113–18. See also Mary E. Bagg to Lucy M. Salmon, September 4, 1889, in Salmon Papers.

questionnaires in Lucy Salmon's survey, leading her to admit that the number of workers interested in such investigations was "infinitesimal" in comparison to their total numbers.[27]

Training schools failed largely because servants refused to attend them. Servants saw no advantage in attending schools when they seldom received higher wages or increased benefits for doing so. Even if anxious to attend classes part time, servants discovered that the hours invested only further diminished their already limited free time. Moreover, they discovered that they were too tired by the end of a day's work to benefit from evening classes. Servants also claimed that the peculiarities of individual employers who wanted housework done their way made formal training useless. Finally, they criticized the instruction offered at training schools. Teachers, servants insisted, never having worked in service, had no conception of the real problems of servants. Whatever their complaints, servants obviously avoided training. One survey showed that only 15 of 156 servants questioned had ever received formal training of any kind.[28]

Servants even agreed with employers on one point: their pessimism about the possibilities of reform. Most proposed reforms were too impractical for servants' tastes, especially those reforms that did little to remove the social stigma. Then too, servants had seen too many once promising reforms wither from neglect. Servants scorned reformers who, entering service for a time as an experiment, "played at being servants." And rightly so. Reformers soon forgot the aches and pains of service, too often remembering their hardships as a "game." As one servant observed, "They don't find out nothin' 'bout livin' out by hiring out."[29]

27. Mary, "Wanted, a Domestic: III," *Old and New*, V (June, 1872), 759–61; "School-Teachers as Vacation 'Home Assistants,'" *Literary Digest*, LXII (August 23, 1919), 60–61; Salmon, *Domestic Service*, ix, and *Progress in the Household*, 24; "Domestic Service Investigation" (MS in Consumers' League of Massachusetts Papers, Schlesinger Library, Radcliffe College), June, 1917, pp. 4–7.
28. Columbian Association of Housekeepers, *Report* (Chicago: n.p. [1893]), 7; Household Aid Company, *Report of a Two Years' Experiment in Social Economics: Boston, 1903–1905* (Boston: n.p., n.d.), 7, 17–18; Henrietta Roelofs, *The Road to Trained Service in the Household*, YWCA Commission on Household Employment Bulletin No. 2 (New York: n.p. [1918]), 10; Elizabeth McCracken, "The Problem of Domestic Service II—from the Standpoint of the Employee," *Outlook*, LXXXVIII (February 29, 1908), 496; I. M. Rubinow and Daniel Durant, "The Depth and Breadth of the Servant Problem," *McClure's Magazine*, XXXIV (March, 1910), 581–82; Gail Laughlin, "Domestic Service," 761.
29. Anne Forsyth, "Seven Times a Servant," *Delineator*, LXXVII (March, 1911), 253; Lillian Pettengill, *Toilers of the Home: The Record of a College Woman's Experi-

Government efforts at reform, being halfhearted and haphazard, did little to reduce the pessimism of either servants or employers. Government bureaus of labor, the branch of state and federal government responsible for investigating and reforming working conditions, were tardy in recognizing domestic service as a legitimate field of labor. The federal government, while studying the most minute aspects of factory and shop employment, snubbed household employment. Influenced by traditional ideas of the home as a religious-cultural training ground, federal economists and labor researchers could not imagine the household or its work as contributing to the national economy. The government excluded servants from its official definition of *working women*: "that class of women who earn their living in occupations calling for manual labor." Only two reports on the condition of domestic servants were published by the federal government before 1920—one in 1901, the other in 1910. Neither one inspired hope of reform.[30]

State governments were somewhat more active. The Massachusetts Bureau of Labor Statistics devoted a portion of its 1872 report to domestic service, and it remained the most active state labor bureau investigating conditions in service. It published useful information on service in several of its annual reports, aided individual reformers, and worked in conjunction with Boston's WEIU to gather and publish information on household labor. Another early contributor to reform was the Minnesota Labor Bureau. In 1888 it published a fairly comprehensive investigation of conditions of service in that state, including data on the age, nativity, education, and conjugal status of servants, as well as reports on wages, hours, and length of time in service. California, Colorado, Indiana, Kansas, Maine, Michigan, and New York soon followed these two examples, although their reports were not always so detailed.[31]

Insofar as reform legislation was concerned, the burden fell on the states. The federal government explained its inactivity by claiming that wide variations in the conditions of service made national regula-

---

ence as a *Domestic Servant* (New York: Doubleday, Page, and Co., 1903), 357; McCracken, "The Problem of Domestic Service II," 493–94.

30. U.S. Bureau of Labor, *Fourth Annual Report of the Commissioner: Working Women in Large Cities* (Washington, D.C.: Government Printing Office, 1888), 9; Flora McDonald Thompson, "The Servant Question," *Cosmopolitan*, XXIX (March, 1900), 521–22; Izola Forrester, "The 'Girl' Problem," *Good Housekeeping*, LV (September, 1912), 376. Gail Laughlin's "Domestic Service" and Sumner's *History of Women in Industry* are the two reports.

31. See Bibliographical Essay for examples of these reports.

tion of such things as wages and hours impossible. But conditions varied widely within states, too, and this, coupled with the late recognition of service as an industrial employment, meant that little was done to reform the occupation. By 1921 thirty-one states had limited the hours of working women to between eight and ten and a half hours daily. Many of these laws included hotel servants in their provisions, but none of them applied to household servants. Indeed, some states, notably Mississippi, New Hampshire, Oklahoma, Pennsylvania, South Dakota, and Tennessee, specifically excluded household workers from their laws. Only thirteen states required that female servants be given adequate time for meals and daily and weekly leisure time, and only two of these states, Oregon and Washington, included both hotel and private servants in their statutes. Only seven states passed minimum-wage laws.[32] Servants' legal protection remained, therefore, limited to custom and to vague laws that were designed to protect American workers generally but were not easily applied to the conditions of domestic service.

And so, the servant problems continued. Nothing could relieve the frustration or the complaints of employers and servants. If one reason for this failure had to be selected above all others, it would be the narrow-mindedness of both groups. Employers and servants were too uncompromising to admit the merits of the other side's protests. But reform was also stalled by an inherent contradiction in the servant problems themselves. Both universal and individual circumstances had molded the servant problems. Reformers who claimed that national and international social and economic changes influenced the nature of domestic service were correct, but so, too, were people who maintained that the servant problems of each household were unique. Since both of these divergent forces—the universal and the individual—had to be considered in order to draft lasting reforms, reformers

32. U.S. Department of Labor, *State Laws Affecting Working Women*, Bulletin of the Women's Bureau No. 16 (Washington, D.C.: Government Printing Office, 1921). See also Oliver E. Lyman, "The Legal Status of Servant-Girls," *Popular Science Monthly*, XXII (April, 1883), 807–813; L. H. Baright, "Woman and Law," *Harper's Bazar*, XXXV (September, 1901), 492–93; Rosalie Loew Whitney, "The Legal Aid Society and Its Work for Households," *Bulletin of Inter-Municipal Committee on Household Research*, I (April, 1905), 11; Margaret M. Burnet, "The Legal Relation of Mistress and Maid, with Some Comment Thereon," *Bulletin of Inter-Municipal Committee on Household Research*, I (December, 1904), 7; Sophronisba Breckinridge, "Housewife and Maid at Law," *Bulletin of Inter-Municipal Committee on Household Research*, I (April, 1905), 7–9.

were, in the end, powerless to solve the problems. They could only point out the many factors which employers and servants ought to consider in reaching their own solutions. Alas, individual judgements required cool consideration and delicate application, two skills that most employers and servants lacked.

CHAPTER TEN

WINDS OF CHANGE
Domestic Service in 1920

Marcel Proust in *Remembrance of Things Past* described perfectly, though unknowingly, the changes wrought by the problems of Americans and their servants by 1920:

> We believe that according to our desire we are able to change the things around us, we believe this because otherwise we can see no favorable solution. We forget the solution that generally comes to pass and is also favorable: we do not succeed in changing things according to our desire, but gradually our desire changes. . . . We have not managed to surmount the obstacle, as we were absolutely determined to do, but life has taken us around it, led us past it, and then if we turn around to gaze at the remote past, we can barely catch sight of it, so imperceptible has it become.[1]

So changed American domestic service—and Americans—in the 120 years following the eighteenth century. During that time, while employers and servants argued and complained and reformers puzzled over what to do, a new system of domestic service slowly, silently, yet resolutely established itself. This new order would not have gone unrecognized in 1800. Indeed, some of its features remained identical to the old order. But if one looked back from the post–World War I era, as had Proust, differences were unmistakable. The problems had not

1. Marcel Proust, *The Sweet Cheat Gone*, trans. C. K. Scott Moncrieff (New York: Random House, 1930), 48–49.

been solved entirely, but changes in the composition of the servant class, the appearance and organization of American households, and methods of housekeeping had certainly altered them. These changes might have occurred anyway, without benefit of the servant problems, but it is certain that the existence of unhappy servants and employers hastened their advent.

The most notable change took place in the composition and size of the servant class. As we have seen, by 1920 the average servant, in contrast to a century earlier, was older, more likely to be supporting or helping to support dependents, and more likely to be Negro. A more significant change, however, was the dwindling size of the servant population. The *percentage* of servants among gainfully employed American workers had been falling steadily since 1890, a trend that had commenced twenty years earlier among female servants alone. U.S. census reports show the following proportional decline of servants among gainfully employed Americans:

1870 . . . . 8.4%   1890 . . . . 7.5%   1910 . . . . 6.0%
1880 . . . . 7.3%   1900 . . . . 6.6%   1920 . . . . 4.5%

The percentage of servants revived briefly in the 1920s to 5.6 percent, but servants, particularly household servants, never again made up as large a share of the work force as they had before 1920. Even more ominously, in 1920 the *number* of servants also dropped for the first time. The servant population declined by over 400,000 between 1910 and 1920 to the lowest figure since 1900. When figures for household servants are separated from those for hotel servants, the decline is even more significant. The supply of household workers was at its lowest level since the 1880s. By 1920 only one servant was available to every sixteen families, a ratio that had exactly doubled since 1870.[2] The number of servants did increase in the 1920s, not to take a final, irreversible plunge until the Great Depression, but by that time the entire system of American service had been transformed.

A significant change among surviving servants was the decreasing number of live-in workers. Daily workers were hardly a twentieth-century invention. Laundresses and charwomen had hired out by the day since the eighteenth century. But with talk of cooperative living, reduction of workers' hours, reorganization of household labor, con-

2. U.S. Bureau of the Census, *Fourteenth Census of the United States: Population* (Washington, D.C.: Government Printing Office, 1921–23), I, 1268–270, and *Population: Occupational Statistics*, IV, 1049–1257.

tractual relationships, and competition with factories and shops for workers, they became an accepted and increasingly popular answer to the servant shortage. Harking back to William Alcott's solution for the servant problems—abolishing servants—modern household reformers like Lucy Salmon, Francis Kellor, and Christine Frederick saw live-out workers as a realistic compromise. Charlotte Perkins Gilman, a grandniece of Catherine Beecher, was the most uncompromising reformer in this respect since William Alcott. Gilman believed that housework, the home, and the family, as organized in 1900, were outmoded social institutions that inhibited social progress. She wanted domestic service and servants to be abolished.[3]

Indeed, day workers, contracted for a limited number of hours, performing specified duties, and returning to their homes each evening, seemed the ideal solution for all concerned. They would spare employers the delicate assignment of keeping strangers in their homes as well as relieve them of a heavy moral responsibility. Employers would have more free time because less supervision would be required of them. Day workers would also cost less. Money wages would admittedly rise in order to pay more efficient workers and to compensate for lost room and board, but employers would still save since they would probably not be paying the full value of lost room and board and would enjoy appreciable monetary savings on light, heat, water, breakage, and general "wear and tear." Servants, too, would profit from the new arrangement. With feudal relationships annihilated, the social stigma and its accompanying sense of inferiority would be significantly reduced. Shorter hours and living out also meant freedom from employer restraints and an end to physical and social isolation. Not surprisingly then, between 1900 and 1920 the number of live-in female servants fell 16 percent. Although this large drop is partly due to the inclusion in the statistical data of waitresses who staffed the burgeoning number of American restaurants, the change is mostly attributable to the growing number of hourly workers in American households.[4]

3. The author of over a dozen books on the subjects of women and the American home, Charlotte Perkins Gilman's two best-known works are *Women and Economics: A Study of the Economic Relation Between Men and Women as a Factor in Social Evolution* (Boston: Small Maynard and Co., 1898) and *The Home: Its Work and Influence* (New York: McClure, Phillips, and Co., 1903). Gilman's most recent biographer is Mary A. Hill, *Charlotte Perkins Gilman: The Making of a Radical Feminist, 1860–1896* (Philadelphia: Temple University Press, 1980).

4. See, for example, Christine Frederick, "Suppose Our Servants Didn't Live with Us," *Ladies' Home Journal*, XXXI (October, 1914), 102, and "Why Should Our Servants Live with Us?" *Ladies' Home Journal*, XXXII (October, 1915), 47, 98; Joseph A. Hill, *Women in Gainful Occupations, 1870–1920*, Monograph No. 9 of the U.S. Census Bu-

Architectural trends and technological innovations, to be discussed below, permitted these changes, but a certain amount of urgency was involved, too. The number of servants declined not just because fewer Americans wanted or needed servants but because fewer workers were willing to labor as domestics. This interesting development resulted from a revolution in American manners, morals, and customs that took place in the second decade of the twentieth century. World War I, especially, challenged the validity of many cherished beliefs. By 1920 older moral standards and laws of etiquette seemed hopelessly puritanical, almost decrepit in their fossilized formality. A new, more flexible system of morals and manners was contrived. *Freedom, individualism,* and *self-expression* took on fresh meaning. Everything was new, vibrant, exciting, unpredictable. A people capable of giving women the vote and outlawing liquor was likely to do anything.

The prospects of working-class women received one of the biggest jolts. American women in general became freer. Uninhibited drinking, smoking, social—and perhaps sexual—intercourse produced the flapper. Women dressed in accordance with the spirit of the new age. In order to accentuate their freedom and youth, they shortened their dresses, bobbed their hair, slimmed their bodies, and flattened their breasts. Everything was shrinking but female boldness, which exploded beyond all expectations. Working-class women, servants perhaps most especially, were captivated by these changes. Freedom being the "fashion," servants quickly adopted it. Wartime labor demands had drawn many girls from service, into factories and offices. Less than a dozen occupations had accounted for female labor opportunities before 1870, and most women worked in half of those job categories. By 1920, though, women were working in dozens of occupations. Workers who might have been forced into service by economic necessity ten or twenty years earlier had new alternatives; they no longer needed to sacrifice their freedom to feudal notions of master-servant relationships. Even women who filled "service" positions as office cleaners and workers in commercial laundries escaped the restrictions of domestic service.[5]

reau (Washington, D.C.: Government Printing Office, 1929), 138–40. U.S. Department of Labor, *The Occupational Progress of Women,* Bulletin of the Women's Bureau No. 27 (Washington, D.C.: Government Printing Office, 1922), 8–10, 28–29 gives several possible reasons for the trend towards daily workers but concludes that the ultimate reason is "a matter of sheer conjecture."

5. James R. McGovern, "The American Woman's Pre–World War I Freedom in Manners and Morals," *Journal of American History,* LV (1968–69), 320–21; Joseph A. Hill, *Women in Gainful Occupations,* 33, 36–39; Clara H. Zillessen, "When Maids Come

Reformers warned employers to brace themselves for the consequences of this change, to be prepared to eliminate the "frills of service." No more being waited on at meals, no more servants on call to
answer telephones and doorbells. Cooking, cleaning, and laundering,
they predicted, were all that could be expected of servants after 1920,
and even at that, families would be expected to help with small housekeeping tasks. Less formal social gatherings also became necessary.
The number of gala public balls and elaborate dinner parties declined.
The cocktail party was a postwar innovation in both middle- and
upper-class homes, symbolizing the end of America's "prolonged afflic-
tion of pretense." The future looked bleak.[6]

The approaching threat to middle-class employers was prefigured in
1918 when the United States Congress took up consideration of a wartime tax on domestic servants. The tax was meant to free unnecessary
servants for the war effort, for work in munitions factories and service
in the armed forces. Americans employing only one servant would be
exempt from the tax since one servant was an "unalienable right of
every American family," but employers of two or more servants would
pay Uncle Sam a certain percentage, ranging from 10 to 100 percent,
of each servant's wages. Such insidious legislation naturally sparked
impassioned debate, and even though nothing came of the scheme, its
mere proposal indicated that the new order was taking command.[7]

Still other alterations in American life confirmed the transformation
of domestic service. American restaurants mushroomed, for example,
and the physical appearance of American households changed greatly.
For some time, the constant trial of bad domestics had so discouraged

Back Again," *House Beautiful*, XLV (April, 1919), 243; Rosalind Richards, "What Is the
Matter with Domestic Service?" *House Beautiful*, XLVI (October, 1919), 248; "The
Passing of the Household Servant," *Literary Digest*, LXXIV (July 8, 1922), 19–20; U.S.
Department of Labor, *The Occupational Progress of Women*, 8–10, 28–29; Mary V.
Dempsey, *The Occupational Progress of Women, 1910–1930*, Bulletin of the Women's
Bureau No. 104 (Washington, D.C.: Government Printing Office, 1933), 27–30, 72–73.
Though not concerned directly with domestic workers, see Maurine W. Greenwald,
*Women, War, and Work: The Impact of World War I on Women Workers in the United
States* (Westport, Conn.: Greenwood, 1980).
    6. "Concerning Mothers' Hinderers," *Outlook*, CXXI (January 15, 1919), 93; Arthur
M. Schlesinger, *Learning How to Behave: A Historical Study of American Etiquette
Books* (New York: Macmillan, 1946), 56–58; Mrs. John King Van Rensselaer, *The Social
Ladder* (New York: Henry Holt and Co., 1924), 210–12.
    7. "Taxes, Servants—and Bliss," *Nation*, LXI (July 20, 1918), 61; Thorstein Veblen,
Essays in Our Changing Order, ed. Leon Ardzrooni (New York: Viking Press, 1943),
267–78; Mary Sargent Potter, "The Proposed Tax on Servants," *North American Re-
view*, CCVIII (November, 1918), 745–48.

some urban families that they fled housekeeping to reside in boarding-houses and "family hotels." This style of living was curious because it so contradicted American reverence for home life. The private household remained an American ideal. Americans would give up home life only under the gravest circumstances, and all who could afford and were capable of managing their own houses maintained them. Yet, beginning even before the Civil War, the number of boarders had been steadily increasing. By 1920 hundreds of thousands of Americans resided in hotels and boardinghouses, havens that became "substitutes for homes."[8]

Of course, the servant malady was not the only reason for boarding out. The heavy expense of housekeeping was another frequently cited cause. The high price of urban land, taxes, and rents made operating one's own household a costly venture. Cost of furnishings, carpeting, utilities, and insurance, not to mention the responsibilities involved, made housekeeping an undertaking not lightly assumed. Newlywed housekeepers, especially, were inexperienced in the art of housewifery and shrank from its mysteries. Yet no reason for boarding was so pervasive or persuasive as the servant problems. Other objections to housekeeping acquired an added dimension when viewed as part of them. Summarizing all complaints, feminist and reformer Charlotte Gilman wrote in 1898, "These [family hotels] are inhabited by people who could afford to 'keep house.' But they do not want to keep house. They are tired of keeping house. It is difficult to keep house, the servant problem is so trying."[9]

Hotels contributed yet another innovation to American home life as they evolved into apartment houses. Apartment living was already common in several European cities by the mid–nineteenth century, the English and French having enjoyed these cozy quarters for years. But American experiments with "French flats" had just begun by that time, constructed first at New York City. Prototype apartments appeared at New Orleans in the 1850s and at Boston ten years later. By the 1870s Boston was imitating New York's more advanced designs. As Chicago rebuilt itself after the Great Fire of 1877, buildings of "flats"

8. See J. Lebovitz, "The Home and the Machine," *Journal of Home Economics*, III (1911), 144–45; I. M. Rubinow, "Household Service as a Labor Problem," *Journal of Home Economics*, III (1911), 517–18. Thomas Butler Gunn, *The Physiology of New York Boarding-Houses* (New York: Mason Brothers, 1857), 12; Henry James, *The American Scene* (New York: Horizon Press, 1967), 101–102.
9. Gilman, *Women and Economics*, 265–66.

met the desires of citizens who wished "to be relieved of house owning and its cares."[10]

America's new apartment buildings were welcomed as a needed "reform of domestic architecture." Architects, it was said, were finally responding to the needs of American housekeepers for compact dwellings. The new domiciles still required care, and some apartment dwellers continued to employ servants for that reason; but the amount of work having been significantly reduced, so, too, were the expense and complications of housekeeping and the number of servants required. Those servants who remained also benefitted from apartment living. Their living conditions were usually no worse in apartments than in houses, and their work was obviously reduced. Most importantly, apartment living increased the feasibility and desirability of live-out servants.[11]

The servant problems affected the architecture of houses even more dramatically. By the early twentieth century, American houses were much smaller and more compact than the large, compartmentalized structures so popular during the nineteenth century. Considerations of health, wealth, and aesthetic taste worked to produce this change, but the need to solve the servant problems by reducing dependency on servants was an undeniable factor.

Some reformers and architects had begun criticizing the interior arrangement of American houses as early as the 1840s. Catherine Beecher was one of the first reformers to speak out. "In deciding upon the size and style of a house," she wrote in *Treatise*, "the health and capacity of the housekeeper, and the probabilities of securing proper domestics, ought to be the very first consideration." Houses, she elaborated, should be designed with the assumption that good servants would be unobtainable and that housekeepers would be performing much of their own work. Once this assumption was made, such obstructions as pantries, servants' quarters, and back stairs could be removed. Andrew Jackson Downing was one architect who agreed. Downing was aware of the servant shortage. He recognized that many housekeepers were being forced to perform their own housework or to

10. Elizabeth Mickle Bacon, "The Growth of Household Conveniences in the United States from 1865 to 1900" (Ph.D. dissertation, Radcliffe College, 1944), 38–40; Roy L. McCardell, "Help! Help! Help!" *Everybody's Magazine*, XV (October, 1906), 483.
11. James Richardson, "The New Homes of New York," *Scribner's Monthly*, VIII (May, 1874), 67–70, 76; Anne L. Vrooman, "The Servant Question in Social Evolution," *Arena*, XXV (June, 1901), 646–48; I. M. Rubinow and Daniel Durant, "The Depth and Breadth of the Servant Problem," *McClure's Magazine*, XXXIV (March, 1910), 584.

operate their households with fewer servants than required. To remedy this situation, he advocated limiting the number of rooms and arranging them with an eye to compactness and utility.[12]

Unfortunately, the nineteenth century was not to be an age of successful architectural reform. Houses remained highly compartmentalized and far too large. Builders saw no contradiction between spacious interiors and functional placement of rooms, no conflict in combining rambling bigness with utilitarian simplicity. Americans wanted big houses, too. Large houses showed a family's material prosperity both because they were costly to construct and because their size obviously required servants. By the mid-1870s even modest middle-class houses had become "luxurious" and laborious to care for. In the early twentieth century, critics were still amazed by the "diffused vagueness" of American households.[13]

But American houses were acquiring a new look in the early twentieth century. As economic catastrophes, such as the depression of 1893–1897 and the birth of the income tax in 1913 (to be imbued with more formidable clout in 1920), combined with the leveling tendencies of World War I, architectural tastes and fashions altered. Pretenses, especially expensive ones, were curbed. Architects, most notably Frank Lloyd Wright, answered the need for simpler life-styles by reviving Andrew Jackson Downing's ideal of the functional house. The house as home—uncluttered, comfortable, sensible—became the goal. Americans could no longer afford houses large enough to be divided between family and servants. Unobstructed space was demanded, and once Americans decided to rid themselves of servants, less rigid designs could supply space without endangering family privacy.[14]

12. Catherine E. Beecher, *A Treatise on Domestic Economy* (New York: Harper and Brothers, 1847), 258–60; Andrew Jackson Downing, *Cottage Residences, Rural Architecture, and Landscape Gardening* (New York: D. Appleton and Co., 1847), 5, and *The Architecture of Country Houses* (New York: D. Appleton and Co., 1850), 39–40, 277. For a good, brief analysis of Downing's work and his influence on both contemporary and later architecture, see Vincent J. Sully, Jr., *The Shingle Style and the Stick Style* (Revised ed.; New Haven: Yale University Press, 1971), xxiii–lix. William D. and Deborah C. Andrews, "Technology and the Housewife in Nineteenth-Century America," *Women's Studies*, II (1974), 309–328, discusses these architectural changes and other technological innovations. The Andrews, however, stress that the purpose of these changes was "to elevate the status and increase the power of the American woman." They make no mention of the servant problems, and they suggest that these changes were proved successful by 1876.
13. James, *The American Scene*, 166.
14. Frank Lloyd Wright, *An Autobiography* (New York: Duell, Sloan, and Pearce, 1962), 140, 142–43; Robert C. Twombly, "Saving the Family: Middle Class Attraction to

The focus of the new plans was the servantless kitchen. The kitchen, the nerve center of housekeeping, was to be placed for easy access to all parts of the house. Women who hoped to manage their own households required convenient, well-planned culinary workshops. Compactness and utilization of space were the goals; "continuous working surfaces," as Catherine Beecher was first to call them, were the remedy. Sink, stove, cupboards, utensils, and working areas placed within easy reach of one another eliminated motion and saved time and energy. Food—its preservation, storage, preparation, and serving—was the primary concern. Energy and time saved in these chores could be applied elsewhere. Kitchen reform had been suggested before but always as a means of reducing work for servants. As such, it had been largely ignored. By 1900 when this same reform was meant to benefit working housekeepers, employer acceptance increased noticeably. Kitchen improvement became an on-going concern, culminating in the 1930s with the "streamlined," servantless kitchen.[15]

Progress towards the servantless home may also be traced in declining use of the isolated dining room. During the nineteenth century, kitchen, dining room, and parlor had been separate rooms with specific functions in socially respectable households. Families employing "servants," as opposed to "helps," distinguished between the preparation of food and enjoyment of meals, thus emphasizing the difference between master and servant. The dining room became a symbol of affluence and status, the kitchen, a place where servants worked, ate, and entertained themselves. But the "new simplicity" of post-world-war America made it convenient and somehow more democratic for families to forsake their dining rooms and eat in the kitchen or an adjoining "dinette." Moreover, kitchens became integrated with the rest of the house to such a degree that it was difficult to tell where they ended and adjacent rooms began. Passage from one room to another was unimpeded, as living room, dining room, kitchen, and other main floor rooms triumphantly merged. The dining room, if remaining at all, was reserved for holiday meals and special occasions.[16]

Wright's Prairie House, 1901–1909," *American Quarterly*, XXVII (1975), 67–68; Siegfried Giedion, *Mechanization Takes Command: A Contribution to Anonymous History* (New York: Oxford University Press, 1948), 620–25. See also Gwendolyn Wright, *Moralism and the Model Home: Domestic Architecture and Cultural Conflict in Chicago, 1873–1913* (Chicago: University of Chicago Press, 1980).

15. Giedion, *Mechanization Takes Command*, 607–620.

16. Frances M. Abbott, "How to Solve the Housekeeping Problem," *Forum*, XIV (February, 1893), 781–82; Katherine Fullerton Gerould, "The New Simplicity," *Harper's*

Changing methods of housekeeping represented the third innovation in American life to affect the servant problems. This process had two phases: reorganization of household work and mechanization of the household. Both changes simplified housekeeping, conserving time and energy and decreasing the housekeeper's dependency on servants. As when advocating better-planned kitchens, reformers had originally recommended these innovations as means of improving the working conditions of servants. But again, public acceptance of such reforms came only after employers had decided or were forced to perform their own housework.

Reorganization of the work process was most obvious in the kitchen. Architectural restructuring of kitchens allowed swift, effortless performance of work. But as workshops, kitchens also needed to be based on principles of efficient organization. Wasted energy was to be eliminated. One reformer, for example, upon analyzing her dishwashing technique, discovered that she made eighty "wrong motions," not counting transgressions in "sorting, wiping, and laying away." Such careless, unscientific procedures had to be remedied if housekeepers were to survive without servants.[17]

Division of household labor in the form of a domestic putting-out system was the next step. Elimination of work from the household had been a long-desired goal of housekeepers. In the eighteenth and early nineteenth centuries, many home industries, such as spinning, weaving, and candlemaking, were eliminated. As the nineteenth century progressed, commercial canning, manufactured clothing, and prepared foods made housekeeping still easier. With the appearance of commercial bakeries, dairies, and laundries towards the close of the century, significant savings of time, energy, and expense resulted.

Yet this was a slow process. Reformers were still urgently demanding more bakeries and laundries in the twentieth century. Difficult problems had to be overcome. One drawback was cost. Some employers believed that hiring inefficient servants was cheaper than paying for the unreliable services of commercial establishments. In 1897 Lucy Salmon still considered the commercial division of household labor to be only a "possible remedy" to the problems of employers and servants. Apprehension and tradition also hindered use of outside means

Monthly, CXXXVIII (December, 1918), 15–16; Giedion, *Mechanization Takes Command,* 620–25.

17. Giedion, *Mechanization Takes Command,* 516–22; Isabel Bevier, *The House: Its Plan, Decoration, and Care* (Chicago: American School of Economics, 1907), 86–87.

of baking, laundering, and preparing foods. In some cases, as with laundries, commercial establishments had reputations for being unsanitary and inefficient. In other instances, employers simply preferred the old ways and were slow to give them up, even when cheaper and more efficient alternatives were available. In any event, it was not until after World War I that a respectable percentage of Americans availed themselves of bakeries, laundries, and prepared foods.[18]

But the quickest means of relief, so far as employers were concerned, was mechanization of household labor. If mechanical and technological advances could be adapted to housework, Americans believed, a savings of time and energy would result. The new inventions were not intended at first for servantless families. People who could not afford servants could not have purchased the expensive new machines. Nor did many people believe mechanical inventions would eliminate servants entirely. Only a few folks foresaw that labor-saving devices, used in conjunction with better planned houses and elimination of traditional household chores, could make the servantless home a reality. But as machines became cheaper, more reliable, and easier to operate, it became apparent that labor-saving innovations could, in the hands of daily workers, go a long way towards rescuing problem-plagued housekeepers from both the dictatorship of the proletariat and the strain of housekeeping. The mechanization of the home was both a cause and an effect of the declining number of servants. The shortage of good servants made mechanization necessary, and as mechanization progressed, it decreased the need for servants.[19]

Architectural innovations and municipal technology were important sources of improvement. Modern plumbing, heating, lighting, and sanitary systems, for example, represented valuable contributions to the reduction of housework. So, too, did such innovations as dumbwaiters

18. Lucy M. Salmon, *Domestic Service* (New York: Macmillan, 1897), 212–13; Helen Ekin Starrett, "The Housekeeping of the Future," *Forum*, VIII (September, 1889), 113; Mary Avery White, "The Removal of Laundry from the Home," *American Kitchen Magazine*, IX (September, 1898), 203–207, and "Can Laundry Work be Removed from the Home Without Increased Expense?" *American Kitchen Magazine*, XVII (April, 1902), 11; George T. Stigler, *Domestic Servants in the United States, 1900–1940*, Occasional Paper No. 24 of the National Bureau of Economic Research (New York: National Bureau of Economic Research, 1946), 26–28. For the continuation of these trends after 1920, see Marilyn P. Goldberg, "Housework as a Production Activity: Changes in the Content and Organization of Household Production" (Ph.D. dissertation, University of California, Berkeley, 1977).

19. Ruth Schwartz Cowan, "The 'Industrial Revolution' in the Home: Household Technology and Social Change in the Twentieth Century," *Technology and Culture*, XVII (1976), 22.

and speaking tubes, which had gained popularity in the 1840s as means of compensating for the shortage of good servants. Most such changes, however, formed part of larger, more complex developments, often divorced from the servant problems, and cannot be detailed here.[20]

Of more immediate concern are the mechanical gadgets and machines inspired by the servant shortage. The story of these labor-saving devices is not one of sweeping, overnight success. Competing innovations were invented, introduced, and accepted or rejected by housekeepers with stuttering inconsistency. The United States Patent Office groaned under the weight of dozens, even hundreds, of patents for the same inventions. Inventions in different stages of development competed side by side for public acceptance. As in architectural change, an overlap was caused by consumers who could not afford, distrusted, or were displeased with early machines.

Cooking stoves were one of the biggest innovations. Cooking was the most time-consuming task of housekeeping. A saving of labor here might free housekeepers from domination by the "lawless autocratic queens" of their kitchens. By the 1830s the cast iron stove, whether wood or coal burning, was a common sight in American kitchens. Yet it was only a beginning. Though an improvement over the open hearth, stoves still required much attention from cooks. Inventors continued to tinker with stoves, making adjustments and improvements, for nearly four decades. Still, their products were dusty, dirty, and time-consuming. Ashes had to be removed every day and fires had to be hand-fed, banked daily, supplied with mountainous quantities of fuel, and watched almost hourly, lest they burn out. There had to be an easier way.

Relief came by mid-century in the form of the gas stove. First used in hotels and very wealthy households, the gas range was clean, efficient, and convenient. It was a potential godsend for all housekeepers, but especially for those who wished to reduce their dependence on servants. Yet not until the 1880s could middle-class Americans afford gas stoves, and even then, in comparison to stoves, servants continued to be cheaper and more plentiful for several decades. Not until 1920

20. Susan L. Kleinberg, "Technology and Women's Work: The Lives of Working Class Women in Pittsburg, 1870–1900," *Labor History*, XVII (1976), 58–72 discusses some of these innovations, and makes the interesting point that the new technology was a demarcation between working-class and middle-class women just as servants had once been. For the period after 1920 see Joann Vanek, "Household Technology and Social Status: Rising Living Standards and Status and Residence Differences in Housework," *Technology and Culture*, XIX (1978), 361–75.

did the odds begin to change, and not until 1940, with over 16 million Americans owning gas stoves and fewer than three million servants at work, were the positions reversed.[21]

Laundry work was the next most important task to receive attention. More patents—over two thousand in 1873 alone—were granted in this household category than in any other. Although the first American patents for laundering and wringing machines dated from 1805, dramatic improvements did not occur until the 1850s and 1860s. Not until 1869 was a recognizably "modern" washing machine patented. The 1869 machine and most that followed it were hand-cranked models. They saved some work, but their operation still required strong arms and backs. Only gradually were they improved to the point where laundresses could be eliminated. Moreover, despite a boom in commercial laundries in the 1870s, widespread mechanization of home laundries did not occur until the second quarter of the twentieth century. Laundresses continued to be the day workers most frequently requested from commercial and reform intelligence offices.[22]

Carpet sweepers were another innovation. There were four types: the totally mechanical variety with rotating brushes, the suction type, the combined brushes and fan, and combined brushes and suction. All four were first patented between 1858 and 1860, and they continued to develop side by side during the remainder of the century. Although the earliest machines were crude, often bulky apparatuses, they generally eliminated more work than they caused. They continued to be improved and by World War I were reaching impressive sales figures.[23]

Numerous miscellaneous gadgets attacked a variety of minor household chores. Throughout the century, various hand tools, most of them kitchen aids, were invented or improved. These included apple parers, pea shellers, fruit seeders, coffee grinders, potato slicers, egg beaters, meat choppers, everything, observed one kitchen worker, but "a contrivance for stringing string-beans." These gadgets eliminated many tedious tasks and, if not banishing servants from kitchens, at least

21. Giedion, *Mechanization Takes Command*, 527–47; Estelle M. H. Merrill, "Electricity in the Kitchen," *American Kitchen Magazine*, IV (November, 1895), 60–63; Stigler, *Domestic Servants in the United States*, 24*n*, 37.

22. Giedion, *Mechanization Takes Command*, 550–53, 561–71; Stigler, *Domestic Servants in the United States*, 24–25; *Bulletin of the Domestic Reform League*, I (March, 1907), n.p.

23. Giedion, *Mechanization Takes Command*, 548–50, 582–95; Stigler, *Domestic Servants in the United States*, 24.

made housekeepers less dependent on them. More elaborate devices were invented, too, such as the mechanized butter churn and portable heat retainer. The latter item was a metal cabinet that stored and kept warm the several courses of a meal. Placed beside the lady of the house during meals, it enabled her to serve dishes as needed without the presence of a waiter. It was less elegant than a waiter but very practical. It also eliminated accident-prone servants and preserved family privacy.[24]

Electricity proved to be the coordinating factor for many household machines, the magic that ultimately allowed mechanization of the entire household. Inventions such as carpet sweepers, irons, and washing machines had been in use for years, but their operation often required more work and inconvenience than they were worth. As households became electrified, labor-saving machinery reached its full potential. Old appliances were made more efficient, old ideas became realities, and new applications became possible. In 1882 the iron was electrified, the sewing machine in 1889, and the stove in 1896. In 1904 the electric attachment plug increased the mobility of all machines. Electricity ultimately made the dishwasher practicable and the vacuum cleaner more efficient and convenient. Electric lighting eliminated many small daily chores required by kerosene, gasoline, and even gas lamps. The electric refrigerator, popular by the mid-1920s, ended many daily chores required by the old ice box. Electric stoves promised to join gas stoves in completing the modernized kitchen, clearing the way still further for the servantless home. Over one-third of America's households were electrified by 1920, including nearly half of the nation's urban and nonrural houses, and electricity revolutionized household labor.[25]

Logically, all of these innovations should have eliminated the need for servants, but then logic should have ended the servant problems long before the advent of the electric stove. As in judging the early

24. Lionel Josaphare, "Hotel Life from Below," *Harper's Weekly*, LVII (April 19, 1913), 12; Giedion, *Mechanization Takes Command*, 553–56; Joseph B. and Laura E. Lyman, *The Philosophy of House-Keeping* (Philadelphia: J. B. Lippincott, 1882), 486–87, 492–96; Hanna Otis Brun, "Household Inventions," *American Kitchen Magazine*, IV (January, 1896), 157–58; Mary Fielding Kalor, "Ourselves and Our Servants," *American Kitchen Magazine*, XIV (October, 1900), 6.

25. Merrill, "Electricity in the Kitchen," 60; Martha Foote Crow, *The American Country Girl* (New York: Frederick A. Stokes, 1915), 123–24; Mary Ormsbee Whitton, *The New Servant: Electricity in the Home* (Garden City: Doubleday, Page, and Co., 1927), v–vi; U.S. Bureau of the Census, *The Statistical History of the United States from Colonial Times to the Present* (New York: Basic Books, 1976), Series S108–19.

effects of commercial laundries and bakeries on housework, it is difficult to estimate the impact of labor-saving devices on servant-employing families. It is probable that by the late 1880s or early 1890s, labor-saving inventions enabled a significant number of housekeepers to escape household cares. But what percentage of housekeepers purchased stoves, carpet sweepers, and washing machines to replace servants is unanswerable. As late as 1930, many observers believed that "mechanical progress" in the household was slower "than in any other line of work," and that servants were not so easily replaced by mechanical devices as were other laborers.[26] Judging from the many Americans who bought labor-saving machines while retaining their servants, many housekeepers lacked the confidence to do without servants entirely. Thus, by 1920 machines, however impressive their increasing number, had not reached their potential. Mechanization made possible the servantless home, but the decision to capitalize on this opportunity rested with individual housekeepers.

In order to understand their obstinacy, one must bear in mind why Americans employed servants. Many employers, perhaps most, tolerated servants in order to spare themselves the exhausting, time-consuming, and boring routine of household labor. These employers were the ones most likely to trade their servants for the latest inventions, provided those inventions were reasonably priced, trustworthy, and truly labor saving. On the other hand, many employers, especially after 1870, employed servants because family tradition and social status required it. These people were most likely to retain both their servants and their machines. To confuse matters further, some employers, who had originally required servants for practical reasons, grew accustomed to having servants and enjoyed the status thus accrued. Keeping servants was chic—none would gainsay that. Even magazine advertisements pictured servants operating the latest household conveniences, serving meals, and generally adding a touch of class to daily life. (After World War I more and more magazines began to portray housekeepers doing their own work.) Thus, whatever their trials in keeping servants, many employers, for any of several reasons, preferred them to machines.[27]

26. Brun, "Household Inventions," 157; Alba M. Edwards, "Composition of the Nation's Labor Force," American Academy of Political and Social Science Annals, CLXXXIV (1936), 19; Giedion, Mechanization Takes Command, 516; "The Passing of the Household Servant," 19–20.
27. Cowan, "The 'Industrial Revolution' in the Home," 9–10.

Household help becomes discouraged and dissatisfied by the heavy labor of cleaning

There is no worry about cleaning in the home where the Arco Wand does the work

Lighten Household Work!

The cleaning of the house is a heavy physical strain and expense for help (if you can get it) as long as you cling to the old, tiresome broom and duster methods of cleaning.

ARCO WAND
VACUUM CLEANER

The Arco Wand Vacuum Cleaner changes weary household cleaning into a few moments of light, quick use of the suction-wand, with no labor and without extra help.

Use the Arco Wand on your floor, carpets, rugs, upholstered furniture, hangings, curtains, mattresses, clothes, furs, shelves, drawers, books, picture frames and mouldings, etc. All will be cleaned instantly, and dust, dirt, and lint piped away into the sealed dust bucket of the machine.

Easily and quickly installed in *old* or *new* residences, apartments, hotels, clubs, theatres, schools, and public and private buildings. Also made mounted on truck for use in factories, and large business buildings. May be purchased on easy payments, if desired, from dealers everywhere.

Send at once for catalog, The ARCO WAND, which gives full descriptions, and illustrates many of its labor and money saving uses.

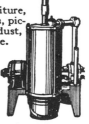

Department C5 AMERICAN RADIATOR COMPANY 816-822 S. Michigan Ave. Chicago

Makers of the world-famous IDEAL Boilers & AMERICAN Radiators

Machine is set in basement or side room. A suction pipe runs to each floor. ARCO WAND Vacuum Cleaners, hose, and tools are sold by all Heating and Plumbing Trade.

Advertisements for household machines stressed the advantage of such labor-saving devices in retaining already scarce help.
Outlook, CXXI (January 1919).

Employers also objected to the new household machines on such practical grounds as cost. Promoters tried to minimize the expense of new equipment, but it was hard to conceal. Even when able to afford modern inventions, many employers remained unconvinced that they saved either time or labor. For example, stoves gave trouble. "Have you caught the cooking stove mania?" a Virginia woman inquired of her sister. All of the woman's neighbors had purchased stoves, and now she planned to buy one, thus, she hoped, freeing herself of servants. Two years later, she had her stove, and although it had been expensive, she admitted that it saved her money in the long run. But stoves also caused many headaches, leading her to confide in her sister, "If I could afford Harriet as cook in an open fire place I never would have consented to the stove." Then there was the woman who upon receiving her mail-order vacuum cleaner discovered it to be so "clumsy of construction" and "awkward to handle" that it required "two strong people at one time to operate it."[28]

Other employers discovered that buying machines was futile because servants refused to use them. Servants were sometimes as reluctant as housekeepers to give up old ways of housework, even when new gadgets and techniques saved labor. "Somehow," marveled one reformer, "servants and washing-machines do not seem to get along well together. . . . The majority . . . do not like them at all, and generally contrive to get them out of order after using them for a few weeks." The same might have been said of stoves, vacuum cleaners, or any other innovation. Some employers and reformers attributed this attitude to stupidity. Servants lacked the intelligence and patience to master machines, they said, and were too dull-witted to appreciate the time and toil machines saved. As late as 1927, reformers were reassuring employers that servants were capable of operating electrical appliances. Perceptive observers realized that servants feared the machines as tools in a conspiracy to force *more* work from them.[29]

Still, increasing numbers of employers welcomed the innovations. They applauded the new machines not as means of easing servants' work but as solutions to a century-old dilemma. Modern conveniences,

28. Mrs. M. Morris to Mary E. Schooler, February 17, 1866 and February 6, 1868, in Mary Eliza Schooler Papers, Perkins Library, Duke University; "Servants and Labor-Saving Devices," *Good Housekeeping*, LV (December, 1912), 860.
29. Frank R. and Marian Stockton, *The Home: Where It Should Be and What to Put in It* (New York: G. P. Putnam and Sons, 1873), 111; "Servants and Labor-Saving Devices," *Good Housekeeping*, LV (November, 1912), 717, and (December, 1912), 859, 860; Whitton, *The New Servant*, 312–26.

American housekeepers discovered, had granted them two wishes hitherto regarded as contradictory: a life free of both domestic drudgery and domestic servants. A housekeeper could now be a club woman, seek self-improvement, care for her family, and still accomplish her housekeeping chores without servants. Or she could compromise by hiring hourly workers, thus avoiding many of the most serious servant problems while still escaping housework.

And so, by 1920 the servantless home had become possible, welcomed, and, with the advent of the modern world, increasingly necessary. A growing number of people believed it to be the only adequate solution to the servant problems, for though some headway had been made, much remained to be done. While a few problems had been resolved, many more had only been reduced in severity or altered in form. The changes, some of them provoked by servants, but most of them consequences of broader changes in American life, had been remarkable only for their leisurely consummation. They represented not a smooth transition from old to new but a jerky, inconsistent replacement of obnoxious circumstances by barely tolerable ones. Americans had not been able to change domestic service as they had originally intended to change it, but as circumstances gradually altered the nature of housekeeping and home life, different, more workable solutions suggested themselves. Unfortunately, no one knew exactly how this had happened or whether the winds of change had blown ill or fair. More unnerving, as Americans gazed into the haze of the 1920s, they were unsure what would happen next. It could be the best of times; it could be the worst of times. It seemed likely that future armies of servants and employers would be smaller, their battles less fierce, and their casualties fewer, but only the foolhardy would predict anything further. One thing and one thing only remained clear, and that uncomfortably so. Americans and their servants would continue to wage war or, as the more civilized would phrase it, to have problems.

BIBLIOGRAPHICAL ESSAY

Letters, Diaries, Reminiscences, and Household Accounts

The letters, diaries, reminiscences, and household accounts of employers and the letters and reminiscences of servants describe the daily lives of Americans as can no other sources. These writings are available in both published and manuscript form, but the most informative documents are generally in manuscript. The letters and diaries of employers are the most plentiful sources of this type, and they abound with details about conditions in service and employer attitudes towards their servant problems. Few letter writers or diarists, particularly housekeepers, could refrain from mentioning their servant woes. Interspaced between comments on the weather, Sally's cold, and the dog's lame paw, housekeepers complained about their domestics and sought remedies for their miseries from friends, relatives, and the Almighty.

After 1890 family letters become progressively less plentiful and, consequently, less valuable. One possible reason for the shortage of later correspondence is the telephone. As telephoning became cheaper and more convenient, people wrote fewer letters than they did in former years. This, however, is probably not so likely an explanation for pre-1920 history as the fact that comparatively little twentieth-century family correspondence has been collected by archivists or collated and published by editors. Numerous collections of letters are probably still in family possession. Also, since progressively fewer American families employed servants, even available correspondence contains fewer references to the servant problems.

The writings of servants, whether in manuscript or printed form, are rare. Servants form part of history's inarticulate mass, those of our ancestors who have left little if any written record of their thoughts, emotions, and deeds. This is not to say that servants could not write. The majority of servants could both read and write, but either they failed to chronicle their lives, or their letters and diaries remain in private hands or have disappeared. Some servants had no incentive to write—no one to write to and no desire to write even if they had a correspondent. Many were too busy to write or too tired at the end of a long work day to bother recording mundane activities. Even when servants did write, their correspondence was less likely to be preserved by friends, relatives, or archivists than the letters of their employers. Most of the surviving servant letters are epistles written to employers and, so, preserved as part of their employers' correspondence.

Several collections and volumes of immigrant letters were also used in this study. These sometimes include letters by servants, but in any case, they provide another perspective on the servant problems. Most immigrants belonged to the working classes, and even if not working as servants themselves, they sometimes had relatives or friends who were servants. Consequently, they were often more intimately acquainted with the realities of a servant's life than were employers and reformers. Their letters provide valuable comments on wages and working conditions, both for servants and for other nonskilled and semiskilled occupations to which the conditions of service may be compared.

For convenience sake, the manuscript collections consulted for this study are listed alphabetically below. It is difficult to say which ones proved most useful. Some collections are much larger than others, and some—not always the largest—were used more extensively than others, but all contain valuable information. On the other hand, few collections can be considered indispensable. They are not unique, and this, I believe, is their great strength. The letters and diaries used here are typical of nineteenth- and early twentieth-century employer and servant writings. The information gleaned from any similarly sized sampling of family papers would very likely yield similar knowledge. Those collections that preserve the writings of servants, being of particular interest, have been designated by an asterisk:

*Adrian (Michigan) Girls' Training School Records, Michigan State Archives, Lansing

Thomas Affleck Papers, State Department of Archives and History, Louisiana State University, Baton Rouge

Samuel A. Agnew Diary, Southern Historical Collection, Library of the University of North Carolina at Chapel Hill

Anderson Family Correspondence (D-1859), Public Records Office of Northern Ireland, Belfast

Anderson Family Correspondence (T-1859), Public Records Office of Northern Ireland, Belfast

John Lancaster Bailey Papers, Southern Historical Collection, Library of the University of North Carolina at Chapel Hill

Charles H. Barry Family Papers, Collection of Regional History, Cornell University, Ithaca, N.Y.

*Beecher-Stowe Collection of Family Papers, Schlesinger Library, Radcliffe College

William H. Bell Diary, New-York Historical Society, New York

Matthew W. Birchard Papers, Burton Historical Collection, Detroit Public Library

Elizabeth DeHart Bleecher Diary, Manuscripts and Archives Division, New York Public Library, Astor, Lenox, and Tilden Foundations

James Bogert, Jr., Account Book with Hired Servants, Museum of the City of New York

James Bogert, Jr., Letters, Museum of the City of New York

*Boltwood Family Papers, Burton Historical Collection, Detroit Public Library

*Bond and Grayson Immigrant Letters, Collection of Regional History, Cornell University, Ithaca, N.Y.

George Y. Bradley Letters, Perkins Library, Duke University, Durham, N.C.

Brayton Family Journals, Collection of Regional History, Cornell University, Ithaca, N.Y.

*Bryan and Minor Papers, Southern Historical Collection, Library of the University of North Carolina at Chapel Hill

Bullock Family Papers, Southern Historical Collection, Library of the University of North Carolina at Chapel Hill

Hugh Cabot Family Papers, Schlesinger Library, Radcliffe College, Cambridge, Mass.

Camp Family Papers, Collection of Regional History, Cornell University, Ithaca, N.Y.

Camp Family Papers (Additional), Collection of Regional History, Cornell University, Ithaca, N.Y.

Campbell Family Papers, Perkins Library, Duke University, Durham, N.C.

Clement C. Clay Papers, Perkins Library, Duke University, Durham, N.C.

Eliza Carolina Clitherall Books, Southern Historical Collection, Library of the University of North Carolina at Chapel Hill

*Ann Thomas Coleman Papers, Perkins Library, Duke University, Durham, N.C.

Colgate-Colby Family Papers, New-York Historical Society, New York

Laura Beecher Comer Diary, Southern Historical Collection, Library of the University of North Carolina at Chapel Hill

Consumers' League of Connecticut Papers, Schlesinger Library, Radcliffe College, Cambridge, Mass.

Consumers' League of Massachusetts Papers, Schlesinger Library, Radcliffe College, Cambridge, Mass.

John Esten Cooke Papers, Perkins Library, Duke University, Durham, N.C.

John Hamilton Cornish Diary, Southern Historical Collection, Library of the University of North Carolina at Chapel Hill

Dana Family Papers, Schlesinger Library, Radcliffe College, Cambridge, Mass.

Edmund Ezra Day Account Books, Southern Historical Collection, Library of the University of North Carolina at Chapel Hill

*James D. B. DeBow Papers, Perkins Library, Duke University, Durham, N.C.

DeRosset Family Papers, Southern Historical Collection, Library of the University of North Carolina at Chapel Hill

Emily Caroline Douglas Papers, State Department of Archives and History, Louisiana State University, Baton Rouge

John Drake, Jr., Diary, Collection of Regional History, Cornell University, Ithaca, N.Y.

Caroline Dunstan Diaries, 1856–70, Manuscripts and Archives Division, New York Public Library, Astor, Lenox, and Tilden Foundations

Edwin Edmunds Account Book, Southern Historical Collection, Library of the University of North Carolina at Chapel Hill

Ellas Family Papers, Collection of Regional History, Cornell University, Ithaca, N.Y.

Grace B. Elmore Diaries, Southern Historical Collection, Library of the University of North Carolina at Chapel Hill

*Emigrant Letters Collection, British Library of Political and Economic Science, London School of Economics

Emigrant Letters from the State of New York, Public Records Office of Northern Ireland, Belfast

Alexander K. Farrar Papers, State Department of Archives and History, Louisiana State University, Baton Rouge

*Federal Writers' Project, Southern Historical Collection, Library of the University of North Carolina at Chapel Hill

Sidney George Fisher Collection, Historical Society of Pennsylvania, Philadelphia

Sidney George Fisher Papers, Historical Society of Pennsylvania, Philadelphia

Fiske Household Accounts, Collection of Regional History, Cornell University, Ithaca, N.Y.

Asa Fitch Collection, Collection of Regional History, Cornell University, Ithaca, N.Y.

Samuel L. Fuqua Account Book, Perkins Library, Duke University, Durham, N.C.

J. H. Furman Plantation Book, Perkins Library, Duke University, Durham, N.C.

Frances Macbeth Glessner Journals, Chicago Historical Society

Gordon Family Papers, Southern Historical Collection, Library of the University of North Carolina at Chapel Hill

Hannah Wright Gould Diary, Collection of Regional History, Cornell University, Ithaca, N.Y.

Grigsby Family Papers, Filson Club, Louisville, Ky.

Grimball Family Papers, Southern Historical Collection, Library of the University of North Carolina at Chapel Hill

John Berkely Grimball Diaries, Southern Historical Collection, Library of the University of North Carolina at Chapel Hill

Meta Grimball Diary, Southern Historical Collection, Library of the University of North Carolina at Chapel Hill

Hall-Stakely Family Papers, Calvin M. McClung Historical Collection, Knoxville–Knox County Public Library, Knoxville, Tenn.

*Hammond, Bryan, and Cumming Families Papers, South Caroliniana Library, University of South Carolina, Columbia

Sarah Catherine Himes Letters, Perkins Library, Duke University, Durham, N.C.

Mebane Hinshaw Papers, Perkins Library, Duke University, Durham, N.C.

Margaret A. Hoard Correspondence, Chicago Historical Society

Houston Family Letters, Public Records Office of Northern Ireland, Belfast

Hubard Family Papers, Southern Historical Collection, Library of the University of North Carolina at Chapel Hill

Huges Family Papers, Southern Historical Collection, Library of the University of North Carolina at Chapel Hill

Christopher Huges Papers, Clements Library, University of Michigan, Ann Arbor

Herman Humphreys Papers, Collection of Regional History, Cornell University

William Hunter Correspondence, Public Records Office of Northern Ireland, Belfast

Henry Hall James Papers, Burton Historical Collection, Detroit Public Library

John Jay Papers, Museum of the City of New York

Jones and Patterson Family Papers, Southern Historical Collection, Library of the University of North Carolina at Chapel Hill

*Mary Susan Ker Diary, Southern Historical Collection, Library of the University of North Carolina at Chapel Hill

Jacob A. Kline Account Books, Southern Historical Collection, Library of the University of North Carolina at Chapel Hill

William D. Lewis Papers, Historical Society of Pennsylvania, Philadelphia

McCall Family Papers, Collection of Regional History, Cornell University, Ithaca, N.Y.

McCann Correspondence (T-1456), Public Records Office of Northern Ireland, Belfast

William Parsons McCorkle Papers, Southern Historical Collection, Library of the University of North Carolina at Chapel Hill

Leander Hamilton McCormick Papers, Chicago Historical Society

McElheny Papers, Collection of Regional History, Cornell University, Ithaca, N.Y.

McGraw Family Papers, Collection of Regional History, Cornell University, Ithaca, N.Y.

Peter Mallett Papers, Southern Historical Collection, Library of the University of North Carolina at Chapel Hill

Henry D. Mandeville and Family Papers, State Department of Archives and History, Louisiana State University, Baton Rouge

May-Goddard Papers, Schlesinger Library, Radcliffe College, Cambridge, Mass.

William Porcher Miles Diary, Southern Historical Collection, Library of the University of North Carolina at Chapel Hill

Minis Family Papers, Southern Historical Collection, Library of the University of North Carolina at Chapel Hill

Mothers' Club of Cambridge, Massachusetts, Papers, Schlesinger Library, Radcliffe College, Cambridge, Mass.

Munford-Ellis Family Papers, Perkins Library, Duke University, Durham, N.C.

*New York House of Refuge Documents, Arents Library, Syracuse University, Syracuse, N.Y.

*John Nolan Letters, Public Records Office of Northern Ireland, Belfast

*Sarah L. Palmer Papers, Collection of Regional History, Cornell University, Ithaca, N.Y.

Park Hotel Registers and Accounts, Collection of Regional History, Cornell University, Ithaca, N.Y.

Frances Pearsall Record Book of Servants' Wages, Museum of the City of New York

Lalla Pelot Papers, Perkins Library, Duke University, Durham, N.C.

Pettigrew Family Papers, Southern Historical Collection, Library of the University of North Carolina at Chapel Hill

Willard Phillips Papers, Massachusetts Historical Society, Boston

Pollack-McClorg Letters, Public Records Office of Northern Ireland, Belfast

Robert Pollack Letters, Collection of Regional History, Cornell University, Ithaca, N.Y.

Octavius T. Porcher Letters, Perkins Library, Duke University, Durham, N.C.

Porter Family Papers, Public Records Office of Northern Ireland, Belfast

Mary Elizabeth Rives Diary, Southern Historical Collection, Library of the University of North Carolina at Chapel Hill

*Lucy Maynard Salmon Papers, Vassar College Library, Poughkeepsie, N.Y.

Abishai Scofield Papers, Burton Historical Collection, Detroit Public Library

Mary Eliza Schooler Papers, Perkins Library, Duke University, Durham, N.C.

Shattuck Family Papers, Massachusetts Historical Society, Boston

Scott Family Papers, Collection of Regional History, Cornell University, Ithaca, N.Y.

Slack Family Papers, Southern Historical Collection, Library of the University of North Carolina at Chapel Hill

Franklin B. Smith Papers, Perkins Library, Duke University, Durham, N.C.

Joseph Belknap Smith Papers, Perkins Library, Duke University, Durham, N.C.

Cornelia Phillips Spencer Papers, Southern Historical Collection, Library of the University of North Carolina at Chapel Hill

John Stanford Household Account Book, New-York Historical Society, New York

Cabell Tavenner and Alexander Scott Withers Papers, Perkins Library, Duke University, Durham, N.C.

Miles Taylor and Family Papers, State Department of Archives and History, Louisiana State University, Baton Rouge

Ella Gertrude Thomas Diary, Perkins Library, Duke University, Durham, N.C.

Thompson Family Correspondence, Public Records Office of Northern Ireland, Belfast

United Services Collection, Archives of Labor History and Urban Affairs, Wayne State University, Detroit
Upson Family Papers, Manuscripts and Archives Division, New York Public Library, Astor, Lenox, and Tilden Foundations
Sarah L. Wadley Diaries, Southern Historical Collection, Library of the University of North Carolina at Chapel Hill
Henry Dana Ward Diary, 1850–57, Manuscripts and Archives Division, New York Public Library, Astor, Lenox, and Tilden Foundations
Abiathar and Emily L. Watkins Papers, Manuscripts and Archives Division, New York Public Library, Astor, Lenox, and Tilden Foundations
Henry Watson, Jr., Papers, Perkins Library, Duke University, Durham, N.C.
David Weeks and Family Papers, State Department of Archives and History, Louisiana State University, Baton Rouge
Katherine Johnstone Wharton Papers, Historical Society of Pennsylvania, Philadelphia
*Calvin Henderson Wiley Papers, Southern Historical Collection, Library of the University of North Carolina at Chapel Hill
Micajah Wilkinson Papers, State Department of Archives and History, Louisiana State University, Baton Rouge
*Josiah Butler Williams Family Papers, Collection of Regional History, Cornell University, Ithaca, N.Y.
Sarah Frances Williams Letters, Southern Historical Collection, Library of the University of North Carolina at Chapel Hill
Women's Educational and Industrial Union Records, Schlesinger Library, Radcliffe College, Cambridge, Mass.
Wyche and Otey Family Papers, Southern Historical Collection, Library of the University of North Carolina at Chapel Hill

Printed employer writings in the form of letters, diaries, and memoirs are plentiful and need not concern us here, but the printed writings of servants are scarce and should be mentioned. When found, servants' writings are often in the form of reminiscences, one of the least reliable of all forms of historical evidence. Still, when used prudently, reminiscences can be valuable. The writings consulted for this study are Mary Anderson, *Woman at Work: The Autobiography of Mary Anderson* (Minneapolis: University of Minnesota Press, 1951); Theodore Blegan (ed.), *Land of Their Choice: The Immigrants Write Home* (Minneapolis: University of Minnesota Press, 1955); Mary Elizabeth Carter, *Millionaire Households and Their Domestic Economy* (New York: D. Appleton and Co., 1903); Rose Cohen, *Out of the Shadows* (New York: Jerome S. Ozer, 1971); Alan Conway (ed.), *The Welsh in America: Letters from the Immigrants* (Minneapolis: University of

Minnesota Press, 1961); Anne Ellis, *The Life of an Ordinary Woman* (New York: Arno Press, 1974); Kyra Goritzina, *Service Entrance: Memoirs of a Park Avenue Cook* (New York: Carrick & Evans, 1939); Irwin Hood Hoover, *Forty-Two Years in the White House* (Boston: Houghton Mifflin, 1934); Georgiana Kirby, *Years of Experience: An Autobiographical Narrative* (New York: G. P. Putnam's Sons, 1887); Mary Lawton, *A Lifetime with Mark Twain: The Memoirs of Kate Leary, for Thirty Years His Faithful and Devoted Servant* (New York: Harcourt, Brace, and Co., 1925); Jay Leyda, "Miss Emily's Maggie," in *New World Writings* (3rd Mentor Selection; New York: New American Library, 1953), 255–67 (contains parts of letters found in the Boltwood Family Papers); Eliza Potter, *A Hairdresser's Experience in High Life* (Cincinnati: n.p., 1859); George P. Rawick (ed.), *The American Slave: A Composite Autobiography* (19 vols.; Westport, Conn.: Greenwood, 1972); Robert Roberts, *The House Servant's Directory* (Boston: Munroe and Francis, 1828); Emmett J. Scott, Jr. (comp.), "Letters of Negro Migrants of 1916–1918," and "Additional Letters of Negro Migrants of 1916–1918," *Journal of Negro History*, IV (1919), 290–340, 412–465.

Traveler Accounts

Historians have waged a considerable debate concerning the research value of traveler accounts. Detractors maintain that travelers, hurriedly scribbling letters and journals as they dashed from town to town, state to state, and coast to coast, tended to record exaggerated and overgeneralized observations. In a sense, this is true, and only the keenest observer can be depended on to place everything he or she witnessed in proper perspective. Many travelers realized that their comments lacked acumen, a few of them wisely referring to their published remarks as impressions, sketches, notes, and glimpses of American life. Shortcomings may be found in the accounts of both foreign and native travelers, but it is the foreign visitor who is most open to criticism. Many foreign travelers, for example, either because they were impressed or repulsed by the democratic nature of American society, exaggerated the egalitarian spirit of American servants. They believed that all servants in the United States were arrogant and independent, and that servants coerced employers into giving them high wages and liberal working conditions. Often they had heard this generalization voiced by American employers.

Nonetheless, if used cautiously, traveler accounts can be valuable. Stripped of rhetoric and naïveté, they provide much useful information. If, for example, a traveler reports a servant as earning five dollars per month in wages, we may accept it as true. Such statements are unlikely to have been influenced by prejudices or generalization.

Likewise, if a traveler reports numerous Irish servants in an ante-bellum New Orleans hotel, we may assume that there were, in truth, many Irish working in that hotel. Such bits of knowledge are trivial in themselves, but when garnered from dozens of accounts, they yield a corpus of material that contributes to a general impression of what service was like. Equally important, nearly all travelers commented to some degree on American servants, especially on hotel servants, with whom they were most often in contact.

The number of published travel accounts written by foreign and native travelers can be intimidating. Luckily, several helpful annotated bibliographical guides are available to aid researchers in evaluating the hundreds of available accounts. The most useful guides are Max Berger, *The British Traveller in America, 1836–1860* (New York: Columbia University Press, 1943); Thomas D. Clark, *Travels in the Old South* (3 vols.; Norman: University of Oklahoma Press, 1956–59), and *Travels in the New South* (2 vols.; Norman: University of Oklahoma Press, 1962); E. Merton Coulter, *Travels in the Confederate States* (Norman: University of Oklahoma Press, 1948); Robert R. Hubach, *Early Midwestern Travel Narratives* (Detroit: Wayne State University Press, 1961); William Matthews, *American Diaries: An Annotated Bibliography of American Diaries Written Prior to the Year 1861* (Berkeley: University of California Press, 1945); Jane Louise Mesick, *The English Traveller in America, 1785–1835* (New York: Columbia University Press, 1922); Allen Nevins, *America Through British Eyes* (New York: Oxford University Press, 1948); Richard L. Rapson, *Britons View America: Travel Commentary, 1860–1935* (Seattle: University of Washington Press, 1971).

Public Documents

Public documents are valuable primarily for the statistical information they provide concerning servants. Details about the number of servants in the work force, age, nativity, race, and conjugal condition can be extracted from these sources. Published decennial United States census returns are the richest and most convenient sources of statistical data, although they must be used with care. Census reports are far from being models of statistical precision, and the quality and type of information they contain vary by decade. Peculiarities within and among censuses make accurate comparisons difficult.

The biggest deficiency of the federal census is its failure to arrive at a consistent definition of *servant*. Census officials could never decide who should be counted a servant, and the word meant something different in nearly every decade. Consequently, comparison of data found in different censuses is hazardous. More confusing, inconsistent interpretation by individual census enumerators of already fuzzy official definitions created startling inconsistencies and inaccuracies within each census. Enumerators counted people as servants who were not servants and excluded others who should have been so counted. The Bureau of the Census was aware of these problems as early as 1870, when it admitted that the organization of American service was so "crude" as to make an accurate count of all service occupations impossible.

Furthering the problems, census data are inconsistent in the type of information they supply about occupations. Not until 1850 were American workers counted and listed by occupation. Even then, only male workers were tabulated, women not being included until 1860. Only after 1870 did census reports provide useful information about the nativity and geographic distribution of workers. Such important details as race, conjugal condition, and unemployment rates were not reported for the nation at large until 1890. Again, categories changed from census to census, making comparison by decade difficult. For example, age divisions used in 1870 and 1880 were rearranged in 1890, significantly retarding efforts to investigate trends in the age of workers. Likewise, the excellent data on literacy gathered in 1890 was not reported in 1910 or 1920. Other problems, such as periodic attempts to correct errors in data thirty to fifty years after its original tabulation, make long-range comparison difficult and insure that the "conspiracy of statistical silence" surrounding domestic service remains largely unbroken.

Other public documents compiled by the federal government combine statistical information with observation, conjecture, and the testimony of servants and employers on the conditions of service. Two official probes dealing with many aspects of domestic service and the servant problems are Gail Laughlin, "Domestic Service," in *Report of the United States Industrial Commission on the Relations of Capital and Labor*, (19 vols.; Washington, D.C.: Government Printing Office, 1901), XIV, 739–67; and Helen L. Sumner, *History of Women in Industry in the United States*, in *Report on the Condition of Woman and Child Wage-Earners in the United States*, *Senate Documents*, 61st Cong., 2nd Sess., No. 645, IX, 177–85. The first of these reports is the more valuable. Other useful publications of the federal government include United States Bureau of Labor, *Third Annual Report of the Commissioner: Strikes and Lockouts* (Washington, D.C.: Government Printing Office, 1887); *Tenth Annual Report of the Commissioner: Strikes and Lockouts* (2 vols.; Washington, D.C.: Government Printing Office, 1894); *Sixteenth Annual Report of the Commissioner: Strikes and Lockouts* (Washington, D.C.: Government Printing Office,

1901); *Twenty-First Annual Report of the Commissioner: Strikes and Lockouts* (Washington, D.C.: Government Printing Office, 1906); United States Department of Labor, *State Laws Affecting Working Women*, Bulletin of the Women's Bureau No. 16 (Washington, D.C.: Government Printing Office, 1921); and *The Occupational Progress of Women*, Bulletin of the Women's Bureau No. 27 (Washington, D.C.: Government Printing Office, 1922); Mary V. Robinson, *Domestic Workers and Their Employment Relations*, Bulletin of the Women's Bureau No. 39 (Washington, D.C.: Government Printing Office, 1924); Mary V. Dempsey, *The Occupational Progress of Women, 1910–1930*, Bulletin of the Women's Bureau No. 104 (Washington, D.C.: Government Printing Office, 1933); *Report on Chinese Immigration, Senate Documents*, 44th Cong., 2nd Sess., No. 689; Joseph A. Hill, *Women in Gainful Occupations, 1870–1920*, Monograph No. 9 of U.S. Census Bureau (Washington, D.C.: Government Printing Office, 1929).

Local and state government documents also provide helpful statistical data and other information. For examples, see Lemuel Shattuck, *Report to the Committee of the City Council Appointed to Obtain the Census of Boston for the Year 1845* (Boston: n.p., 1846); Massachusetts Bureau of Statistics of Labor, *Annual Report for 1872* (Boston: n.p., 1872), *Annual Report for 1884* (Boston: n.p., 1884), *Annual Report for 1887* (Boston: n.p., 1887), *Trained and Supplemental Employees for Domestic Service*, Part II of *Annual Report for 1906* (Boston: n.p., 1906). The bureau's report for 1884 was later republished by Carroll D. Wright as *The Working Girls of Boston* (Boston: Wright & Potter, 1889). The bureau also published the *Massachusetts Labor Bulletin*, which contains valuable articles on domestic service. See, for example, "Hours of Labor in Domestic Service," Bulletin No. 8 (October, 1898), 1–27, "Social Conditions in Domestic Service," Bulletin No. 13 (February, 1900), 1–16, and "Social Statistics of Working Women," Bulletin No. 18 (May, 1901), 29–49. Those state bureaus of labor mentioned in Chapter Nine as taking an interest in domestic service sometimes included helpful information in their annual reports after 1880. See especially California Bureau of Labor Statistics, *Second Biennial Report* (Sacramento: n.p., 1887), *Third Biennial Report* (Sacramento: n.p., 1888); Kansas Bureau of Labor and Industry, *Tenth Annual Report* (Topeka: n.p., 1895); Maine Bureau of Industrial and Labor Statistics, *Annual Report for 1888* (Augusta: n.p., 1889), *Annual Report for 1892* (Augusta: n.p., 1893), *Annual Report for 1910* (Augusta: n.p., 1910); Michigan Bureau of Labor and Industrial Statistics, *Twelfth Annual Report* (Lansing: n.p., 1895); Minnesota Bureau of Labor Statistics, *Biennial Report* (n.p., 1887); New York Bureau of Labor Statistics, *Third Annual Report* (Albany: n.p., 1886), *Fourteenth An-*

nual Report (Albany: n.p., 1897), *Report of Special Committee of the Assembly Appointed to Investigate the Condition of Female Labor in the City of New York* (New York: n.p., 1896). Another potentially valuable source is the manuscript census rolls. I have not used these reports extensively, but they offer an excellent means of testing general conclusions at the local level.

Magazines and Newspapers

Period magazines are most useful for studying the ideas of reformers. A striking division occurs, however, in both the quality and quantity of these writings at about 1870. Antebellum magazines are not very useful. Even ladies' magazines, the form of periodical literature one would suppose most likely to discuss household problems, were too esoteric and genteel to succumb to a public debate on servants. Antebellum servant-reform writings are limited to a few editorials, essays, and letters to editors complaining about the state of domestic service from the employer's point of view. Blaine Edward McKinley, who makes extensive use of periodical literature in his dissertation, has formed this same conclusion. The most useful pre-1870 magazines are *Arthur's Home Magazine* (1852–1898), *Harper's Monthly* (1850–1920), *Harper's Weekly* (1857–1916), *Knickerbocker* (1833–1865), and to a lesser degree, *Ladies' Magazine* (1827–1836) and *Godey's Lady's Book* (1830–1898). The best guide to these magazines is Frank Luther Mott's definitive work *A History of American Magazines* (5 vols.; Cambridge: Harvard University Press, 1930–68).

The situation is more complex for the 1870–1920 period. During this half century, a larger number and a wider variety of American magazines published an increasing amount of material on the servant problems. General news magazines, household journals, and women's magazines exploded in number and greatly expanded their coverage of the servant question. Joining them were several new types of periodical, including professional journals and magazines devoted to household and social reform. Some of these magazines, such as *Harper's Monthly* and *Harper's Weekly*, continued from the antebellum period, but most of them were established after 1865. The most useful of the new periodicals for studying the servant problems are *American Journal of Sociology* (1895–1920), *Arena* (1889–1909), *Atlantic Monthly* (1857–1920), *Charities* (1897–1907), *Collier's Magazine* (1888–1920), *Cosmopolitan* (1886–1920), *Delineator* (1873–1920), *Forum* (1886–1920), *Harper's Bazar* (1867–1920), *Hotel Bulletin* (1910–1920), *Hotel Management* (1922), *Hotel Monthly* (1892–1920), *Independent* (1848–1916), *Ladies' Home Journal* (1883–1920), *Lippincott's Magazine* (1868–1916), *McClure's Magazine* (1893–1920), *Nation* (1848–1920),

New England Kitchen Magazine (1894–1895; between 1895 and 1903 this was published as *American Kitchen Magazine*, and between 1903 and 1908, it was continued under a variety of titles), *North American Review* (1815–1920), *Old and New* (1870–1875), *Outlook* (1870–1920), *Scribner's Magazine* (1887–1920), and *Scribner's Monthly* (1870–1920).

Popular magazines also add to our repository of servants' writings. First-person narratives by servants and former servants, either in the form of articles or letters to editors, appear in several post-1870 publications. These accounts vary in credibility, some of them apparently having been polished and enlivened by ghost writers. Most of these accounts, however, are useful when prudently used. They include, by magazine, "A Servant on the Servant Problem," *American Magazine*, LXVIII (September, 1909), 502–504; "Waitress Work in Summer Hotels," *American Kitchen Magazine*, XIII (June, 1900), 85–88; Annie Bezanson, "The Disadvantages of Housework," *American Kitchen Magazine*, XVIII (January, 1903), 139–40; H. H., "A Houseworker's Experience," *American Kitchen Magazine*, XVIII (February, 1903), 191–92; Mary Alden Hopkins and A. O. C., "A Letter and a Reply on the Servant Question," *Collier's Magazine*, XLVII (April 22, 1911), 36; Edith J. R. Isaacs, "Why Maids Leave Home: Real Letters That Also Show How They Might Be Induced to Stay," *Delineator*, LXXXIV (January, 1914), 5, 46; Louisa May Alcott, "How I Went Out to Service," *Independent*, XXVI (June 4, 1874), 1–3; "A Servant Girl's Letter," *Independent*, LIV (January 2, 1902), 36–37; James Samuel Stemons, "Tipping—the Other Side," *Independent*, LV (March 26, 1903), 725–29; Agnes M., "The True Life Story of a Nurse Girl," *Independent*, LV (September 24, 1903), 2261–266; "A Washerwoman," *Independent*, LVII (November 10, 1904), 1073–1076; "The Story of an Irish Cook," *Independent*, LIX (March 30, 1905), 715–17; "Confessions of a Japanese Servant," *Independent*, LIX (September 21, 1905), 661–68; "A Butler's Life Story," *Independent*, LXIX (July 14, 1910), 76–82; A Negro Nurse, "More Slavery at the South," *Independent*, LXXII (January 25, 1912), 196–200; Maud Younger, "The Diary of an Amateur Waitress: An Industrial Problem from the Worker's Point of View," *McClure's Magazine*, XXVIII (March, 1907), 543–52 and (April, 1907), 665–77; Mary, "Wanted, A Domestic: III," *Old and New*, V (June, 1872), 759–61; "The Experiences of a Hired Girl," *Outlook*, C (April 6, 1912), 778–80; "An Ideal Mistress," *Outlook*, CI (August 10, 1912), 91–94. See also C. S. Angstan, "The Story of a Housekeeper," *Independent*, LXIII (July 11, 1907), 91–94. While this is only a reported conversation between an employer and her servant, it has the ring of truth.

Additionally, several reformers who had worked as servants published accounts of their experiences. The most comprehensive of these accounts appeared in Lillian Pettengill, *Toilers of the Home: The Record of a College Woman's Experience as a Domestic Servant* (New York: Doubleday, Page, and Co., 1903), but most reformers revealed their adventures in magazine articles. These afford useful information on the conditions of service but should be considered apart from the accounts of servants. See Amy E. Tanner, "Glimpses at the Mind of a Waitress," *American Journal of Sociology*, XIII (July, 1907), 48–55; Jane Seymour Klink, "Put Yourself in Her Place," *Atlantic Monthly*, XCV (February, 1905), 169–77, and "The Housekeeper's Responsibility," *Atlantic Monthly* (March, 1905), 372–81; a series of seven articles by Anne Forsyth, "Seven Times a Servant," in *Delineator*, LXXVI (September, 1910), 157–58, (October, 1910), 252–53, (November, 1910), 358–59, 437–38, (December, 1910), 469–70, 574, LXXVII, (January, 1911), 13–14, 64, (February, 1911), 92–93, and (March, 1911), 173, 252–54; Inez A. Goodman, "Ten Weeks in a Kitchen," *Independent*, LIII (October 17, 1901), 2459–464; A Novelist, "At Service in A Millionaire's Family," *Scribner's Magazine*, LXX (October, 1921), 493–503, and "Being a Waitress in a Broadway Hotel," *Scribner's Magazine*, LXX (September, 1921), 314–25.

Only limited use was made of newspapers in this study. They were used primarily for the data to be gleaned from their want ads and for the articles and editorials that occasionally appear in their columns. Yet newspapers are a potentially important source. See, for example, the use made of newspapers in Alice C. Hanson and Paul H. Douglas, "The Wages of Domestic Labor in Chicago, 1890–1929," *Journal of the American Statistical Association*, XXV (1930), 47–50. Newspapers also printed letters to editors written by servants. Again, prudence is required in using some of these letters, but examples are found in the New York *Times*, December 5, 1872, p. 3; March 26, 1875, p. 5; May 5, 1875, p. 6; March 9, 1879, p. 9; March 16, 1879, p. 9; March 30, 1879, p. 9.

Records and Publications of Reform Societies

Manuscript records of reformers and reform organizations provide not only correspondence but surveys, pamphlets, and society documents, all of which provide a comprehensive account of reform methods and activities. These collections are listed in this bibliography under the subheading Letters, Diaries, Reminiscences, and Household Accounts. In addition, several of the largest reform organizations published reports and periodical literature describing plans for reform and the progress of reform efforts. The most complete collection of such reports, pamphlets, and journals, some of them relatively rare, are the Women's Educational and Industrial Union Records and the Lucy Maynard Salmon Papers. Copies of most of the reports of the antebellum New York and Philadelphia societies for encouraging faithful service are found in the New York Public Library, New-York Historical Society, Historical Society of Philadelphia, and the American Antiquarian Society.

Servant Manuals, Household Manuals, and Etiquette Books

The importance of these materials has been described in Chapter Eight and Chapter Nine, and many examples are given in the accompanying notes. The manuals provide excellent examples of the attitudes of employers and servants toward one another, and many post-1870 household manuals give good descriptions of servants' daily duties. These sources also illustrate, as shown in Chapter One, popular images of the housekeeper, the lady, and the home. There are no guides or directories to servant manuals, but for household manuals and etiquette books, the following can be useful: Russell Lynes, *The Domesticated Americans* (New York: Harper and Row, 1963); Dixon Wecter, *The Saga of American Society* (New York: Charles Scribner's Sons, 1937); Arthur M. Schlesinger, *Learning How to Behave: A Historical Study of American Etiquette Books* (New York: Macmillan, 1946); Mary Reed Bobbitt, *Bibliography of Etiquette Books Before 1900* (New York: New York Public Library, 1947); Waldo Lincoln, "Bibliography of American Cookery Books, 1742–1860," *Proceedings of the American Antiquarian Society*, XXXIX (1929), 85–225.

Collected Essays, Pamphlets, and Monographs

These cover many and varied aspects of the servant problems, including wages, servants' working and living conditions, economic and social conditions of the working classes, place and role of women in American life, immigration, nativism, social attitudes towards servants and the home, and plans for servant and household reform. Many volumes of such material are available. Those I found most helpful are mentioned in the notes, but several deserve to be singled out. Two detailed appraisals of the lives of black domestics during the late nineteenth and early twentieth centuries are Isabel Eaton, "Special Report on Negro Domestic Service in the Seventh Ward," in W. E. B. DuBois, *The Philadelphia Negro: A Social Study* (New York: Benjamin Blom, 1899), 425–509; and Elizabeth Ross Haynes, "Negroes in Domestic Service in the United States," *Journal of Negro History*, VIII (1923), 384–442. The number of people with surefire solutions to the servant problems is overwhelming, but see Charlotte Perkins Gilman, *The Home: Its Work and Influence* (New York: McClure, Phillips, and Co., 1903); Mrs. A. J. [Margaret] Graves, *Woman in America* (New York: Harper and Brothers, 1843); Maria J. McIntosh, *Woman in America: Her Work and Her Reward* (New York: D. Appleton and Co., 1850); Scott and Nellie Nearing, *Woman and Social Progress* (New York: Macmillan, 1912); Griffith A. Nicholas [Elizabeth Strong Worthington], *The Biddy Club* (Chicago: A. C. McClurg and Co., 1888); Mary A. Ripley, *An Essay on Household Service* (Buffalo: Women's Educational and Industrial Union of Buffalo, 1889); Catherine M. Sedgwick, *Live and Let Live; or, Domestic Service Illustrated* (New York: Harper and Brothers, 1837); Ruth Sergel (ed.), *The Woman in the House: Stories of Household Employment* (New York: The Woman's Press, 1938); Harriet Prescott Spofford, *The Servant Girl Question* (Boston: Houghton Mifflin, 1881); Mrs. C. H. Stone, *The Problem of Domestic Service* (St. Louis: Nelson Printing, 1892); and Ida M. Tarbell, *The Business of Being a Woman* (New York: Macmillan, 1912).

A rather specialized but significant type of contemporary printed material is the architectural monograph, handbook, or design book. Again, these are far too numerous to conveniently list, but a good collection of such materials is available at the University of Michigan Libraries. A serviceable guide is Henry R. Hitchcock, *American Architectural Books: A List of Books, Portfolios, and Pamphlets on Architecture and Related Subjects Published in America Before 1895* (New York: DaCapo Press, 1975). Among the century's most popular works were Lewis Falley Allen, *Rural Architecture: Being a Complete Description of Farm Houses, Cottages, and Out Buildings* (New York: C. M. Saxton, 1852); George F. Barber, *Modern Dwellings* (London: Gresham, 1905); Henry W. Cleaveland, William Backus, and Samuel D. Backus, *Village and Farm Cottages* (New York: D. Appleton and Co., 1856); Andrew Jackson Downing, *The Architecture of Country Houses* (New York: D. Appleton and Co., 1850); Eugene Clarence Gardner, *Illustrated Homes: A Series of Papers Describing Real Homes and Real People* (Boston: James R. Osgood, 1875); Greta Gray, *House and Home: A Manual and Text-Book of Practical House Planning* (Philadelphia: J. B. Lippincott, 1923); John Hall, *A Series of Select and Original Modern Designs for Dwelling Houses* (Baltimore: John Murphy, 1840); H. Hudson Holly, *Modern Dwellings in Town and Country Adapted to American Wants and Climate* (New York: Harper and Brothers, 1878); Hermann Valentin von Holst, *Modern American Homes* (Chicago: American Technical Society, 1918); David H. Jacques, *The House: A Manual of Rural Architecture* (New York: George E. and F. W. Woodward, 1867); Charles D. Lakey, *Lakey's Vil-*

lage and Country Houses; or, Cheap Homes for All Classes (New York: American Builder, 1875); Francis Osborne, *The Family House* (Philadelphia: Penn, 1910); George Palliser and Charles Palliser, *Palliser's Model Homes* (Bridgeport, Conn.: Palliser and Palliser, 1878); John W. Ritch, *The American Architect: Comprising Original Designs of Cheap Country and Village Residences* (2 vols.; New York: C. M. Saxton, 1849); John Calvin Stevens and Albert Winslow Cobb, *Examples of American Domestic Architecture* (New York: William T. Comstock, 1889); Gustav Stickley, *Craftsman Homes* (New York: Craftsman, 1909); Russell Sturgis *et al.*, *Homes in City and Country* (New York: Charles Scribner's Sons, 1893); T. Thomas, Jr., *The Working-Man's Cottage Architecture, Containing Plans, Elevations, and Details for the Erection of Cheap, Comfortable, and Neat Cottages* (New York: R. Martin, 1848); Calvert Vaux, *Villas and Cottages* (New York: Harper and Brothers, 1857); Ekin Wallick, *The Small House for a Moderate Income* (New York: Heart's International, 1915); Gervase Wheeler, *Homes for the People, in Suburbs and Country; the Villa, the Mansion, and the Cottage* (New York: Charles Scribner, 1855); George Everton Woodward and Francis W. Woodward, *Woodward's Country Houses* (New York: George E. and F. W. Woodward, 1865); Richardson Wright, *Low Cost Suburban Homes: A Book of Suggestions for the Man with the Moderate Purse* (New York: Robert M. McBride, 1920). Useful articles and house plans also appear in contemporary journals and magazines, such as *American Homes* (1895–1904), *American Homes and Gardens* (1903–1920), *Architects' and Builders' Magazine* (1900–1920), *Architectural Record* (1891–1920), *Country Life in America* (1901–1920); *House and Garden* (1901–1920), and *House Beautiful* (1896–1920).

The plight of working women was a popular topic after 1870. The literature portraying their lives provides useful information on working and living conditions among laboring women generally, and it sometimes touches on domestic service and servants. See, especially, Edith Abbott, *Women in Industry* (New York: D. Appleton and Co., 1910); Louise Marion Bosworth, *The Living Wage of Women Workers* (New York: Longmans, Green, and Co., 1911); Elisabeth B. Butler, *Saleswomen in Mercantile Stores* (New York: Charities Publication Committee, 1913), and *Women and the Trades* (New York: Charities Publication Committee, 1909); Helen Campbell's several books on the subject, including *Prisoners of Poverty: Woman Wage-Workers, Their Trades and Their Lives* (Boston: Robert Brothers, 1887), and *Women Wage-Earners: Their Past, Their Present, and Their Future* (Boston: Robert Brothers, 1893); Gwendolyn Salisbury Hughes, *Mothers in Industry: Wage-Earning by Mothers in Philadelphia* (New York: Arno

Press, 1977); Lee Meriwether, *The Tramp at Home* (New York: Harper and Brothers, 1889); Virginia Penny, *How Women Can Make Money* (Springfield, Mass.: D. E. Fisk and Co., 1870), and *Think and Act: A Series of Articles Pertaining to Men and Women, Work and Wages* (Philadelphia: Claxton, Remsen, and Hoffelfinger, 1869); and Robert A. Woods and Albert J. Kennedy (eds.), *Young Working Girls: A Summary of Evidence from Two Thousand Social Workers* (Kennebunkport, Me.: Milford House, 1974). For an interesting view of an occupation that became an alternative to domestic service for many women by 1920, that of the restaurant waitress, see Frances Donovan, *The Woman Who Waits* (Boston: Richard G. Badger, 1920).

Secondary Works on Domestic Service

The purpose of this essay has been to explain the merits of those primary sources used in researching the servant problems. Helpful secondary works are cited in the notes. I would, however, like to comment on those secondary sources pertaining directly to domestic service. The standard work on the subject for many years was Lucy Maynard Salmon, *Domestic Service* (New York: Macmillan, 1897). Her book remains valuable for its portrayal of service in the 1890s and its excellent presentation of contemporary reform programs. But Miss Salmon, though a capable historian, was also a servant reformer, an unfortunate coincidence that colored her interpretation of the history of service and detracts from her book's usefulness as history. George J. Stigler's monograph *Domestic Servants in the United States, 1900–1940*, Occasional Paper No. 24 of the National Bureau of Economic Research (New York: National Bureau of Economic Research, 1946) was the next serious examination of American service to appear, carrying the story forward into the twentieth century. Stigler's brief and largely statistical view of service was one in a series of studies on American labor and industry sponsored by the National Bureau of Economic Research. It deals primarily with the impersonal economic consequences of service as an occupation, though Stigler does provide useful quantitative information on many aspects of household labor as they relate to the national economy and work force.

A pair of popular histories, both of them overly anecdotal and tending to reinforce old myths and misconceptions, was published in the late 1950s and early 1960s. First came Russell Lynes, *The Domesticated Americans* (New York: Harper and Row, 1957, 1963). Lynes devotes a chapter of his history of the American home and American home life to domestic service. Although he hints at important ramifications of the servant problems—such as architecture—his discussion is superficial. Similar is Ernest Sackville Turner, *What the Butler Saw:*

Two Hundred Years of the Servant Problem (London: Michael Joseph, 1962), principally a study of English service, but including a chapter on the United States.

Scholarly analysis of domestic service was saved from the popularization of "social historians" towards the end of the 1960s by Blaine Edward McKinley, " 'Strangers in the Gates': Employer Reactions Towards Domestic Servants in America, 1825–1875" (Ph.D. dissertation, Michigan State University, 1969). McKinley's work is limited, however, by his concentration on employers and reformers, his focus on service in the Northeast and Midwest, and his failure to carry analysis beyond 1875. David E. Schob then contributed to our knowledge of rural help before the Civil War in *Hired Hands and Plowboys: Farm Labor in the Midwest, 1815–1860* (Urbana: University of Illinois Press, 1975). An interesting account of the relations between employers and servants in a Chicago family has been provided by Helen C. Callahan in "Upstairs-Downstairs in Chicago, 1870–1907: The Glessner Household," *Chicago History*, VI (1977–78), 195–209. Most recently, David M. Katzman, *Seven Days a Week: Women and Domestic Service in Industrializing America* (New York: Oxford University Press, 1978), has sought to describe service between 1870 and 1920. His is the most comprehensive account to date, but he tends to concentrate on blacks as the typical servant. Moreover, Katzman confuses social history with "historical sociology" (vii–viii) and is, like Salmon, an admitted reformer. His approach requires that readers be wary of some of Katzman's interpretations. A general criticism of all of the above-mentioned authors is their failure to use manuscript collections and unpublished period writings more extensively than they do. A subject so intensely personal and "domestic" as household service requires the use of such sources to balance the pronouncements of government reports and published remarks on the servant problems.

Background for the study of nineteenth-century domestic service may be found in several good works on the colonial period. Especially useful are James Curtis Ballagh, *White Servitude in the Colony of Virginia* (New York: Burt Franklin, 1969); John Spencer Bassett, *Slavery and Servitude* in the Colony of North Carolina (Baltimore: Johns Hopkins University Press); John Demos, *A Little Commonwealth: Family Life in Plymouth Colony* (New York: Oxford University Press, 1971); Lorenzo Greene, *The Negro in Colonial New England* (New York: Atheneum, 1969); Cheesman A. Herrick, *White Servitude in Pennsylvania: Indentured and Redemption Labor in Colony and Commonwealth* (New York: Negro Universities Press, 1969); Marcus Wilson Jernegan, *Laboring and Dependent Classes in Colonial America, 1607–1783* (Chicago: University of Chicago Press, 1931); Winthrop D.

Jordan, *White over Black: American Attitudes Toward the Negro, 1550–1812* (Baltimore: Johns Hopkins University Press, 1969); Samuel McKee, Jr., *Labor in Colonial New York, 1664–1776* (New York: Columbia University Press, 1935); Edgar J. McManus, *Black Bondage in the North* (New York: Syracuse University Press, 1973); Albert Matthews, "Hired Man and Help," *Publications of the Colonial Society of Massachusetts*, V, *Transactions* (1897–98), 225–56; William Miller, "The Effects of the American Revolution on Indentured Servitude," *Pennsylvania History*, VII (1940), 131–41; Edmund Morgan, *The Puritan Family: Religion and Domestic Relations in Seventeenth Century New England* (New York: Harper and Row, 1966); Richard B. Morris, *Government and Labor in Early America* (New York: Columbia University Press, 1946); John H. Russell, *The Free Negro in Virginia, 1619–1865* (Baltimore: Johns Hopkins University Press, 1913); Abbott Emerson Smith, *Colonists in Bondage: White Servitude and Convict Labor in America, 1607–1776* (Chapel Hill: University of North Carolina Press, 1947); Warren B. Smith, *White Servitude in Colonial South Carolina* (Columbia: University of South Carolina Press, 1961); Julia Cherry Spruill, *Women's Life and Work in the Southern Colonies* (Chapel Hill: University of North Carolina Press, 1938); Laurence W. Towner, " 'A Fondness for Freedom': Servant Protest in Puritan Society," *William and Mary Quarterly*, XIX (1962), 201–219.

Also helpful in evaluating American service are several studies of British domestic service, the source of so many American assumptions and traditions concerning household labor. Here again, one encounters both popular and scholarly works. The best and most recent of the popular histories is Frank Dawes, *Not in Front of the Servants: Domestic Service in England, 1850–1939* (London: Wayland, 1973). More serious works include Dorothy Marshall, *The English Domestic Servant in History* (London: The Historical Association, 1949); Joseph Jean Hecht, *The Domestic Servant Class in Eighteenth-Century England* (London: Routledge and Kegan Paul, 1956); Leonore Davidoff, "Mastered for Life: Servant and Wife in Victorian and Edwardian England," *Journal of Social History*, VII (1974), 406–428; Joan W. Scott and Louise A. Tilly, "Women's Work and the Family in Nineteenth Century Europe," in Charles E. Rosenberg (ed.), *The Family in History* (Philadelphia: University of Pennsylvania Press, 1975), 145–78, dealing with European as well as English service; Pamela Horn, *The Rise and Fall of the Victorian Servant* (Dublin: Gill and Macmillan, 1975); and Theresa M. McBride, *The Domestic Revolution: The Modernisation of Household Service in England and France, 1820–1920* (New York: Holmes and Meier, 1976). McBride attempts to draw comparisons between American and English service, but she falls short of an effective or convincing analysis. She does not appear to be familiar enough with the American experience in service, and she is too dedicated to sociological models to appreciate the differences between American and European life. Further comparative studies, if deemed necessary, must rely on more extensive research to do the subject justice.

INDEX

English: as servants, 42, 51–53, 58–59
Ettiquette books, 24, 149–51

Factory work: compared to service,
101–102, 109–110
Fall River. Massachusetts, 46–47
Family hotels, 186–87
Farrar, Eliza W., 151
*Father's Advice to His Daughter on
Going Out to Service*, 154
Followers, 76
Footmen: duties of, 90–91
Foreign-born servants. *See* Immigrants
Forum, 169–70
Franklin, Benjamin, 154
Frederick, Christine, 165, 183–84
French: as servants, 51–52, 56–57
"French flats," 187–88
"French leave," 130

Gadsby's Hotel, 52–53
General Federation of Women's Clubs,
172
German Housewives Society, 171
Germans: as servants, 42, 49, 51–53,
56–57, 58–59
Gilded Age, 13–14, 129
Gilman, Charlotte Perkins, 165, 183–84,
184n
Girls' Lodging House, 156
Glenn, Jane, 144
Golden age: myth of, 6–7, 47–48, 54–55,
139; in South, 6–7
Good Housekeeping, 169–70
Great Awakening, 147–48
Griffiths, Solomon, 19
Griscom, John, 152

Hale, Sarah J., 151, 157
Hale, Susan, 18
Hampton Institute, 165
Harper's Bazar, 169–70
Hartford, Connecticut: employers in, 23
Hawthorne, Nathaniel, 151
Health of servants, 42, 99–100, 138–39
Help: as euphemism for servant, 47–48,
54–55, 125–26
Herrick, Christine, 165
Holyoke, Massachusetts: servant union
in, 134
Home industries: elimination of, 88,
191–92

Honesty: servant lack of, 64–67; among
servants, 69–70. *See also* Moral behavior
Hotel and Restaurant Employees' Union,
132–33
Hotel Bulletin, 169–70
Hotel living. *See* Boarding-out
Hotel Mail, 169–70
Hotel Monthly, 169–70
Hotel servants, 38, 48–49, 51–52, 97
Hourly workers, 168, 183–84
Hours of labor: of household servants,
97–99; of hotel servants, 99; as complaint of servants, 99–102
Household labor: as reason for employing
servants, 10–11; specialization of,
83–84, 88, 167; reorganization of,
191–92
Household manuals, 149–51
Household technology: advances in, 88,
192–95, 198–99; resistance to, 195–98
Household Union, 134
Housekeeper: defined as employer,
11–12; as servant, 88–89
Housing: of Negro servants, 34; of all servants, 113–19
Hungarians: as servants, 59

Illinois: servants in, 49
Immigrants: as servants, 4–5, 16–17,
49–50, 51–53. *See also* "New immigration"; specific nationalities
Indentured servants, 3–4
Independent, 169–70
Indiana: employer in, 7; servants in,
56–57; investigation of service, 179
Indians: as servants, 49
Industrial Workers of the World, 137
Intelligence of servants, 63–64
Intelligence offices: as means of acquiring
servants, 19–21; description of, 19–20,
72–73; unflattering reputation of,
20–21; influence on servants, 71–74;
efforts to reform, 152–53, 155
Intemperance among servants, 77–78
Inter-Municipal Committee on Household
Research, 171–72
Iowa: servants in, 56–57
Irish: as servants, 4–5, 40, 49, 51–53,
56–57, 58–59; as servant stereotype,
40, 50
Irish Pioneer Emigration Fund, 16